Reelecting Bill Clinton

Reelecting Bill Clinton
*Why America Chose a
"New" Democrat*

John Hohenberg

Syracuse University Press

Copyright © 1997 by John Hohenberg
All Rights Reserved

First Edition 1997
97 98 99 00 01 02   6 5 4 3 2 1

The paper used in this publication meets the minimum requirements of American National Standard for Information Sciences—Permanence of Paper for Printed Library Materials, ANSI Z39.48-1984. ♾™

Library of Congress Cataloging-in-Publication Data
Hohenberg, John.
    Reelecting Bill Clinton : why America chose a "new" democrat / John Hohenberg. — 1st ed.
        p.   cm.
    Includes index.
    ISBN 0-8156-0491-2 (alk. paper)
    1. Presidents—United States—Elections—1996. 2. Clinton, Bill, 1946–   . 3. United States—Politics and government—1993–
I. Title.
E888.H65   1997
324.973'0929—DC21   97-8381

Manufactured in the United States of America

For JoAnn, as always

John Hohenberg, a distinguished journalist and political and diplomatic correspondent in New York, Washington, D.C., the United Nations, and abroad, was Professor of Journalism, Columbia Graduate School of Journalism, from 1950 to 1976. From 1954 to 1976, he also served as the Administrator of the Pulitzer Prizes and Secretary of the Pulitzer board. He is the author of *The Bill Clinton Story* (Syracuse University Press, 1994), *Foreign Correspondence: The Great Reporters and Their Times,* 2d edition (Syracuse University Press, 1995), *The Pulitzer Diaries: Inside America's Greatest Prize* (Syracuse University Press, 1997) *The Professional Journalist, Free Press/Free People,* and three books on the Pulitzer Prizes, among others. He also holds a Pulitzer Prize Special Award for his services to American journalism.

Contents

To Help Us Believe Again   ix

PART ONE **The Rivals**
1. Shutdown   3
2. "It's the Economy, Stupid!"   13
3. Dole's Problems   20
4. Clinton Cools It   27
5. The Outsiders   35
6. Tip-off in Iowa   42
7. The Long, Long Trail   48
8. Dole as Challenger   54

PART TWO **Changes of Front**
9. Black Hole   63
10. Emergency!   70
11. The "New" Democrat   77
12. Dole Quits the Senate   84
13. A One-Two Punch for Clinton   90
14. Guns in June   96
15. State of the Campaign   104

PART THREE Purposes and Principles

16. Big Tobacco   113
17. Clinton and Russia   120
18. Perot Redux   127
19. The War on Terror, I   135
20. "Of the People, by the People . . . "   142
21. Dole's Rescue Operation   149
22. Show Time in San Diego   156
23. The Hapless Warrior   165
24. Clinton at Fifty   172
25. Return to Chicago   180

PART FOUR The Fall Campaign

26. Labor Day Kickoff   193
27. Advantage: Clinton   201
28. Rehearsal for A.D. 2000?   207
29. The Republican Dilemma   215
30. The War on Terror, II   222
31. The Race Tightens   229
32. Congress Goes Home   237
33. Clinton Bids for Peace   244
34. The Debates   251

PART FIVE The Election

35. Ending the Campaign   261
36. The Presidential Election   268
37. State of the Union   276

Appendix: The 1996 Presidential Election Results   289
Index   291

To Help Us Believe Again

In concluding my account of the presidential election of 1992 with Bill Clinton's victory,* I wrote that the president-elect was "the product of a different age, one in which the country itself was changing, even though Congress and the two-party system were slow to change with it."

Such problems were emphasized once again in 1996, when President Clinton became the first Democrat to be reelected to the highest office in the land since Franklin Roosevelt won sixty years ago. The difference, however, was that the American electorate toward century's end also chose to confront Clinton with the leadership of a divided government by retaining a Republican-controlled Congress with broad powers to investigate the White House.

That this clash of opposite values was also the most expensive campaign in our history became an additional reason for a detailed examination of its merits and demerits, the purpose of this book. As to my theme, a somewhat muted plea for patience, faith, and understanding of the democratic process, my colleague James Reston said it best:

> Somewhere, there is a line where the old publish-and-be-damned tradition of the press may converge with the new intelligence and the new duties and responsibilities of this rising generation.
>
> I wish I knew how to find it . . . for it could help us to believe again in this age of tricks and techniques that may be our greatest need.*

But as this narrative demonstrates, the public's doubts about the rectitude of government still have not been laid to rest after being aroused by the conduct of the Vietnam War, the Watergate affair, and the Nixon resignation — the central issue that still confronts the presi-

---

* *The Bill Clinton Story: Winning the Presidency* (Syracuse Univ. Press, 1994), 272.

* The quote is from Reston's speech at the fiftieth anniversary celebration of the Pulitzer Prizes.

dent and Congress at the end of this benighted century. Continued strife, therefore, would scarcely seem to be the best way to resolve the troubles discussed herein. It is to be hoped that this work is a modest contribution toward that end.

Once again, I am grateful to Syracuse University Press to publish so promptly and so effectively this detailed account of Bill Clinton's second campaign, which, like the first, demonstrates to the American public that this is indeed a presidency in transition toward century's end—a lead-in to the monumental changes that are increasingly likely in the next century. I owe the deepest thanks as well to the press's executive editor, Cynthia Maude-Gembler, for the editing and added preparation of this volume for publication in 1997.

Dedicating the book to JoAnn F. Hohenberg, as always, is the only way I have to show how much I appreciate her constant encouragement and her wise counsel, which enabled me to complete this work in time for our eighteenth wedding anniversary this last Thanksgiving Day.

PART ONE
The Rivals

1 Shutdown

Late fall 1995 was an embarrassing time for sensible government in Washington. D.C. Although a November chill heralded the coming holiday season, Thanksgiving it wasn't. The Christmas spirit, too, would be curdled that year, particularly for 800,000 government employees on unpaid vacations. The presidential campaign of 1996 was approaching amid signs of disarray and utter confusion in the nation's capital.

At an isolated White House, a mordant air of crisis seeped to a wondering public from a crowded press room, where television reporters, among others, continually broadcast the non-news that the president was meeting with his advisers in the Oval Office. In the absence of any immediate announcement to rally the nation, however, the crepe-hangers—always a force in the news business—concluded that the president had lost control and America was adrift.

The scene was quite the opposite at the other end of Pennsylvania Avenue, where congressional leaders, too, were awaiting the outcome of the Oval Office conference. While comment from that eminence was also tightly reserved, there was a barely suppressed air of jubilation that contrasted oddly with the obvious distress at the White House.

These two of the three branches of the federal government had been in a struggle for power. That much appeared evident, but there was no certainty at the moment which one would emerge dominant. The issue was known. For this Congress, the one hundred–fourth since the first in George Washington's time, had just made history that clammy and disagreeable November 14, 1995. By refusing to grant funds to the president to meet federal government payrolls, among other necessary expenses of a great self-governing nation, the national legislature had caused the 800,000 federal employees to be sent home that day without pay until further notice.

In effect, that decision—to which the president strenuously objected—had caused Congress to shut down almost the entire basis of the federal government itself, headed by all the offices of the president's cabinet, the Pentagon, the budget office, and most others of importance. Quite naturally, the workers were as confused — and as angry — as their leaders. Few dared even guess how it would all end. And as for the public at large, the very word *crisis* in government affairs had been used so often in this sorely tried administration of President William Jefferson Clinton, forty-second of the line, that the very word had lost its meaning.

To be sure, the United States had survived wars, pestilence, and many another calamity from the burning of the White House and other public offices in Washington by British invaders in 1814 to Herbert Hoover's despair for the future of the republic after the stock market collapse of 1929. But this, alas, was the first time the federal government had been dealt so powerful a blow in so controversial a manner. Even with secession and the War Between the States, President Abraham Lincoln had kept his government functioning and the Union's armies on the march.

But this time, toward century's end, the attack came not from any foreign foe or domestic rebellion or even the fateful wreckage of a flawed economy but from the inability of President Clinton and the Congress to work together for the benefit of the 263 million American people, who expected them to perform their sworn duties no matter what.

In the time of the thirty-second president, Franklin Delano Roosevelt, he had revived the flagging spirit of a prostrate and well-nigh bankrupt nation in the pit of the Great Depression. Many an elderly American still alive, and I among them, can remember crowding around radios at work and at home to hear that commanding voice holding out hope to the American people in these well-remembered terms in his first inaugural address of March 4, 1933:

> The money-changers have fled from the temple of our civilization. There must be an end to conduct in banking and business which too often has given to a sacred trust the likeness of callous and selfish wrong-doing. This nation calls for action now.

Action, surely, is what FDR won from that Congress of sixty-two years ago, allied as it was to a president of the same Democratic Party. In the "hundred days" of 1933, during which the New Deal was thrown together in a sprawling bundle of legislation that went to the White House for signature, that president and that Congress together headed a distraught nation toward ultimate recovery and world power.

Now, at last, there was more news from Washington on that November day in 1995. This time, it came from the congressional leaders who were awaiting President Clinton's collapse—his expected agreement to their principal demand after the Republican revolution of 1994 gave that party control of both houses of Congress for the first time in forty years. It was, briefly and forcefully put, a balanced budget and a return to fiscal probity by a Democratic president who, so Republicans believed, was on the point of yielding to their shutdown of government.

Only, this time at least, President Clinton didn't collapse. At the end of his conference with his advisers in the Oval Office, the message that had been sent to an opposition Congress prepared for a victory celebration was, in effect, "No surrender!" Now, it was the congressional leaders, Speaker Newt Gingrich of the House and Senator Bob Dole, majority leader of the Senate, who had to be concerned. But as Speaker Gingrich himself confirmed long afterward, he still expected President Clinton to give in to the Republican crusade for a balanced budget.

And why not? From the Republican point of view, it was dishonest of a Democratic administration to continue to play the game of deficit spending to maintain costly social services such as Social Security, Medicare, and Medicaid, among others, when the nation's income wasn't sufficient to support them at the level placed by Democrats.

That, in fact, was why the carefully designed plan to close the federal government had been adopted and orchestrated with credible efficiency. This was the way the opposition had chosen to put into effect its "contract with America," with which they had won the midterm elections, control of Congress, and, so they believed, immense power over the White House.

As the first few days passed slowly toward the latter part of November and there still was no sign from the White House that the president would give up, there seemed to be slight movement among his opponents. It came about when Senator Dole, the leading candidate for the Republican nomination against President Clinton's reelection in 1996, no longer appeared to be taking a major part in promoting the continued shutdown. It was not that he was deserting his forceful comrade, Speaker Gingrich, the Georgia firecracker who had had such confidence that the president's stamina could be broken. But now Dole was simply not as much in evidence in the daily briefings for the press by the congressional leadership.

And so Speaker Gingrich alone had to take the heat of reporters' sharp questions over how long the Republicans proposed to prevent the federal government from functioning. Little by little, even the opposition press began to show editorial disapproval of the Republican revolution for a balanced budget.

An equally slow and cautious reevaluation of President Clinton's position was also evident in the all-important TV news broadcasts and commentary on the shutdown, along with a clamor of disapproval of the Republican strategy from defiant Democratic editorial pages. What the Democratic minority in Congress and the Democratic press argued was that the Republicans wanted a tax cut as well as a balanced budget to benefit mostly people who had no need of either.

Gradually, before a week had passed, it appeared that the Republicans had been put in a losing position through their own daring, although none of their leaders would admit it. The most zealous among the Republican majority, the seventy-three conservative House freshmen who were particularly loyal to Speaker Gingrich, were the most insistent on rejecting any thought of giving up the shutdown. What the usually moderate Senator Dole thought of the new problems of the Republican Congress never became publicly known at the time because Speaker Gingrich was kept out front all by himself; and as a result, his ratings in the polls fell disastrously. Probably, Dole was more motivated against prolonging the shutdown because some of the older conservatives of the party, especially Senator Phil Gramm of Texas, were ready to challenge him in the forthcoming primary elections that would determine the Republican nominee for president in 1996.

At seventy-two, this was Dole's last chance for the presidency, having tried twice before and failed. With twenty-eight years of service in the Senate, six more in the House, and a distinguished record as a soldier in World War II, he seemed to be in a strong position to challenge President Clinton. Moreover, in August 1995, he had, for a short time, been leading Clinton in the polls.

But it now had become clear that the public, as shown in the polls, did not support the Republican government shutdown and Dole, as a presumptive presidential candidate, began changing his outlook. Not surprisingly, near the end of the first five days of the shutdown, the White House's resistance stiffened; and so now, if there ever had been any disposition on the president's part to meet Republican demands for a balanced budget, the prospect vanished.

Moderate Republicans dropped away from Gingrich's side along with Dole. And soon, only the seventy-three rabid freshmen conservatives in the House remained as the Speaker's loyal supporters. After six days, therefore, it finally was Gingrich who had to surrender. Possibly, Dole and his more moderate supporters in the Senate had helped bring about an early end to this particular test of strength; certainly, with only a slim six-seat majority in the one-hundred-member Senate with one-third of its membership facing reelection in 1996, there was more reason for concern than in the House, where the Republicans held a larger lead.

This is how I noted the conclusion of the six-day government crisis in my diary:

Nov. 20—The U.S. government shutdown was resolved overnight with a typical series of political promises to put 800,000 Federal employees back to work with full restoration of pay. President Clinton agreed to balance the Federal budget by the year 2002 if the Republican majority in Congress satisfied him with safeguards for Medicare, Medicaid, Social Security, the environment, education, etc. Senator Dole also accepted, after which his main conservative rival for the Republican Presidential nomination, Senator Gramm of Texas, called it "a sellout."

In the renewed bargaining with the president that followed, however, the Republican lines stiffened once again. Even though Speaker Gingrich had yielded to Dole and the other Senate moderates to reopen the federal government on November 20, he seemed unable to get over the notion that the White House could still be forced to yield—that Clinton himself was so weak a character that he would cave in to Republican demands for a balanced budget and the all-important added tax cut.

Within less than one month, therefore, Gingrich once again was throwing the congressional switch toward another shutdown that would be longer, tougher, and uglier than the first. This time, under the Speaker's management, the 800,000 federal employees were sent home for an indefinite period once again; but now, they had a payless Christmas and a payless New Year to add to their trials. No matter. Despite Dole, Gingrich again had his way. That closure lasted more than three times as long as the first shutdown and created even more public animosity toward the brash Republican conservatives in general and Gingrich in particular. These were my diary entries at the time beginning in the last weeks of 1995:

> Dec. 16—More woe. The Republicans have closed down the government again to try to force bigger cuts in services and give themselves a tax break.
>
> Dec. 18—The New York Stock Exchange broke open, down 101 points, tipped by the latest government blockade and a general belief after the shutdown that the Federal Reserve won't cut interest rates very soon.
>
> Jan. 10—It's snowing. Washington and the government are still closed down.

On January 10, for the second time, Gingrich had to give up; and this time, he was really licked and admitted it. To an interviewer a few days later, he confessed that he had underestimated President Clinton's resolve. What the Speaker did not refer to, however, was the undoubted pressure that Dole and the senatorial moderates had put on him and the seventy-three House hard liners to reopen the government — and promptly.

Confronted with the consequences of a second failure to force a presidential surrender, Gingrich told his young zealots that the Republican leadership (meaning Dole) had made its decision and that the government shutdown would have to end. The Speaker refused to listen to frantic pleas for reconsideration. And that — at last — was how the Republican rebellion ended for a second time just a few days before President Clinton, in effect, opened his own mild offensive on January 23 with his fourth State of the Union message.

Before a joint session of Congress, he offered conciliation that night to the beaten Republican majority before him to the accompaniment of continual cheering and handclapping from the resurgent Democratic minority that dominated the nationally broadcast proceedings.

Far from demanding immediate action to resolve the nation's problems in the challenging manner of Franklin Roosevelt, what this fifty-year-old latter-day president had to do was to reflect soberly on the way in which his authority had been circumscribed in quite a different time in the nation's history. He seemed to make it a particular point to admit that the power and the glory of the chief executive in the governance of the nation had eluded him. The confession was genuine enough, even heartfelt, as he conceded, "The era of big government is over."

How his Republican foes, with their corporate constituencies, roared their approval at that unexpected admission — and particularly the president's follow-up in describing the outlook for the new federalism of the next century:

> It will have to be smaller and less bureaucratic; it will have to focus more on results than rules; it will have to work more in partnership with state and local governments, community groups, and the private sector. And [this with what seemed to some among his audience like a heartfelt sigh] it will have to earn the respect and the trust of the American people.

Well! Whether or not Clinton meant it and would put up with it in a second term, if reelected, is beside the point now as it was that night. The presidential utterance of 1996 at face value constituted quite a comedown from Franklin Roosevelt's image of the presidency at the bottom of the Great Depression. But then, this was quite a different America from the one that had turned so eagerly to FDR and his Congress — a much greater nation now caught in the savage gridlock of a bitterly divided government.

If I couldn't understand Dole's behind-the-scenes compromises with

Gingrich and his wrecking crew of seventy-three young conservatives, I was just as much put off by President Clinton's well-meant efforts to ease the strain of his relations with a hostile Congress. I should have thought that the president would have known that his plea for a more merciful congressional approach to the fears of the deprived and the dispossessed would have been rejected with scorn, which was exactly what happened.

As he ended his hour-long defense of his administration in his State of the Union address, in which he had hoped to ease the strain of his relations with a hostile Congress, all he heard was the stage-managed cheering and hand-clapping of the Democratic minority. The Republicans, for the most part, sat on their hands or walked out.

Since the previous September 30, when the president's last federal budget funds had run out and Congress had failed to vote its usual renewal, the voters realized that the White House had been forced to get along on minimal amounts of money ladled out by the Republicans a few weeks at a time. In effect, the position was paralyzing, and there was no sign of imminent change.

In the strange ways of American politics, Senator Dole was assigned the task of responding to President Clinton in public, but he was given only ten minutes of TV time for it. Moreover, the response was recorded in advance from a studio, so that, when released, it reached perhaps one-tenth or fewer of the 20 million households that were estimated to have heard the president's live delivery. No matter what the senator might have said, his comments would have had relatively little effect on the body politic. Knowing that, he seemed to have hurried through the script that had been prepared for him and thereby drew criticism on himself by some of the eight candidates who opposed him for the Republican presidential nomination.

Dole's critique had been fairly standard stuff in the Republican lexicon. The president, so the senator said, had the same limited view of America as "the country's elite — a nation of special groups." He went on:

> We must rein in our runaway government, return power to the people, reduce the tax burden, put parents back in charge of our schools, untie the hands of our police, restore justice to our courts and put faith once again in the basic goodness, wisdom and self-reliance of our people.

Right away, Dole's chief conservative rival for the presidential nomination, Senator Gramm, struck back with a discouraging comment. "It is clear to me that we are not going to beat Bill Clinton by matching our empty rhetoric with his." To that, a Republican county chairman in Iowa, Roger Linn, added, "If this is the beginning of the campaign, Clinton could quit right now because he's got it!"

There was a lot more of this at high Republican Party levels and low, to which Dole responded mildly that he'd had only a few minutes for his response to the president and had done the best he could with his time. It was a break that Clinton could not have anticipated, mainly because it foreshadowed an outburst of rebellion against Dole's leadership while he was campaigning for the party's presidential nomination.

But Clinton, ruminating that night at the White House on his boxed-in position without adequate funds to operate the government, was scarcely in a position to anticipate an eventual wide-open break in the Republican campaign of gridlock against both his administration and his policies for the nation's future.

The president had reason for his concern over the state of the union despite the adverse reaction among the more extreme Republican conservatives against Dole's mild criticism of the presidential address before Congress. What the nation did not know then was that the Republicans were still threatening a third government shutdown, plus a financial crisis that would affect all federal debt obligations.

The day before Clinton's speech to the joint session of Congress, he had authorized Secretary of the Treasury Robert E. Rubin to warn publicly of what amounted to a weakening in the value of federal long-term bonds and other government obligations. Rubin had already served notice on the financial community that the Treasury would have no choice other than to default on its financial obligations after the end of February, now only a little more than a month off, if Congress failed to raise the national debt limit by that time. Even that move was not widely reported. It indicated that a separate congressional resolution in support of government securities was urgently needed in addition to the usual continuing small grant of funds by congressional authorization that, in effect, kept the government running for only a few weeks at a time.

The threat to government securities in itself turned out to be a shocker to Wall Street. It was one thing, certainly, to anticipate a default by some poorly governed little country in the Andes or the Himalayas. But this was the United States of America that was being shoved to the brink of insolvency by admission of its chief financial officer, the former head of the renowned Wall Street brokerage firm Goldman, Sachs.

There was no secret about the facts in the case. On November 15, 1995, just one day after the first shutdown of the federal government, the nation's statutory debt limit of $4.9 trillion had been reached. But no move had been made in Congress that day or even later to increase the nation's debt limit so that more securities could be issued by the federal government.

Consequently, Secretary Rubin hadn't enough money left in the US Treasury to buy his morning cup of coffee. Shutdown or not—and obviously with the president's approval—what he did then to keep the federal government going and to meet expenses beyond the relatively small sums Congress granted a few weeks at a time was to borrow from various statutory funds of the government covering pensions.

But as any housewife knows quite well when operating on a self-imposed budget, there is a limit to this kind of questionable emergency borrowing. Secretary Rubin, in his own tight spot, had already told Wall Street that his internal borrowing deadline was February 29. It followed that not only would Congress have to stop threatening the president with a third shutdown but a prompt vote to extend the national debt limit was also urgently needed.

To emphasize the nature of the emergency (and Secretary Rubin may well have shrewdly calculated that something like this would happen), a leading Wall Street credit-rating service, Moody's, announced the morning after the president's State of the Union address that it was considering lowering the rating (the ability to pay) for $387 billion in Treasury securities. If anything would cause even the most radical among the Republicans to run for cover, so the White House calculated, that would be it.

For good measure, the Republicans took another jab from unnamed Wall Street authorities who hinted to financial news services that Moody's announcement might well drive down the price of government bonds. After all, the New York *Times*'s Republican among its columnists, William Safire, weighed in with this denunciation of "a little willful group of House Republicans":

> It's a foolish and wrongheaded method of pressure. You don't play a game of chicken with the American dollar. If you are not prepared to carry out a threat, you should never make it, and anyone prepared to carry out the first national default is as crazy as Nero.

Although Speaker Gingrich and his Republican backers weren't directly named, there was no doubt about the identity of the authors of the threatened default. And when President Clinton said that he and Gingrich had had an "agreeable" telephone talk, any questions about the source of the newest attack were removed.

Gingrich, at a news conference next day with Senator Dole, encouraged the notion that he was willing to compromise on outstanding issues, after which Dole sent what was billed as a confirming letter to the president. But what happened after further negotiations soon fell into the familiar gridlock between a Republican Congress and a Democratic White House. As for the public perception of events, every major poll now reflected declining public confidence in Congress, with Gingrich's approval rating falling to only 29 percent.

In due course, the Republicans finally shelved their threat against government securities and continued thereafter to extend limited funds for immediate government use. But the effect on the president and his negotiators was a slow though very definite decline in appropriations for the most necessary of the government's social services to those most dependent on them as well as further cuts in educational and environmental funds.

Before Senator Dole had faced his eight challengers in the first party primary elections for the leadership of the Republican ticket, President Clinton had begun an advance in the earliest polls of that presidential election year. But the cost already seemed prohibitively high. Still, Clinton had overcome far greater odds in his 1992 race against President Bush, who at one juncture was a seventeen-point favorite but in the end was badly beaten in his second and last run for the highest office in the land.

2 "It's the Economy, Stupid!"

Although President Clinton was unopposed for renomination as the Democratic candidate, his campaign for reelection in 1996 was bound to be a tough sell at the outset. This time, it was no joke, as it had been in 1992, when he poked fun at his foes in the Bush administration with his bumper stickers that read It's the Economy, Stupid!

The economy remained a dominant issue for an exceedingly nervous electorate, still shaken by the billion-dollar corporate downsizing movement that had been so unsettling to the working class and the poor. Clinton argued, to begin with, that the New York Stock Exchange was operating at its highest levels in history while the nation's "misery index" — the figures for inflation and unemployment — were at their lowest ebb in a quarter of a century.

Also, he was not exaggerating when he contended that he had cut the nation's budgetary deficit almost in half in his first four years, with fewer people out of work than at any time since the Eisenhower administration. He claimed, in fact, that his administration had created more than 10 million new jobs.

But despite all the good news, as the president himself admitted, at least half of America's families had seen their incomes shrinking in terms of real purchasing power. In a report entitled "A Brief Look at Postwar U.S. Income Inequality," the Census Bureau demonstrated that, from 1968 to 1994, the top 20 percent of American households increased their share of the country's aggregate income from 40.5 percent to 46.9 percent. As for the other 80 percent, statistics indicated that their share either remained stationary or dropped.

Put in dollars and cents, the Census Bureau determined that households in the top 20 percent gained $32,191 on average by leaping from $73,754 in 1968 to $105,945 in 1994, or 44 percent upon adjustment for inflation. But for the same period, households in the lowest 20 percent gained only $560, moving from $7,202 to $7,762. And when it is realized that the poverty level was officially more than twice as much as the average lower-household income in 1994, it says a great deal about the condition of poor American families then.

That, in brief, was the position as the 1996 presidential campaign was about to begin, with Clinton calling for a rise in the minimum wage of 90 cents an hour and his prospective Republican rival, Senator Dole, refusing to support even that paltry offering.

True, there were improvements later in the year, when the Census Bureau announced that the number of poor people in America had dropped by 1.6 million in 1995 and that family income had risen for the first time since 1989. In its report of September 26, 1996, the bureau said that the percentage of the nation's poor had been cut to 13.8 in 1995, from 14.5 the previous year, mainly showing small benefits for blacks and old people.

As for the gain in household incomes, according to the report, half of the nation's households boosted their income by 2.7 percent over the previous year to at least $34,074. But the report also indicated that this improvement was accomplished because there were at least two workers in most households — and their wages on average showed a decline. That, too, became a part of the campaign at a later date — still emphasizing the importance of the economic issue.

Nothing about Clinton's beginnings foretold his rise in the nation. He was born August 19, 1945, in Hope, Arkansas, soon after his father, William Blythe, died in an automobile accident. When his widowed mother remarried, this time choosing a family friend, Roger Clinton, the youth, then sixteen, adopted his stepfather's name, later obtained a BS degree in international affairs from Georgetown University and a two-year Rhodes scholarship at Oxford.

Exactly when he made known his views against the war in Vietnam isn't certain, but there is no doubt that he was in the forefront of the college students protesting the conflict. That activity, however, never seemed to interfere with his three-year studies at Yale Law School, where he met Hillary Rodham, whom he married on October 11, 1975, two years after both received their law degrees. He was teaching then at the University of Arkansas, and she was practicing with the Rose law firm in Little Rock.

Soon afterward, Clinton's political career skyrocketed. He became Arkansas's attorney general in 1977 and won his first two-year term as governor in 1979. After losing the gubernatorial election in 1981, he was reelected governor four more times and then called himself "the Comeback Kid." In 1992, after winning the Democratic presidential nomination, he seemed like a one-hundred-to-one shot to beat an overly confident President Bush—a little-known Arkansas governor challenging a sitting Republican president.

Still worse, Clinton ran into big trouble when the grocery-checkout-counter tabloid *Star* linked him to a twelve-year extramarital romance with an actress, Gennifer Flowers. After the Republican high command saw to it that his tale was amplified nationwide, Clinton and Hillary appeared together on CBS's *60 Minutes,* then the top-rated Sunday-night TV show, and denied the allegations.

Bush, meanwhile, had a run of bad luck. The economy, which had been fueled by Ronald Reagan's $2-trillion investment in national defense, took a sharp downturn in the middle of Bush's reelection drive. And at just about the same time, billionaire H. Ross Perot was making an effective independent run for votes as an unexpected third candidate—votes, as it turned out, that were drawn more from Bush than from Clinton.

That is when the familiar bumper stickers developed into an advantage for what had been thought of as an ineffective Democratic pitch for the presidency. On election day, Clinton could once again call himself "the Comeback Kid." With almost 45 million votes to Bush's 39 million and Perot's unexpectedly high 18.7 million, Clinton, at age forty-six, became the third youngest elected president of the United States, after John F. Kennedy and Theodore Roosevelt. His electoral tally was 370 to 168.

But before Clinton was through—stupid or not—he would also be wrestling with the economy and no doubt wondering all the while why there were so few haves and so many have nots in the land of the free and the home of the brave.

Even with the help of Democratic majorities in both houses of Congress that went back forty years to the Eisenhower administration, the new president's legislative performance in his first two years (1993–1994) fell short of his lofty expectations.

Primarily, that disappointment was attributed to the failure of his comprehensive programs of health insurance for all Americans—the principal objective of his administration once he assumed office. Although such health protection for all citizens had been accepted for years as an obligation of some of Europe's major governments, that kind of guarantee had never existed in the United States. It had been President Clinton's dearest wish, therefore, to formulate and propose that his Democratic Congress in 1993 should enact such all-embracing legislation.

With Hillary Clinton's enthusiastic help and the support of so major a figure as Senator Edward Kennedy, among others, the president had great hope for his revolutionary health insurance plan. But, as so often happens with such ambitious innovations in the American system, the Clinton administration attempted too much. Either that or the anti-health-insurance lobbyists and their persuasive tactics sidetracked the administration's efforts. In any case, the health program failed of passage.

President Clinton did better in those first two years with the passage of other legislation: the North American Free Trade Agreement; a gun-control law establishing a five-day waiting period for prospective gun buyers, pending a check of their backgrounds; a "motor voter" law linking voters' applications to automobile license renewals; and a $500 billion reduction in the federal budget deficit.

The administration's biggest accomplishment while Congress was still under Democratic control was the president's omnibus $30 billion crime-prevention law that included life sentences for thrice-convicted criminals and a ban on the sale of nineteen types of semiautomatic weapons. This statute, coupled with another law for the appointment of 100,000 new police across the land, was credited with stemming an increase in crime-connected violence, fatalities, and associated outrages.

President Clinton's debits, however, remained to haunt him. From the outset of his administration, he and Hillary Rodham Clinton became the targets of Republican-initiated inquiries into their investments in Whitewater real estate in Arkansas, to which they repeatedly responded that their only failing had been that they had lost money through a risky investment. No crime was charged against the Clintons. And yet, a special prosecutor and a Senate committee, headed by Senator Alfonse d'Amato (N.Y.), kept digging into the Whitewater matter in the apparent hope that something incriminating them might turn up.

Given time, this situation developed into a separate inquiry, also under Republican sponsorship, to determine what part, if any, the president and the first lady had played in the collapse of the Madison Guaranty Savings and Loan of Little Rock that had been headed by James B. McDougal, who had also been a partner of the Clintons in their Whitewater real estate venture. The Senate committee also inquired about the situation when Madison Guaranty went into bankruptcy in 1985 and regulators appointed by then Governor Clinton took charge, especially when it became known that Hillary Rodham Clinton had, for a brief time, previously represented the firm. Still, at the time, not the slightest evidence of wrongdoing on the part of the Clintons came to public notice.

The Republicans also made an issue out of the dismissal of all seven employees of the White House Travel Office shortly after the Clintons moved into the mansion. There was much to-do over Mrs. Clinton's role in the dismissals, what had happened to some missing documents, and the reason for the suicide of the deputy White House counsel, Vincent Foster. At the request of the special prosecutor, the White House eventually had to produce 40,000 pages of official documents for the inquiry.

The Republican strategy soon became clear. By harping on Whitewater, travelgate, and associated matters for the first two years of the Clinton regime, the party leaders hoped to make a comeback in the 1994 congressional midterm elections. First, they saw the Democratic leadership sinking in the polls. And soon even Clinton's own ratings began to suffer.

Therefore, it was a shattering defeat when the Republicans, for the first time in forty years, took control of both houses of Congress in 1994, forcing the Democratic leadership into the unfamiliar role of the minority opposition—the first step in the Republican plan to recapture the White House in 1996. There is no doubt that the youthful and inexperienced President Clinton was confused. Few then would have ventured to gamble on his continued success as "the Comeback Kid." Even the taunt, "It's the Economy, Stupid!" seemed to have been turned against its authors.

The price the nation paid, however, was very high. For the Republican comeback, gridlock, the paralysis of Congress, had been successfully used by Senator Bob Dole, now the majority leader of the upper house. But it was also apparent that the minority Democrats could play the same game. When it happened, Dole soon discovered that he and his Republican-dominated Congress were being hurled back on the defensive by another of those strange well-nigh mercurial shifts of public opinion that were so lamentably characteristic of the antigovernment mood in American during the last years of the century—a hangover from the divisiveness of the Vietnam era. With President Clinton's refusal to bow to the pressures of two successive Republican shutdowns of much of the federal government by a wildly uncontrolled Congress, a New York *Times*–CBS poll that winter of 1995 put the Republican Party's approval rating at only 41 percent, the lowest in the poll's history.

That low rating, however, didn't mean that the Democrats had more than an outside chance of regaining control of the upcoming One hundred-fifth Congress or that President Clinton was assured of reelection. The Republican-led Senate inquiry into the role of President and Mrs. Clinton in the Whitewater affair was still going on. And there were also too many other issues that were being left unresolved. The most important remained the feeling of almost despairing doubt that dominated the lives of so many of the hard-pressed middle class and the working poor.

Despite the advance in his political fortunes, as indicated by his rise in the polls, President Clinton was still deeply aware of the difficulties that lay ahead of him before election day. The ever-present taint of scandal, implicit in the Senate and court actions arising from the Whitewater and the linked Madison Guaranty bankruptcy, were tough enough for both the president and the first lady to face day by day. Even so, there was no way to avoid the even more daunting task of raising the enormous sums it would take to finance his return to the White House for another four years, let alone the slimmer chance of the election of a Democratic majority in both houses of Congress.

How much money would it take? More than nine months from election day, with all the expense of devising advertising campaigns and determining when and where to air them before the nation, plus Clinton's own speeches, the sky seemed to be the limit. There were reports from the Federal Election Commission (FEC), published together with lists of contributions for 1995, in which the Republican presidential campaign already had its first $100 million added to its treasury, with much of it pledged to or already spent by various candidates.

President Clinton and his campaign staff, sequestered in their war room in the White House basement, could only hope to do as well once the country realized he now seemed to have better than an even chance of reelection. But given public anxiety, he also knew those odds could rapidly shift in unpleasant directions.

Taking congressional reports to the FEC separately for 1995 as an indication of what the president could expect, Republican congressional candidates admitted receiving $34.7 million, as compared with only $10.9 million for Democrats, a ratio of better than three to one favoring the Republicans.

In preparing for the run for the presidency, the official Republican figures reported in 1995 showed that Senator Dole, as the leading candidate, already had received $20.4 million; Senator Phil Gramm, $19.2 million; and financial magazine publisher Steve Forbes, as a newcomer, $17.9 million, all of it his own money, with his expectation that he would eventually exceed that total in 1996 in what appeared to be a quixotic effort to become the party's presidential nominee.

By comparison, as Clinton and his White House staff began intensifying their own fund-raising appeals, he was obliged to admit publicly that he was in essence at a low point in his personal resources.

He blamed the immense legal expense of defending the first lady and himself in court actions and congressional and other inquiries into Whitewater, Madison Guaranty, and the disappearance of documents from the White House Travel Office when its seven-member staff was fired.

This admission by the president came about in an article published by *Money* magazine early in 1996 that suggested the president could be on the verge of personal bankruptcy. The article had been called to the president's attention during an impromptu news conference at the White House amid preparations for the opening of his reelection campaign.

Clinton didn't seem at all surprised. He was quoted as having responded to the magazine's estimate of his low net worth by saying, "I guess that's just about right." Strange? To be sure, it was; particularly so, just before the beginning of what had been billed well in advance as the longest and most expensive presidential campaign in the nation's history.

At the time, the president of the United States was being voted an annual salary of $200,000 that was taxable, plus an allowance of $50,000 to help defray expenses attributed specifically to his official duties. For travel expenses that were nontaxable, the president was also allowed an additional $100,000, plus $20,000 for official entertainment within the Executive Office of the President.

Despite what would seem to the average citizen to be a generous reward for a chief executive, President Clinton had to admit being close to broke going into what would be, in all probability, the costliest reelection campaign of the century. And so, as it turned out, there was an ironic meaning even for the president himself in the old bumper sticker that read It's the Economy, Stupid! He and his party were likely to be more dependent on maintaining economic growth at least through election day, if they expected to raise the millions necessary for his campaign.

With the coming of the election year, fortunately, the president's numbers were slowly showing improvement in the polls, mainly because of adverse public reactions to the government shutdowns by the opposition. Through a gaping hole in the nation's election laws, as well, both Republicans and Democrats were gathering huge corporate contributions to each political party that could then be assigned pretty much where the money was needed most. And so even though Dole was strapped and Clinton personally was nearly broke, the money people already were placing their bets—and the incumbent president had an advantage there. That was the position as the presidential campaign of 1996 was taking shape.

3   Dole's Problems

Although Senator Dole was heavily favored for the Republican presidential nomination over his eight rivals, his problems were also mounting as President Clinton's prospective challenger. As the wrathful public reaction to most polls had already indicated, blame for the federal government closings of late 1995 and early 1996 had been placed squarely on the Republican-dominated Congress. Among individuals, the one who suffered most was Speaker of the House Newt Gingrich, as became evident in a shattering reduction in his approval rating to 24 percent—and falling.

Moreover, with a continuing rise in President Clinton's standing, Dole's candidacy was being hurt, too, although not as severely as Gingrich's reputation as the third-highest public official in the land. From within the moderate element of the Republican Party, the Senator was being advised discreetly to distance himself from Speaker Gingrich, whose own role in the campaign, meanwhile, had been sharply diminished.

But was it really practical for the Senate majority leader to distance himself from the Speaker of the House, being the two dominant officials of the Congress of the United States? And as for the Speaker at the same time adopting a low profile for the entire presidential campaign on behalf of Senator Dole, another bit of sage advice from some of the party's strategists, that also would have amounted to an inversion of character.

No, it already had occurred to some of Dole's closest friends—and even to the candidate himself—that he was being put in the impossible position, as Clinton's strongest prospective challenger, of daily directing the intricate operations of the Senate while campaigning for his party's highest honor and, ultimately, the presidency itself. How would he do both for the better part of nine months?

Obviously, until he had locked up the Republican presidential nomination, Dole couldn't make a decision on either taking a leave of absence from the Senate or otherwise freeing himself for what would almost certainly be an uphill battle against a sitting president — and a tough young one at that.

As for Gingrich, he certainly was scarcely someone the party's presumptive presidential candidate could afford to offend, much less ignore. Like Clinton, the Georgian, who was only three years older than the president, had completed his education during the Vietnam War era, with a B.A. from Emory in 1965, an M.A. from Tulane in 1968, and a Ph.D. in European history from Tulane in 1971.

Gingrich was too ambitious to be satisfied with academic life, however. In 1977, after teaching for six years at Northern Georgia College, he turned to politics with almost immediate success.

While serving in the House from the Ninety-sixth to the One hundred-third Congresses, he helped develop the ultraconservative strategy of continual attack, through which he and his fellow-Republicans ended Democratic control of Congress in 1994. Mainly, this minority political offensive was based on the military principle of outflanking the enemy wherever possible by using the power of delay, obstruction, and confusion.

It was under these circumstances, too, that the Republican faithful developed the notion of attaching impossible opposing bills to almost any measure the Democrats introduced in Congress. The result, in most cases, was gridlock; if the Democratic majority up to 1994 seemed about to achieve a meaningful victory, the Republicans, as a last resort, would stage a filibuster that could be broken only by a two-thirds majority.

By stalling the legislative process through gridlock so that Congress failed to enact Clinton's most important program (health care reform) in his first two years as president, the Republicans took control in 1995 and were then in a position to aim at the White House in 1996.

But now the gridlock strategy was seized upon by the minority Democrats to plague their conquerors, which was something Messrs. Gingrich and Dole hadn't anticipated. The result for Congress was just as devastating, beginning in early 1995. The Democratic leaders in the House and Senate operated with such skill that the Republican-controlled One hundred-fourth Congress couldn't even pass its own program pledged to America's future.

If Gingrich now felt frustrated and Dole fumed, there was nothing that they could conceivably do about it at the start of the presidential election year. Besides, Dole had yet to win the presidential nomination in the primaries that were scheduled from mid-February through the spring.

It was then that the Republicans tried to force their notions of a balanced budget and complementary legislation on the White House with disastrous results. Between Clinton with his vetoes and the obstructive Democratic tactics in Congress, the Republican idea of a federal budget was no closer to being balanced than it had been before the onset of the Republican revolution of 1994.

The odd-man-out in this turnabout between Republicans and Democrats, however unexpectedly, became Senator Dole, even though Speaker Gingrich bore the brunt of the public's disapproval of a legislature that couldn't legislate and a chief executive whose role was sharply and even cruelly limited. What could a frustrated public possibly think of a federal government that was twice shut down and, for any meaningful public action, bottled up thereafter?

Senator Dole thereby found himself beleaguered by obstructionist Democrats in his role as the Senate majority leader. Worse still, it became increasingly difficult for him to make the mandatory speaking appearances in states where Republican primaries were being held and his rivals were belaboring him with jabs at his age, his record as a conservative, and even the few times in the dim past when he had approved a Democratic initiative.

And so it was not only the Republican Congress that became as vulnerable as its Democratic precedessor to delay, obstruction, confusion, and filibuster. Even as he aspired to the Republican presidential nomination, Dole, in effect, became the captive of a congressional system that had let itself be broken down without any immediate possibility of substantial repair.

Of course, when his friends and sympathizers in Congress saw his position linked so closely to Gingrich's in this mirror image of Harry Truman's "Do Nothing" Eightieth Congress, Dole's well-wishers rushed to TV and recorded in print their suggestion that the Kansan should take a leave of absence from his Senate leadership. But if Dole had done so then, while facing eight opponents in the primaries, he could have been hurt; it might even have proved an embarrassment to his chances for the presidential nomination.

At that juncture, Gingrich was no help either. In addition to his responsibilities for the shutdowns, the Speaker also was having his troubles with an Ethics Committee whose members he had helped select; and there had been muttering ever since about the speedy disposition of a complaint against him. The issue, to put it bluntly, had been his joyful acceptance of a $4.5 million advance payment against royalties on his best-selling book, entitled *To Renew America*.

The Georgia firecracker's patron for this literary largesse had been Rupert Murdoch, the Australian book publisher, newspaper and TV owner, and influential internationalist. As the members of the Ethics Committee had sadly reminded the Speaker, Murdoch, as a power in America, could well have had influence on issues before this Republican-controlled House that might conceivably create the impression of a conflict of interest affecting the Speaker himself.

Gingrich promptly saw the point and returned the $4.5-million advance in favor of a $1.00 payment accepted in good faith. But nevertheless, in his first summer in authority in Congress, his book made the best-seller list of the New York *Times,* and so his profits were obviously considerable.

All of these events may have been pushed far back in public memory during the spectacular course of events in Congress during Gingrich's first two years as Speaker. Still, as the influence of President Clinton and his congressional minorities increased in the wake of Republican difficulties and Senator Dole's preoccupation with campaigning, Speaker Gingrich became a decidedly unpopular figure in the nation's capital, and his "Contract with America" was all but forgotten.

Because Gingrich himself had participated in a quasi-criminal procedure against former Democratic Speaker Jim Wright, who was forced in 1989 to resign his high office, the possibility of such a reversal at the hands of a prospective enemy majority was no mere theory. If a disenchanted American public voted to return a Democratic president and Congress to power in 1996, there was no telling what might happen next.

Dole considered Senator Phil Gramm of Texas to be the most important, the smartest, the best financed, and therefore the most dangerous of those who contested his candidacy for the party's presidential nomination. Gramm was already calling himself "the most electable conservative" in the country and looked the part, being a graying, fifty-four-year-old former economics professor at Texas A & M.

The Texan also based his campaign on his adherence to the platform of a religious organization called the Christian Coalition, which had considerable power in parts of the South, particularly Texas. He also criticized Dole as "too moderate a Republican." The weakness in Gramm's position, however, was that the Christian Coalition had that year spread its favors between him and Dole, with an outside show of support for the former TV commentator Pat Buchanan.

Had Gramm shown signs of battling with Dole all the way for the party's presidential nomination, perhaps the Senate's majority leader might have had cause for concern. But the Texan was also up for reelection to another six-year Senate term in 1997, of which he was reasonably certain, so he wasn't likely to waste his war chest, supposedly as large as Dole's, if he failed to beat the Kansan in an early primary. That, finally, was the incentive that led Dole to center his opposition on Gramm.

Lamar Alexander, a former governor of Tennessee, was quite a different candidate—a moderate who also professed sympathy for the Kansan but concluded he was too old, out of date, bereft of new ideas, and without either the will or the strength to inspire the electorate. In response to criticism of the wealth he seemed to have acquired while in the State House at Nashville, Alexander merely laughed off such suspicions, which did not satisfy his critics.

At fifty-five, what Andrew Lamar Alexander had going for him far more than anything else was the relative scarcity of talent with public appeal at the top level of the Republican Party. His professional background was solid—a B.A. from Vanderbilt and a law degree from New York University, together with membership in Phi Beta Kappa. After practicing law in Tennessee with Senator Howard Baker's firm until 1978, Alexander had served successive terms as governor of the state, then became president of the University of Tennessee in 1988, and secretary of education in the Bush administration.

In the opening stages of the Republican primaries, Alexander was hampered as a contender against Dole because his moderate position on many issues seemed not to have won him many friends on the religious right. That group still exercised a surprising amount of influence in the party.

One other senator was in contention—Richard Green Lugar of Indiana, the chairman of the Senate Foreign Relations Committee and a member of the upper house for almost twenty years. At sixty-four, Lugar was trim, fit-looking, outspoken, an expert in foreign affairs, a former Rhodes scholar, and a member of Phi Beta Kappa. Except for a diffident manner and the public's unfamiliarity with his career, this insider might have been a serious contender for the nomination. But before the primaries began, he was regarded within his own party as an anchor man, the old reliable in the unlikely event that a deadlock developed over the nomination between Dole and his leading challengers.

Among the newcomers in the field, the most interesting was Steve Forbes, the financial magazine publisher who announced that his pet project was a flat 17-percent tax on all incomes—high, medium, and low—that would scrap the federal income tax as it now exists. A rival candidate at once called the Forbes approach to income taxes a "truly nutty idea" because it would place the greatest strain on low-income people, who were least able to bear the 17-percent rate, while letting the wealthiest, Forbes included, benefit from the relatively low flat rate for their level.

Such criticism, however, didn't bother Malcolm Stevenson Forbes Jr., who had inherited a fortune publicly estimated at $438 million from his father, the founder of the publishing house headed by the *Forbes* financial magazine. It probably hurt the forty-eight-year-old president, CEO, and editor-in-chief a great deal more than his tax critics when his rival, *Fortune* magazine, made light of his bid for a presidential nomination by attributing it merely to his unoriginal idea of how to sell more financial magazines. In any event, Dole was interested enough in the idea of a flat tax to interview Forbes eventually on the scheme, but he didn't seem in any great rush to climb aboard a 17 percent flat rate for all comers.

The Kansan didn't seem worried, either, by the last four in the field—Pat Buchanan, whom he dismissed as an extremist; Congressman Robert Dornan of California; a former ambassador, Alan Keyes; and businessman Morrie Taylor. At the beginning of the primary elections, therefore, Dole seemed to have the advantage over his rivals; but he also had to find a solution to the seemingly insuperable handicap of being virtually a prisoner of the Senate if he emerged later in the spring as the presumptive Republican presidential candidate—a role the party's national convention in August would speedily confirm.

Overshadowing all these purely political considerations and the thing that really handicapped Dole as Clinton's prospective opponent was the fantastic performance of the Dow-Jones averages to more than double that of the Reagan years—evidence of the financial community's belief in the nation's economic strength. Barring the unlikely event of a financial setback during the ensuing presidential campaign, that strength would deprive the Republicans of their most powerful issue against a Democratic president seeking reelection. And because Clinton had also been able to maneuver the nation's armed forces into peacekeeping assignments rather than all-out war in the style of Bush's Persian Gulf offensive, that issue also could not fairly be used against the Clinton White House.

It appeared, therefore, that if Dole became the party's standard-bearer, he would be limited to what he called the "character issue" against the president—everything from the suspicions over Whitewater and the Madison Guaranty scandals to the allegations of the successor to Gennifer Flowers, a former campaign worker named Paula Corbin Jones, who had lodged a sexual harassment law suit against the president. In a few words, a dirty campaign in which mud could fly in all directions.

Despite the favorable outlook for the economy, however, there was no reason to believe that the lords of Wall Street would be able to spread their riches across the land. Nor was there any guarantee, even among the politically elect, that the conditions of the hard-pressed working class and the desperation of the poor could be relieved to any marked degree.

The corporate down-sizing movement was continuing to cost veteran workers tens of thousands of jobs, even though the administration boasted of more new jobs than those that were being lost. Yet, rather than encourage the working class by supporting the administration's proposal for a 90-cent-an-hour increase in the minimum wage to $5.15, Dole was still putting up strenuous objections. And as for the poor, he was all for clamping down on public welfare at the federal level.

The truth of the position of the financial community, therefore, seemed to be that the lords of Wall Street were first taking care of their own. Under the circumstances that dreadfully stormy winter, what the president was doing often on his trips to disaster-stricken areas was to deliver federal funds to places where the need was greatest. For that, he didn't need congressional approval.

As a result in that presidential election year, the Republican outcry against presidential disaster relief was greater than usual. The accusation against the White House was that Clinton was delivering grants of emergency aid to areas of political importance to him—such as California, Texas, Florida, and the New England states.

The charges, so the Democrats responded, begged the question. What, they asked, was the president to do? Withhold help from hard-hit parts of the country? But the uproar continued, together with rising outcries for help, as the damage from winter storms increased and presidential visits with emergency funds became a part of the American scene.

This is what it was like in America at the outset of that election year, with Senator Dole campaigning for the Republican nomination and trailing President Clinton in the polls. The fortunate still earned vast profits in Wall Street, and the majority still viewed a government too deadlocked to help them very much, except for disaster relief.

4 Clinton Cools It

President Clinton decided to delay opening his campaign for reelection early in 1996 while Senator Dole was occupied in always-costly primary battles. With a continuing drop in the public view of the Republican-controlled Congress, what the president apparently decided to do was to remain aloof from the opposition party's troubles. Instead, he not only took to looking presidential—his presence was always impressive—but he also acted the part with his increasingly frequent trips around the country and abroad.

Few could seriously criticize him for biding his time. According to the political gospel handed down by James Aloysius Farley in Franklin Roosevelt's era, the public doesn't pay much attention to presidential campaigns until the day after Labor Day anyway. And so far, the Republicans seemed to have tied themselves up as well.

At any rate, Clinton's journeys around the country on disaster relief that winter gave him the appearance of a caring chief executive who could deal effectively with the public's hopes for job security and protection of the family at home while also seeking to preserve peace abroad. But for all his affability and openhearted manner, the president was too much of a realist to assume that he could carry his early advantage in the polls into the fall over an old campaigner like Senator Dole, with thirty-five years' congressional experience behind him. In addition, a cautious White House publicity machine had tried from the outset to discourage the notion held by more enthusiastic Democrats that they were now in a position to recapture control of Congress and to reelect the president.

After all, the Republican lead in the House was more than five times as large as the party's six-vote advantage in the Senate; and considerably more Democrats than Republicans were retiring from Congress that year, with few Democratic replacements expected. Furthermore, no matter how far down in the polls Speaker Gingrich and his ultraconservative freshmen House members might sink, they still retained important constituencies across the land, beginning with the once-Democratic Solid South.

True, despite the damage done by the private corporate campaign of downsizing, the Clinton administration still contended that it had been able to create far more new jobs in its first four years, halve the nation's deficit, cut the cost of government, provide an earned income tax credit for working families, establish family medical leave, and bar illegal immigration that threatened American employment.

In approaching his reelection drive, moreover, the president had an opportunity to salvage his cherished program for universal health care for all American families that the Republicans had been able to block in Congress. Together with his pledge to "reform welfare as we know it," the Clinton health bill defeat had been accounted his most costly failure since his election in 1992. It was believed that both would be at the heart of his reelection drive once he decided it was time to act.

As for the long struggle over a balanced budget the Republicans had forced on Clinton with their two government shutdowns and renewed threats for worse tests yet to come, he had at least obliged a hostile Congress to back off for the time being. What the White House had won through the president's stubborn resistance to political blackmail was an agreement with the opposition to fund the federal government through election day in return for Democratic assurances of more cuts in appropriations for functions other than Social Security, Medicare, and Medicaid.

The reason that the Republicans had finally come to terms was self-evident. Congress, under Republican control, now had plunged to an all-time low of only 25 percent approval ratings in the latest polls, and as mentioned earlier, with Speaker Gingrich finishing a point lower.

To try to meet Republican demands for a less expensive program of federally financed public welfare, what President Clinton had done early that year, when pressed, was to resort to his familiar campaign tactic, adopting the substance of a Republican-approved position. In this instance, the White House had publicly embraced a radical program developed by a Republican governor of Wisconsin, Tommy Thompson, who was also trying to reform "welfare as we know it." The Thompson plan was tough. It offered wage subsidies in place of federal cash help for working single mothers, but only to those who found a job and went to work regularly.

Still, in his first public announcement, Clinton had apparently decided to make the Wisconsin Workfare program a part of his own revision of the welfare law, under which federal waivers would be granted to states willing to conduct their own policies in the field. The reaction, however, was far more critical than the president had expected. Senator Dole criticized him for having vetoed two previous Republican welfare proposals at the national level. And child welfare advocates assailed him for making it necessary for single mothers to find a job before they and their babies could be offered state support.

It therefore became apparent that revising "welfare as we know it" might well become a campaign issue in the fall. And in the end, the president eventually had to qualify his approval of Wisconsin Workfare, pending agreement on a method of seeking jobs for poor mothers plus an added provision that made fathers as well as single mothers responsible for their offspring.

From his earliest plans for his reelection campaign, the president emphasized his interest in promoting what he called family values, which necessarily cut across a number of issues and sometimes gave added meaning to important legislation that had been intended by a business-minded Congress to support industrial expansion. The president's handling of the Federal Telecommunications Act, hailed by Congress as a way of reducing consumer rates for telephones, cable TV, and electric utilities, also demonstrated the White House's interest in family values.

At about the same time, there had been renewed agitation by public-interest groups to curb TV violence as a means of reducing child crime. Ordinarily, this might have seemed to be of little consequence in a presidential campaign, but Clinton seized upon it at once to advance his own cause.

In announcing on TV the signing of the Telecommunications Act, he held up a small gadget in one hand, calling it a V-chip, then explained to the viewing audience across the nation that it could be used by parents to prevent children from seeing increasingly violent, crime-inciting programs on TV. The V-chip, as the president pointed out, would be required as a TV part to be inserted in any set manufactured for public use once the new law took effect.

The president also served notice that he would soon call on the TV industry as a whole to adopt the same type of code for categorizing sex and crime programs that the movie industry had been obliged to accept for many years. It was noticeable that the networks in particular didn't take very long to use such warnings for parents at the beginning of most sex and crime shows; but whether that warning deterred younger viewers is doubtful, although there did continue to be a decline in overall crime statistics nationally.

Once the president convened his White House conference on TV violence, as promised, he began with a stern lecture to the participants for further protection for the public from both crime and risque material in support of his concept of family values. That, with the V-chip, became a part of the White House reform program for TV; but overall, there still seemed to be no marked decline in the kind of objectionable material being broadcast. And as for the new computer-run Internet, there was no limit to the sordid sex scenes that were available, mainly to perverts.

Still, the president remained more in tune with public taste than the TV and Internet moguls; and so, given time, a certain amount of change in such programming was bound to come about. As an incidental commentary on Congress's special interest in the Telecommunications Act, it should be pointed out that a little-noted feature of the legislation removed all limitation on the ownership of radio broadcasting companies in the United States. Predictably, that lack of control set off an immediate urge for radio chain ownership and profits for the larger companies, which also had something to do with family values, even if it wasn't what the president had in mind.

Another piece of major legislation that was bound to attract attention in a presidential year was a White House panel's proposal to strengthen environmental standards against what was called a dangerous rise of polluted water and air in the United States. Although the Republican-dominated Congress since 1995 had been accused of chipping away at environmental standards for clean water and air, the latest panel report called for much stronger action across the land to stem the rise of polluted home surroundings and particularly polluted drinking water in some of the largest cities in the land.

Nobody who has ever lived in such metropolitan centers as New York City and Los Angeles, Chicago and Washington, D.C., had to be warned of filth in air and water at home and at work that was a real part of the menace to a decent life. Financial incentives to clear the air and to purify drinking water were at the root of the latest White House environmental report, but many of the proposed remedial measures appeared to be theoretical.

The most practical suggestion, and one that immediately attracted President Clinton's attention, was a panel plan for lower tax rates that might be offered to business and industry to promote greater participation to protect the public from the spread of foul air and dirty water. But mainly, their report was regarded as a counter to Congress's apparent indifference toward maintaining basic environmental safeguards and increasing legal inspection and control in heavily populated areas across the land.

The one part of the environmental crusade that was bound to grip public attention was the broadened anti-tobacco-smoking campaign that also had strong presidential support. In an election year, this support was of particular interest to women's organizations and other anti-tobacco groups, on the one hand, and to worried tobacco farmers in the multimillion-dollar industry, on the other.

As for the billion-dollar companies, always so ready with excuses and self-defense despite a record of 400,000 tobacco-related deaths annually in America, the spreading warfare produced stepped-up contributions to the campaigns of friendly officeholders in Congress and elsewhere. In the latest attack on tobacco-related fatalities on teenage smoking, a congressional inquiry disclosed that cigarette companies in some instances had deliberately increased the nicotine content of cigarettes. Those who so testified were, in the main, former tobacco employees who were promptly dubbed whistle-blowers, to which a solid line of tobacco executives swore, with raised hands, that the charge was false.*

The anti-tobacco witnesses contended before Congress, however, that the secretly conducted nicotine boost in cigarettes had been intended to hook more youngsters of tender years into smoking cigarettes, something that the cigarette companies' representatives also denied under oath at public hearings of the congressional investigative committee. Still, more former tobacco employees with knowledge of the truth kept insisting before the investigators that Big Tobacco was at fault; and in consequence, the Food and Drug Administration kept threatening to declare nicotine a dangerous drug.

Before long, Philip Morris, the largest of the accused group of industrialists in this carnival of smoking deaths, made an extremely limited offer to cooperate with President Clinton's proposal to protect teenagers from the smoking habit: A Philip Morris executive agreed to the president's proposal to keep cigarette billboard advertising at a certain distance from schools.

It really wasn't much of a concession, given the government's verified claims of steadily increasing deaths by the hundreds of thousands that were attributed to the use of tobacco and its derivatives. But it was at least a small sign that Big Tobacco was taking this campaign seriously, although its claims of virtue continued unchecked and its profits still soared into the billions. And despite governmental threats to outlaw nicotine as a poisonous drug, nothing happened.

The evidence against Big Tobacco mounted, however, to such an extent that more than a score of states filed class-action suits against

---

* Later in that presidential election year, according to an ABC-TV report, most if not all the oath-taking executives had been replaced some months after they returned to work.

various tobacco companies to recoup payments of Medicaid and other expenses of its citizens who were suffering from illnesses induced by tobacco smoking. True, such legal offensives had been filed by individuals and government agencies for half a century or more without result; but now the evidence was frighteningly clear, and there seemed to be a better chance for damage suits.

Still, the outlook remained mixed. On the side of Big Tobacco, the Supreme Court early in that presidential year had rejected one large class-action suit. But on the side of the public, the Liggett group, one of the smallest of the Big Tobacco group of companies, was reported to have settled another such class-action suit without going to trial. In return for being freed of the legal threat, Liggett's lawyers contended that their agreement was so qualified that it would be difficult to enforce.

Aside from these legal actions, President Clinton, in his enthusiasm for defending family values, continued to be a major player in the effort to reduce teenage smoking through pressure on Big Tobacco to refrain from campaigns to induce children to acquire a habit that so often proved to be fatal. Of course, it didn't win Clinton any votes from such small potential victims; but the president did earn the gratitude of grateful parents. As for Senator Dole's part in these proceedings, he appeared to be too busy with his primary election campaign to pay much attention to anything else. But eventually, he was in trouble.

President Clinton wasn't able to keep his cool quite as easily early in that campaign year when he began bumping across potholes along the often-difficult highways and byways of foreign affairs. He discovered first of all that exhibiting American support for a favored foreign client facing a tough election wasn't always the best way to promote American policies abroad. When the president warmly embraced the cause of Prime Minister Shimon Peres on a visit to Israel early in 1996, knowing that Peres faced a difficult campaign against his Likud Party rival, Benjamin Netanyahu, it didn't bolster the always-shaky, American-suported peace arrangements with Israel's Arab neighbors. Four fanatical Arabs had turned themselves into human bombs by blowing themselves up and taking more than sixty Israeli villagers to death with them.

Despite the president's continued support of Peres, the Arab outrage strengthened Netanyahu's bid for power when he made the dominant issue Israeli security rather than peace in return for land, the latter being the Labor Party's program. Encouraged by Clinton's support, Peres warned Israeli voters that his defeat would endanger the American-brokered peace with the militant Arab states.

Similarly, President Clinton's support for a greatly weakened Boris

Yeltsin in Russia, whose presidency was endangered by a Communist comeback in another pending election, seemed at first only to add to Yeltsin's troubles. While Clinton was on his trip abroad early that year, he didn't give Yeltsin the kind of personal backing he offered to Prime Minister Peres; what the beleaguered Russian president did receive was a quick American-sponsored course in how to campaign for reelection on Russian TV that set him to singing and dancing as well as orating against his Communist rival.

Clinton was in a much better position to win support at home when he strengthened the American role in the far Pacific, which had been long overdue in view of the American bases in the area and the added military commitments, which included 45,000 troops in Japan and 35,000 in South Korea.

In yet another intervention early in 1996, the president visited the American peace-keeping forces in Bosnia-Herzegovina, part of a larger operation under UN auspices that was created to protect Bosnia's Muslims from renewed Serbian attack. This, however, was something more than a "show the flag" trip because Clinton had previously authorized the participation of American bomber aircraft in the first NATO air attack in the organization's history—an act that forced back the attackers and made possible, with American assistance, more effective UN peace-keeping.

On the way home from that trip, which had begun with the first Egyptian "antiterrorist" conference of 1996 and the campaign visit to Israel, President Clinton had stopped off in London and Ireland to try to repair that peace arrangement, which had been shattered by renewed bombings by the Irish Republican Army. Unfortunately, he didn't get very far with his pleas for peace there.

Even after the President returned home from these and other adventures, the extent to which he was committed to foreign affairs continued to take time and effort without much to show for either. When France insisted on new atomic tests in the Pacific following Chinese atomic blasts for the same indefinite political purpose, both American allies and client states sought American action to end such activities. But France, like the Communists in Beijing, paid no attention to American appeals, which were sidetracked even faster than Washington's protests.

But when the elderly Chinese mandarins began shooting missiles toward much smaller Taiwan across Taiwan Strait to try to influence a presidential election there, Clinton took stronger action. He ordered a Pacific fleet carrier task force into the strait between Taiwan and the Chinese coast. As a result, the missile attack halted, Taiwan elected an anti-Communist as its first president, and peace was preserved in the Pacific.

Just for good measure, American authorities then smashed a Chinese Communist arms-smuggling ring in the United States with at least two Beijing government officials included in a roundup of arrests. And some weeks later, the Communist state, under threat of a $2 billion American trade boycott, shut down domestic factories that were pirating American pop records and other entertainment.

It was in the midst of the Chinese missile offensive that President Clinton decided on his Pacific visit to encourage Japan's return as a military power and later also visited South Korea to insure continued peace there. Soon after his return home from that expedition, he had a welcome surprise when his protest to the United Nations was upheld against the violent action of Cuban fighter pilots who shot down an unarmed private aircraft in international waters, far off the Cuban coast, and killed four Cuban American civilians.

What spared the president further distractions abroad as he prepared toward spring for the opening of his reelection campaign was the reticence of Senator Dole to involve himself in all but the most necessary foreign issues that affected American interests. It was Dole's position as the presumptive Republican presidential candidate that Clinton's domestic record had to be the first and most likely subject of attack. The one nondomestic issue he emphasized was a refusal to endorse a new five-year term for the elderly Egyptian Secretary General of the United Nations, Boutros Boutros-Ghali, a position with which President Clinton agreed. The international community thereupon criticized both as well as the continual American refusal to pay about $1 billion in back UN membership costs and other fees. As far as the presidential campaign was concerned, at least in its earliest stages, political disagreements between the candidates still stopped at the water's edge. But even that seemingly unofficial truce was likely to be broken once the rivalry between the president and the senator took stronger shape in the fall.

Under the fervor of the mounting Republican attack, there was a limit to how long Bill Clinton could afford to cool it by maintaining an assumption of calm at the White House. It was one thing to hold off on endorsing the secretary general and shoring up an overly expensive and far too large international organization like the United Nations and quite another to continue to ignore an increasingly aggressive rival like Bob Dole. Before long, the president would have to come out fighting.

5   The Outsiders

Just before the primaries began in February, a mysterious boomlet developed for General Colin L. Powell as a more desirable presidential choice than either Bill Clinton or Bob Dole. Although the former chairman of the Joint Chiefs of Staff gave no encouragement to his amateur backers, the publicity barrage in his favor soon reached national proportions. Nobody had to ask, "Who's he?"

The Powell candidacy (it was of course assumed he'd want to run) was quite seriously discussed on TV's Sunday talk shows, the op ed page columns of the big-city newspapers, and many a home and fireside. Nothing quite like it had been seen in this country since the trustees of Columbia University invited General Dwight David Eisenhower to become the university's president as a prelude to his triumphal ascent to the White House as the Republican nominee in 1952.

In the case of General Powell, the argument for pitting him against Dole and his rivals for the Republican nomination was that no one had opposed President Clinton for the Democratic renomination, and it was too late now to try. And anyway, Powell's amateur promoters insisted, he was a natural for Republicans at a critical time, very much as Ike had been in 1952. Here, at last, they concluded, was another "great outsider" who had the background, the ability, the authority, and — most of all — the popularity to set the ills of government and the nation to rights. Besides, and this usually in an undertone of confidentiality, "Powell, y'know, had nothing to do with the crazy business of twice shutting down the government."

That, to sum up, was what strengthened the sudden campaign to elevate this latest potent military figure to the highest office in the land as the country's first black chief executive by grace of the Republican Party. And what about Dole? There were various answers plus the usual, being "too old"; and besides, he could go right on being the Senate majority leader, couldn't he? From then on, pending the opening of the primaries in which Dole already was widely picked as a hands-down winner, there were expert TV examinations of the general's position on the Republican ultraconservative religious agenda, with mixed results among TV debaters.

Some of the general's known beliefs were especially troublesome to the faithful, particularly his support of a woman's right to have an abortion if she wanted one. And while the Christian far right hemmed and hawed as usual over so advanced a position on women's rights in the United States toward the end of the twentieth century, a gallant attempt was made by influential Republican moderates to gloss over that embarrassment in the urge to find a gold-plated outsider like General Powell to rout Clinton and his Democrats from the citadel of government in Washington, D.C.

But it finally became necessary to determine whether the general was willing to run on the Republican ticket with a congealed platform and a plank that bound the party and its candidates to reject abortions for all women regardless of circumstances—a position that repeated polls had shown that women themselves opposed by more than 2–1. Apparently sensing that the time had come to make his own position clear in the matter of contesting with Senator Dole and others for the party's presidential nomination, General Powell—without giving any reason—gracefully removed himself from contention by declining to become a candidate for the presidency at the age of fifty-eight.

That, however, did not entirely discourage the promoters of the Powell boom. Now they turned to the possibility of linking him to the Dole presidential race as a candidate for vice-president. Dole took the suggestion with becoming seriousness, even journeying to Virginia early on during the primary election season when he learned that the general was active in supporting the candidacy of Republican Senator John W. Warner for reelection.

Although the meeting between the senator and the general appeared to have been courteous, it didn't last long. Powell wasn't interested in running for vice-president, either, as Senator Dole regretfully conceded to an inquiring reporter. The troublesome issue appeared to be the no-no to abortion in any form that the religious right had inserted in the Republican platform. As Senator Dole observed after his meeting with General and Mrs. Powell, there was little chance of the general's agreement to a vice-presidential candidacy because his wife strongly supported women's rights.

It was after the visit with the Powells that the senator, in the course of the primary campaign, decided to insert a provision in the Republican platform that recognized the vast differences within the party about a woman's right of choice for an abortion. But even though Dole himself still supported the outright party ban on abortion while conceding there was a strong opposing view, the religious right threatened a floor fight at the Republican National Convention. Accordingly, Dole's standing in the polls continued to show him trailing President Clinton long before the conclusion of the Republican primaries.

Even so, there continued to be efforts to link General Powell in some manner to the Dole candidacy. Bob Woodward of the Washington *Post,* in a book about American politics, raised the possibility that Dole, if elected president, would ask General Powell to become his secretary of state. Without confirmation from either source at the time, and given Dole's unfavorable standing in the polls, that appeared to be the longest of long shots. But that, too, was a part of the Powell mystique at a time when Republican chances for the fall campaign were faltering.

In the early stages of Dole's presidential campaign, the view from Texas also became important to him and his supporters for the Republican nomination. It was there, at his Dallas headquarters, that H. Ross Perot was calculating the chances of his partly organized Reform Party in November to register and perhaps exceed the 18.9 percent share of the total vote he had received in the 1992 election. Most public intelligence at that stage in the proceedings concluded that this nascent third-party movement was laboring through various stages of confusion ranging from mild to total.

Still, based on Perot's close to 20 million vote in 1992, he himself was entitled to collect $32 million in federal funds if he decided to run again, this time presumably as his party's candidate. The question was whether the federal authorities would let him pass that chunk of public financing to any other presidential choice of the Reform Party's convention—a decision that would have to be made by the Federal Election Commission.

But there were two certainties for the Reform Party and Perot long before its scheduled August convention. First, it would take much more than the federal money to finance a realistic run for a third-party candidate and, despite a steady flow of small contributions from its more that 1 million members, Perot himself would again have to decide how much more he could spend on another presidential campaign. Even though he still was worth several billions, his people were now continually appealing for outside contributions.

Among political insiders in both major parties, and particularly the anxious Republicans, the question was repeatedly raised again, as it had been in 1992, "What can Perot hope to accomplish?" The answer after four years was just as difficult to determine as it had been in the sixty-six-year-old Texan's first campaign. Once again, rumors surfaced that Perot's motive was a grudge fight against Republican chances because of a sour relationship he had had years ago with George Bush in Texas before Bush was elected vice-president under President Reagan in 1988. But now, Bush was far removed from the scene, and Senator Dole seemed to be as conservative as Perot himself, except for a difference in the degree of their opposition to abortion. And even there, both having at times been quoted as favoring abortion if it involved saving the life of the mother, little basis seemed to exist for ill feeling. Nor was the difference in age significant, Dole being only six years older. As elderly politicians, both seemed regrettably set in their ways and open to few suggestions for change. Nevertheless, Perot gave no indication of dropping his third-party movement.

What effect he might have on a 1996 campaign between Clinton and Dole at that early stage could be mere guesswork. In the first stage of his 1992 campaign before he suddenly quit on July 16, the Texan had had a temporary advantage when he led both major-party candidates in a few public public opinion polls. But when he returned to the race just as suddenly on October 1, he had to start all over again as a single-digit independent candidate.

Even so, he made a respectable showing in presidential debates against his major-party rivals, until his audiences perceived that he was seemingly obsessed with the notion that Republicans under Bush had been "playing dirty tricks" on him. He followed up with a story that was first published in the Boston *Herald* on October 23 and elaborated on the following Sunday, October 25, on the CBS show, *60 Minutes*. During the broadcast, he charged that unnamed Republicans had tried to disrupt the wedding of his daughter Caroline on August 23. Later, he was reported to have told the FBI that the same unnamed foes had planned to tap his six telephones and office equipment in Dallas. President Bush called the charges "crazy."

Despite so incredible a performance at the climax of the 1992 campaign, a total of 19,741,065 people voted for Perot as an independent against 39,102,343 for Bush and 44,908,254 for Clinton. Perot may not have won any electoral votes, which were being divided 270–168 between Clinton and Bush; but despite his strange accusations and his on-and-off campaign, the Texan still brought to the polls 12 million people more than the total who had voted for Ronald Reagan in 1984 against Democrat Walter Mondale—no mean achievement in itself.

In a warm-up for the 1996 campaign, a Reform Party convention in California heard an insurgent Democrat, former Governor Richard D. Lamm of Colorado, deliver a keynote address. Throughout, Lamm was also critical of his fellow Democrats and urged Coloradans and Californians to qualify as Reform Party members. Still, neither President Clinton nor his Democratic campaign staff showed concern over a threatened third-party race by a former New Dealer. At the time, the Reform Party had qualified for a line on the presidential ballot in only about twenty-five states.

A little later when the Reform Party's arrangements for a vote on a presidential ticket became public, it appeared that only two candidates, Perot and Lamm, had then received sufficient support to be listed as contenders for the party's presidential nomination. Arrangements were later made to send mail ballots to all the million or so members, from which the presidential candidate would be chosen. The result was scheduled to be announced at the opening of the Reform Party's convention in Long Beach, California, on August 11, the day before the Republican convention in San Diego, with speeches scheduled by the Reform candidates. After that, there were to be more mail ballots for the membership to choose the candidates for president and presumably vice-president, whose identities were scheduled to be announced when the party's delegates reconvened August 18 at Valley Forge, Pennsylvania.

Early on, the only acknowledged candidates were Perot and Lamm; but August was a long way off, and given Perot's key role as organizer and chief financier, together with his reputation for sudden changes in plan, it would have been hazardous to try to predict the outcome. But with the formality of the Democrats' renomination of President Clinton scheduled at their Chicago convention in early August and the proposed spread of the Reform convention to dates immediately before and after the Republican convention, it was apparent that the Reform ticket, if there was one, would be influenced by whatever developed at the Republican meeting.

During the interim, what Perot and his staff were trying to do was to form alliances with splinter parties in various states that already had places on one or more state ballots so that the Reform Party, with a change in name, could be listed on more state ballots. What happened in New York State was a guide for the future when Reform and an Independence Party joined forces after the latter gained a listing on the state ballot. Similar combinations were arranged by Reform with other small parties that already had listings in Minnesota, Oregon, and Virginia.

Perot seemed to be preparing for a battle in which he seemed to believe the Reform Party might change the course of the election by concentrating its influence against one of the two major party candidates in some of the key states—California, Texas, Florida, and New York among them. Just why he might be spending so much of his own money and making such elaborate plans for the growth of his Reform Party remained a major question for both the Republican and the Democratic Party campaigns. But to a somewhat greater extent, it was the Republicans rather than the Democrats who appeared to have the most to fear from this on-and-off, third-party movement, should it be able to field a credible presidential candidate and spend the money to make him more than a mere figurehead in the outcome.

For those who did not take Perot's charges of Republican "dirty tricks" seriously in 1992, the disclosure that year of illegal passport searches affecting then President-elect Clinton, his mother, and Perot are worth recalling, together with President Bush's subsequent embarrassment. What happened may not in any sense have upheld Perot's panicky accusations during the campaign, but the result of a postcampaign investigation demonstrated inexcusable tampering with passport files within the custody of the State Department.

The passport searches evidently had been based on a Republican suspicion late in the campaign that Clinton, then the leader in the 1992 presidential election polls, may have done some strange things while he was at Oxford during the latter part of the Vietnam War and had visited Moscow. Subsequent evidence revealed that the illegal inspection of his files may have had to do with a rumor that, at one point, he was so embittered by the Vietnam War that he sought to change his citizenship.

No support for the rumor could be found, however, either in the State Department files or in those of the British Passport Office. Just why Clinton's mother, Mrs. Virginia Kelley, and Perot also had their files illegally examined was never made clear. But after a postelection inquiry by State Department Inspector General Sherman M. Funk, Assistant Secretary of State for Consular Affairs Elizabeth M. Tamposi was accused of having ordered the illegal passport searches. Although she denied responsibility, President Bush summarily dismissed her just before the end of his term, even though she pleaded that she had acted on the basis of press requests under the Freedom of Information Act. After learning of the late-night private examination of his files, President-elect Clinton vowed that if anything like that happened under his administration, he wouldn't wait until election day to fire the culprit. To that vow, Perot soberly agreed, on the ground that the passport search constituted a "gross abuse of federal power."

In Perot's summation of his 1992 campaign at the end of his third and last debate with his major-party rivals, which was broadcast to the nation, he said:

> The question is, "Can we govern?" The "we" is you and me. You bet your hat we can govern because we will be in there together and we will figure out what to do and you won't tolerate gridlock, you won't tolerate endless meandering and wandering around, and you won't tolerate nonperformance. And believe me, anybody that knows me understands that I have a very low tolerance for nonperformance also. Together, we can get anything done. The president mentioned that you need the right person in a crisis. Well, folks, we got one. And that crisis is a financial crisis.

The independent candidate's conclusion in 1992 wasn't phrased and delivered with oratorical flourishes, but it evidently pleased the millions of people who voted for the Texan with the deep pockets. That very well may have had more to do with Bush's defeat than anything else; but the eventual result, Clinton's election, made a 100–1 shot the president of the United States. As he had said in that last debate of 1992:

> We can do better. And it's not tax-and-spend economics. It's invest and grow, put our people first, control health care costs, and provide basic health care to all Americans. Have an education system second to none and revitalize the private economy. That's my commitment to you.

No matter how well-meaning candidate Clinton may have been, President Clinton couldn't deliver on that grand layout of promises made at the end of the 1992 campaign. Voters who mused over past promises were entitled to ask during the 1996 campaign whether the president would be able to do any better in four more years. A part of the answer had already come from General Powell, who wouldn't accept Senator Dole's vice-presidential bid for the Republican ticket, and Ross Perot's promotion of a third party that was also bound to affect Dole's chances to send Clinton back to Arkansas. The outsiders would have much to do with the result of the presidential election of 1996.

6　Tip-off in Iowa

Bob Dole was still the front-runner for the Republican presidential nomination when about 100,000 Iowans straggled to their caucuses on February 12. Six days before, there had been a slight hitch in the proceedings when his conservative rival, Senator Phil Gramm of Texas, had lost a majority of neighboring Louisiana's delegates to the TV figure, Pat Buchanan, who took thirteen out of the twenty-one at stake. All other major contenders had paid no attention to Louisiana, however; and only 21,000 people had made the decision there at forty-two caucus sites, and so the vote wasn't considered significant.

Gramm himself had rallied his Iowa supporters for what was considered to be the first real test for all the candidates by trumpeting the challenge. "I am the only candidate who can bring together the social conservatives and the economic conservatives and beat Bill Clinton."

There were reports from Louisiana that David Duke, the former Ku Klux Klan leader, had supported Buchanan; but the TV orator refused to acknowledge KKK backing—something that made him seem an even more unlikely entry in the Republican sweepstakes. Gramm, at any rate, appeared to believe that his excellent Texas academic and political background, together with the $20 million or so he had raised for this campaign, would be enough to give him a good chance against Dole.

As he put the position to his supporters in Iowa before the caucuses began: "If I can run in the top three in Iowa, we're very much in this race. If I don't run in the top three, we're out of this race. So it's clear-cut." As for Louisiana, Gramm had no alibis. He did argue that Dole had turned on the heat against him, although he wasn't explicit about how and with whom his Senate colleague had injured him. And as for Buchanan, Gramm was specific in blaming the former KKK leader, Duke, and his racist followers for helping turn the religious far right against him. Duke then eagerly claimed Buchanan as his candidate.

Buchanan, at the time an unknown quantity in the race for the

Republican presidential nomination, was upbeat about his chances in Iowa — and in the nation as well. He said to reporters while the caucuses were under way, "Pat Buchanan can win this nomination and put together a coalition to win his election."

Steve Forbes and his $4 million war chest for Iowa alone was attracting more attention as a potential purchaser of the Republican nomination, however; and former Governor Lamar Alexander of Tennessee was being taken more seriously than Buchanan, the rank outsider, as Iowans prepared to give their verdict. A few of the news crowd showed nervousness over Dole's chances, even though their consensus was that he'd win that first important test in Iowa. Still, some like Peter Jennings of ABC-TV wound up their precaucus newscasts by guessing for the benefit of their millions of viewers that there might very well be surprises when the returns came in. That is what happened.

Although Dole took first place when the respondents from caucuses in the state's 2,142 precincts made known their choices, it wasn't by much; and the surprise that Jennings had anticipated was Buchanan's strong second-place showing in the crowded field. With 23 percent of the tally, the TV commentator was right at the heels of the Kansan, the majority leader of the Senate, who was only 4 percentage points ahead of him.

While Alexander finished third with 18 percent and immediately claimed that the party's presidential nomination was now narrowed to Dole and himself, the Republican leadership in the nation's capital didn't seem to be taking him too seriously just then. Buchanan had suddenly become a bogeyman — a far right extremist, as Dole called him, who was counting on scare tactics and the America First battle cry of another era to bring him victory. Unfortunately for Senator Gramm, the religious far right on which he'd counted for victory actually did split its vote between Dole, Buchanan, and himself; and so the Texan finished a distant fifth, with only 9 percent of the caucus vote. Even Forbes, whose campaign was estimated to have cost $400 a vote, came in ahead of him by 1 percentage point.

Senator Richard Lugar was buried in the field with only 4 percent, 3 points behind former Ambassador Alan Keyes and barely ahead of the also-rans — Congressman Robert Dornan and businessman Morrie Taylor, whose share of the vote was only 1 percent.

The prize in these caucuses supposedly was twenty-five delegates to the Republican National Convention, but Dole wasn't sure of all of them. More important, the nation as a whole now knew that Dole would not have an easy time of it in his third and presumably last bid for his party's presidential nomination. For if so few Iowa Republicans and independents thought enough of him to support him in the caucuses and brought in Messrs. Buchanan and Alexander as close rivals, then the Kansan's bid for the highest office in the land was already in trouble.

The forthcoming primary election in New Hampshire, therefore, might not settle much of anything; but it surely would show whether Buchanan was just an accident and Alexander an also-ran. And of equal value, New Hampshire would demonstrate whether Dole, after two previous losses in presidential primary years there, now at last would have major appeal to the state's Republican and independent voters.

The biggest loser in Iowa was Senator Gramm, who withdrew from the contest two days after his fifth-place finish saying, "When the voter speaks, I listen, especially when the voter is saying someone else's name." The name he was referring to was Dole's in the apparent belief that the contest for the conservative vote and the church vote lay entirely between him and his Senate colleague. Evidently, he hadn't learned from his mistake in brushing off Buchanan in Louisiana that the blustering TV broadcaster was in the process of attracting the bulk of the conservative vote that wasn't already committed to Dole.

To the end, Gramm believed — as he put it — that he was "the only conservative alternative to Dole." And even Dole, despite Buchanan's close second-place finish in Iowa, still appeared more concerned about Forbes and his millions than the colorful and embattled Buchanan. The unpalatable truth was that the earnest, owlish, graying Gramm — despite his war chest — hadn't lit any bonfires among a worried electorate. He'd preached the conservative gospel of balancing the budget and so on, when Iowans, who feared for their jobs in the corporate "downsizing" of America wanted somebody to speak up for them. Even Dole had failed to address the issue that was attracting so much of the blue-collar and lunatic fringe vote to Buchanan, who had nearly caught him in the caucus vote.

"In the end, people opted for the more fiery presentation of their views that Buchanan gives," said Charles Black, one of Gramm's chief campaigners. Consequently, it was likely that Gramm would need both his best efforts and the remains of his war chest in the fall reelection campaign for his Senate seat, probably the determining factor in his decision to drop out of the presidential contest.

By contrast on the day Gramm withdrew, the way in which Buchanan attracted the attention of both the fearful and the malcontents among the voters demonstrated how anger and passion, even at this late date in America, can sway dissatisfied and, at the fringes, even panicky people. Dashing into Manchester immediately after throwing a scare into Dole in Iowa, the TV figure electrified a New Hampshire audience by shouting, "Look what's going on in our country, my friends. When

AT&T lops off 40,000 jobs, the executioner that does it, he's a big hero on the cover of one of those magazines and AT&T stock soars."

As the crowd roared its approval of Buchanan's attack on big business, he followed up, "We got to have a new conservatism of the heart that looks upon all Americans as brothers and sisters. We got to be concerned about all of our folks." What did the candidate propose to make more jobs at better pay, cause homes to be more secure, and keep the national economy from slowing? Once again, he resorted to the simple and wrong-headed approach of the America First orators of the 1930s. He proposed fencing in America quite literally to keep illegal aliens, mainly Mexicans, from seizing American jobs; halting the loss of jobs to other foreign competition by slapping import taxes on uncooperative countries, specifically Japan and China; repealing American membership in world trade groups like the North American Free Trade Agreement; and lifting the burden of taxation from the middle class.

This was red meat compared to the puffed rice that Dole, for one, had been offering his audiences. But such oratory was not without appeal as well to the bigots — white supremacists and other extremists who were flocking to Buchanan's standard, even though he professed to discourage them by dropping campaign operatives who were known members of such groups as well as professional anti-Semites.

He also hacked away at basic conservative themes — antiabortion; prayer in the schools; and down with gays, lesbians, and big government, among other standard positions of the far right. But above all, he was a crowd pleaser, as he had already proved in Iowa and was carrying on at once in the New Hampshire campaign. When he wasn't peppering Dole, Alexander, and their supporters, he was tearing into President Clinton and the first lady with humorous intent. There was no doubt that the usually conservative crowds loved it when he mocked Clinton for adopting several conservative positions. "Next week, he'll be up here in New Hampshire with the gunowners, holding an assault weapon over his head, wearing one of those camouflage outfits, and saying, 'Don't try to take may fahr-arms away from me.'"

Such performances as these put him in a class with some of the old America First and hate crowd of another day — Huey Long, Father Charles Edward Coughlin, and the rest of their kind who surged to public prominence in the FDR era before World War II. But it was a part of Buchanan's routine to deny such associations, just as he so frequently had to deny Facist and anti-Semitic views, the latter originating mainly because he advocated American reversal of the recognition of Israel.

But for all that was held against him, his opponents soon realized in New Hampshire, as they already had discovered to their cost in Iowa, that this intensely active and colorful stump speaker was a personality who had to be reckoned with in this 1996 presidential campaign. Mistrust him or not, he had crowd appeal; he knew how to get steady publicity, even from TV and newspaper moguls who hated his guts; and he considered himself a match for President Clinton as a campaigner.

After Iowa, so did the third-place finisher, Lamar Alexander, who now repeated the line that Dole, though a distinguished American, was too old for the job. It wasn't a view that caught on with either the Republican party officials in Washington, the party's faithful across the land, and certainly not with the senator himself. He wasn't about to step aside to let this Tennessee politician take over a moderately conservative position as the nominee who would oppose President Clinton in the fall. Moreover, to a lot of Alexander's critics in Tennessee, he still had some explaining to do to account for the money he had accumulated while in the highest office in the state.

It was also strange that the former governor heaped abuse on Senator Dole and otherwise pursued the negative course he denied he had adopted because he usually spoke in gentle, even wheedling tones. For a seasoned politician and a former university president, he was a study in opposites in both what he did and what he said.

His position on public welfare was an example of the oddities of his approach as a candidate for the Republican nomination. What he proposed for welfare, so he said in his first campaign appearance in New Hampshire, was to do away with federal welfare funding altogether and to distribute it to the states. There, he added, welfare funds "would be spent at home through neighborhood charities, through girls' and boys' clubs, through emergency shelters. It takes a much bigger heart to say 'I will help you' than to say, 'I will hire the government to help you.'" The absurdity of putting children to work for needy families by authorizing them to dispense welfare funds, let alone the creation of still more emergency shelters for the poor and homeless in the hands of private charities, did not seem to register with Alexander.

It was also his notion that, if he didn't pay any attention to Buchanan, the TV orator would go away and leave the contest mainly to Dole and the former governor. But Buchanan wasn't about to disappear. On the contrary, he let Alexander have a few jabs now and then, to which the latter responded in kind. "The future," Alexander said of his campaign, "represents new ideas. Senator Dole represents not many ideas, and Buchanan represents the wrong ideas."

That, in brief, was how he came to be accused of running a negative compaign while denying that he was doing so. It didn't seem to be going over very well in New Hampshire to begin with. But Alexander's biggest problem, aside from how he earned his own fortune, was that he seemed to be extremely short of campaign funds; and his continual suggestions that Dole step down didn't bring him any help from the leaders of his party. It seemed obvious that Alexander would have to win a few primaries fairly soon or see his hopes for the Republican nomination dissolve.

For Forbes, the other multimillionaire who headed for New Hampshire after failing to make headway in Iowa, the position there seemed even weaker. In a televised interview shortly after hearing the bad news in Des Moines, Forbes candidly admitted that he had adopted the wrong strategy in trying to flood the air waves with negative ads disparaging Senator Dole and others seeking the nomination. He pledged reform, but that didn't necessarily mean sweetness and light.

As an amateur politician, he now looked the part instead of pretending to be the tough outsider who would bowl over all the career politicians, get himself elected to Washington with an advertising campaign, and then somehow put through his 17-percent-flat-tax notion. The first thing that seemed to be downplayed in the "new" Forbes campaign, in fact, was the flat tax that had been so violently criticized as a way of letting the rich keep their profits and inheritances.

Instead, three new commercials were unveiled in New Hampshire for TV use in Forbes's campaign there, dealing respectively with the problems of education, parents, and health care. Although all were crisp, commercial thirty-second spots, they didn't seem to do very much to advance the multimillionaire's chances for the Republican nomination. What the ads did was to try to change his image from that of a ferocious anti-Washington magazine publisher to a rather mild-looking, middle-aged candidate with a shy, often mechanical smile, a hesitant handshake, and not very much of a prospect for the highest office in the land.

The only candidate of the nine seeking the nomination who fared worse was Senator Richard Lugar, the insider in the field who could honestly and fairly be depicted as an expert on American foreign policy. But that, too, was the way American politics worked during presidential elections toward century's end.

7 The Long, Long Trail

It is an American tradition, born mainly through Yankee stubbornness and local pride, that the first votes for presidential nominees are cast in New Hampshire. To stay ahead of rivals for the honor among the other forty-nine states, including the largest and most powerful, the little Granite State has steadily advanced the date of its choices for Democratic and Republican leadership until the length of the entire campaign exceeded nine months toward century's end.

For 1996, it is true, Iowa's caucuses stole the lead in the weary march down the long, long political trail by a few days in February; but there was consolation for New Hampshire because the caucuses were said to be only straw votes. The *real* first test at the voting machines, so the argument went in the middle of Yankeeland, would be on February 20, when New Hampshire would announce to the nation at large whom it favored for the Republican presidential nomination—Senator Dole, Buchanan, Alexander, Forbes, or their four lesser rivals. The last, Senator Gramm, had already been knocked out in Iowa.

The Democrats, still watching the Republicans cut each other up, were solidly behind President Clinton for reelection; but the wary Clinton, viewing developments from the White House, continued campaigning in his own style by picking up the indications from Iowa of public anxiety over jobs and an economy that favored the rich while penalizing the hard-working middle class and pauperizing the even less fortunate across the land.

It was reasonably clear, therefore, that the furious battle between the president and the new Republican Congress over budget balancing had, in the end, amounted to very little. The public at large had been too busy trying to make ends meet, except, of course, for the lucky ones who shared in Wall Street's gigantic profits.

If the reaction of the people in the nation's news business meant anything, hundreds of them had converged on New Hampshire to see what Dole could do with such unexpected rivals as Buchanan and Alexander. Elsewhere, many millions of prospective voters across the country were also watching the Granite State's vote. This is not to say that New Hampshire would influence the other forty-nine states in any decisive manner; that kind of reaction was more likely to come from California, Texas, or Florida.

Still, first impressions could not be discounted in a presidential year, especially when it was emphasized that no Republican had ever won the presidency without first winning in New Hampshire. Moreover, New Hampshire was also being blamed for lengthening the presidential campaign by moving up its balloting and thereby extending the battle to what would have been unbelievable lengths in earlier years. Now, this extended campaign period would place enormous stress on Bob Dole as an elderly politician and send the cost of running for president to new highs.

But whatever the penalties, New Hampshire — with only 4 electoral votes out of the 270 required for a majority in the electoral college — was leading the parade. And although a large part of New England was buried in snow along with mid-America that harsh winter, the attention of a considerable part of the nation was on New Hampshire for first returns on the Republican nomination.

Dole should have felt at home in New Hampshire while campaigning for the primary despite the closeness of his finish in Iowa. But to the veterans in the news business who watched him working the voters from day to day, he seemed curiously ill at ease, even inarticulate, at a time when he should have been in top form. Instead of rousing his audiences in a state that had gone heavily Republican in presidential elections from 1976 through 1988 and narrowly went for Clinton in 1992 only because Ross Perot drained off a part of the Republican vote, the Senate majority leader seemed listless and uninspired. Often, he gave way to platitudes where he should have clearly outlined his position.

By comparison, Buchanan and Alexander, who had finished so close to him in Iowa, were working the electorate with their own brand of politics. Buchanan quickly found a ready response to his America First isolationist line, although Alfred M. Landon had tried it without success sixty years earlier, only to be buried by the 1936 Roosevelt avalanche of forty-six states to two. As for the more moderate Alexander, he put on a red-and-brown-plaid shirt and tried walking across the state in the snow to attract attention. The other candidates lagged for the time being, including Forbes, with his $4 million designated for the state campaign.

Dole's lack of spirit in his own drive was attributed by some of his well-wishers to uninspired speech writers. Others believed him to be overly cautious while trying to control his celebrated temper. Even so, he *did* draw largely sympathetic crowds; but all too often, he seemed far too defensive as a supposed front-runner. All in all, it was an awkward position, not only for the senator but even more so for the Republican leadership that was counting so heavily on him to challenge and turn back President Clinton's bid for reelection. The opinion polls had already indicated that none of his rivals for the party's nomination were given much chance of putting Clinton down. And now, near a critical point in the New Hampshire primary, Dole himself generally finished at less than 50 percent in polls that matched him against Clinton. Clearly, something had gone wrong; but nobody in the Dole camp seemed to have any suggestion for putting more zip into the aging senator.

This was the position when all eight remaining candidates for the Republican nomination appeared live at a local Manchester TV station, a broadcast that was spread nationally by CNN five days before the state's electorate would vote. Here, at last, Dole had a chance to put down the pesky Buchanan and the softer-voiced but no less aggressive Alexander. The others seemed to be so much background, despite the political eminence of some and the enormous wealth of Forbes.

But it required no partisan of Buchanan's prejudices, which were so widely known among those with whom he associated, to concede that he made an impression in foreign affairs only by attacking American membership in foreign trade organizations—an area from which the country draws one-third of its income. He also professed not to be saying mean things about Senator Dole and former Governor Alexander; but he whipped back at them for bad mouthing him and criticized these imagined faults. "No heart, no thought, just attack, attack, attack."

What Buchanan seemed to resent more than anything else was Dole's frequent charge of extremism, based on the broadcaster's white supremacist and anti-Semitic associations, including his nasty habit of mocking Jewish officeholders in the federal government by stretching out their names as if even they were objectionable to him. He also lumped Latin Americans into a group, with a contemptuous reference to "José," as if that name in itself were a condemnation of sorts. But when he was called a racist, he cried foul. To such attitudes as these, repeatedly exhibited on the stump and echoed in that night's appearance with the others, Dole commented toward the end of the program, "Pat's really gotten carried away tonight.... Did you have a bad day or something?"

Dole himself took off in a mild way at some early Forbes commercials in which pictures of the senator's wife and dog were used. He gave photos of each to Forbes, with a request that he use decent likenesses if he persisted in sponsoring negative advertising. Then came this shot from the senator to the multimillionaire, who had never held public office. "I know your problem. You have lot of money. You want to buy this election. But this election is not for sale."

To Alexander, who also complained as another target of Dole's negative advertising, the senator retorted, "I didn't know anything about negative advertising until I saw you use it against Pete Wilson [the governor of California]." Yet, Alexander gamely tried to show that he also had positive attitudes with some laudatory remarks about the benefits he promoted in education and job training when he was secretary of education. He also dwelt on his proposal to form a new unit of the armed forces to be assigned to border patrol to keep out unwanted Mexicans.

But neither Buchanan nor Alexander, as the second- and third-place finishers in Iowa, showed any brilliant insights as qualifications for high elective office. Both looked like overly anxious politicians trying to act presidential before a big vote in a small state.

Buchanan had still another problem. On the night of the broadcast in Manchester, he had to get rid of his cochairman, Larry Pratt, who had been publicly identified as a regular participant in white supremacist and anti-Semitic meetings. Pratt argued implausibly that he didn't know the purpose of such meetings and said that he despised hate groups; but the act was unconvincing. Exit Pratt.

As for Alexander, the *Wall Street Journal,* with the largest daily circulation in America, critically examined some of his expenditures as governor of Tennessee; and the Associated Press looked into his rise as a multimillionaire while in public office. The candidate responded that he had done nothing wrong.

All that activity was preliminary to the news out of New Hampshire on February 20 that Buchanan beat Dole by 2,000 votes for the state's Republican delegates, with Alexander as a strong third, Forbes a distant fourth, and the rest of the candidates in single-digit percentages of a vote by substantially fewer than 200,000 people — less that a quarter of the eligible electorate. Buchanan could not be blamed for bubbling over as he savored his upset victory over the supposed front-runner. "Nothing as significant as this has happened within my lifetime." A more serious estimate came from one of the most distinguished Republicans in the nation, former Senator Howard H. Baker Jr. of Tennessee, who had been Alexander's campaign manager. "We Republicans are tearing ourselves apart."

The outmaneuvered Dole, in refusing at first to concede defeat, predicted nevertheless,

> It's going to be a one-man race before long, but right now it's a two-man race. We know that we're in a fight for the heart and soul of the Republican Party. That's what this race is going to be all about.
>
> We will decide if we are the party of fear or of hope, if we are the party that keeps people out or brings people in, and if we are angry about the present or optimistic about the future.

Whatever Dole said, however, he could scarcely conceal the blow that someone coming out of nowhere like Buchanan had dealt to the Republican Party and its leadership. Even so, despite the Democrats' gratification over the slump in the opposition's fortunes, President Clinton reacted with caution. Commenting on Buchanan's victory, he said merely, "This country doesn't need another pundit."

As for the Republican leadership, former Senator Baker had said it all. No one high in the party was supporting Buchanan at that juncture. Instead, General Powell, who had declined to be a candidate for the nomination, now took to viewing the party's prospects in November with concern. With regard to Buchanan's New Hampshire triumph, he said, "Pat sometimes gives out messages that are of intolerance, which I think is very unfortunate. This is not the time for intolerance. This is the time for inclusion." And in regard to Buchanan's thesis of renewed isolationism, including the fencing in of the entire Mexican border, General Powell responded, "We can't pull up our drawbridges and withdraw back into our own continent."

The rest of the party's leaders seemed divided between accepting Buchanan's mob appeal as a reality and preparing for him as a possible presidential nominee or fighting him to the bitter end, no matter what happened to the party. Some also warned that a hostile Buchanan might make another third-party run like the Perot independent race in 1992 that put Clinton in the White House. It was truly an extraordinary position for the party of Lincoln, Theodore Roosevelt, and Dwight David Eisenhower so early in the 1996 presidential election year, with election day far removed on November 5. It wasn't as if the Democrats were rallying behind FDR, Truman, or John F. Kennedy; Clinton, first-rate campaigner though he had proved himself to be, had not yet established himself as a popular president, although he was slowly rising in the polls as the Republicans were declining.

What had happened as the field approached the fateful four weeks of March, when the largest and most important primaries would decide the nominee, was that the Republican presidential nomination was up for grabs. With the retirement of Senator Gramm, Buchanan now had the extreme conservative position all to himself. But Dole, as a moderate and still the choice of the party's leaders, had to share his constituency with Alexander and Senator Lugar as the decisive primary tests approached. Both these rivals refused to drop out; and even more critical, Forbes's multimillion-dollar ad attacks were beginning seriously to hurt Dole's chances.

Thus Dole had to do something in this extremity in order to stay in the race. Caught between the improbable combination of Buchanan, Alexander, Lugar, and Forbes after less than one month of campaigning, the senator rearranged his staff toward the end of February. Although he retained Scott Reed as his campaign manager, he brought in a new deputy in charge of strategy and advertising, Don Sipple, who formerly had worked for Governor Pete Wilson of California, and switched his staff of pollsters. The reason for the shift, he said, was that his message, whatever it was, hadn't been getting out; also, his ads had been too negative and his opinion polls too optimistic.

It did appear from the outside that Dole was particularly concerned over the damage being done to his chances by Forbes's negative advertising. At one point, he was quoted as saying, "Sooner or later, we've got to get out of these states where Forbes has spent a ton of money."

But Forbes was now beginning to emerge from the pack as a contender. On February 24, he scored his first primary victory in little Delaware, after spending about $400,000 in advertising there, beating Dole by 33 percent to 27 percent of the vote, with Buchanan a distant third. The publisher's first victory, however, won him very little respect from the rest of the field because he and the black diplomat, Alan Keyes, were the only ones who had bothered to show up in Delaware.

Three days later, with more massive spending on TV attacks against Dole, Forbes won again in Arizona and picked up another thirty-nine delegates; but the Kansan still topped him by winning seventy-five additional delegates in North and South Dakota. As the campaign developed, even though the senator never again had to worry about any critical loss of delegates to his opposition, the mounting effect of all the negative TV exposure took its toll on his lowered standing against President Clinton in successive public opinion polls.

Yet, Dole kept on winning primaries, regardless of his chances of victory in the general election in November. For better or worse, he was clearly the Republican's candidate for president.

8   Dole as Challenger

Senator Dole became the likely Republican nominee to oppose President Clinton's reelection in a brisk, six-week campaign with a string of primary election victories over a lackluster field. It wasn't so much a political triumph for him as it was a virtual abdication by the opposition.

The elderly senator still trailed the youthful president in the polls, however, without any break in sight. The Senate's long Whitewater inquiry into the Clintons' failed Arkansas land deal remained bogged down, and the court action in the case was weeks away from a verdict. But for all their wealth and bluster, the Republicans were getting nowhere in reversing the pro-Clinton trend in the campaign; and the White House was smugly, even recklessly overconfident.

As Congress took its spring break in early April, some of Dole's advisers were now insisting that the candidate should propose a leave of absence to reverse the trend in the presidential campaign; but neither he nor Mrs. Dole signaled any immediate decision.

Even though Dole had mounted to the peak of power in his party, his approval rating as a presidential candidate was still declining to disastrous levels against the president; political Washington knew something would have to be done soon or, in effect, the Republicans would have to concede the presidency to the Democrats, fight to retain control of Congress, and continue the debilitating status of gridlock.

As might have been expected, the White House had adopted a sardonic outlook toward the confused opposition and Dole's own reduced stature as a challenger early that spring. Even though President Clinton was in Egypt at the time, attending what turned out to be the first of a series of antiterrorist conferences among Arab leaders (actually, the purpose was anti-Israel), Vice-President Al Gore commented as follows on the Republican position:

> They're at each others' throats over ideology. Their statements are not aimed at mainstream voters. The performance of the Gingrich-Dole

Congress and the Buchanan-Dole-Forbes presidential race have by themselves put on vivid display the division and the rancor of the Republican Party. It is real hard for them to say no to the extremist elements.

The strategy of the Clinton campaign was simple enough. What the Democrats were doing, by linking Dole with the unpopular Speaker Gingrich and the almost as troublesome far-right candidacies of Forbes and Buchanan, was to use an impatient, deadlocked Congress as the center of their attack. Much the same approach had brought a hard-earned and entirely unexpected victory in 1948 to President Harry Truman, when he made a "Do-Nothing Eightieth Congress" the issue in his race against his overly confident Republican challenger, Thomas E. Dewey, then the governor of New York.

The difference forty-eight years later was that, regardless of Senator Dole's troubles with Speaker Gingrich's shutdowns by the One hundred-fourth Congress, Bill Clinton had yet to prove himself to be a gut fighter of Truman's character who could make possible his own reelection and a Democratic return to congressional power only two years after a lamentable loss to Republicans at midterm in 1994.

Clinton's "nice guy" image alone wouldn't be enough. Nor could he count on a virtual abdication of Republican efforts to stop his reelection, a hazy theory based on Dole's seemingly helpless attitude toward an uphill national campaign at the end of the primary season. It would have been a mistake for the Democrats to regard Dole's seventy-two years as a distressingly old age at a time when many an American male was living longer and enjoying it more, not to overlook the even greater life-span of American women toward century's end.

The Democrats also couldn't count on having everything their own way for the greater part of that excessively long and exceedingly expensive presidential election year. To be sure, the press clippings in early spring made agreeable reading for a relaxed White House that hadn't yet been put to a real test of its effectiveness in the 1996 campaign. But would it be able to match, much less outlast, the kind of blustering, no-holds-barred TV advertising attack of which the Republicans were capable in the climactic weeks of the fall? That, in effect, was the real problem.

The story of Dole's successes in his primary election drive for the Republican presidential nomination may be summed up, in political terms, as superior organization. Senator Gramm's religious following on the far right had been more sanctimonious. Forbes had had much more money (but probably less political sense) than anybody else, spending between $3 and $4 million in some states in an effort to buy Republican voters' loyalty. And Buchanan had wangled more TV time for his far-right oratory, so prejudiced and so ineffective after his few early successes. The others had just trudged along, as Alexander in particular chose to do by walking across some of the states in the apparent hope of gaining votes out of sympathy.

Altogether, the way in which the Republican primary spectacle was presented to the American public, it wasn't a particularly inspiring view of party politics in America toward the end of the century. Had Dole faced tougher opposition in his own party, his early mistakes beginning in New Hampshire might have been fatal to his campaign for the presidential nomination.

He would have been vulnerable, as later events demonstrated, had any of his opponents dared challenge him to try to change the Republican platform plank barring all compromise with its extreme position against abortion. The same was true of his early inflexible position against raising the minimum wage by 90 cents an hour. And on environmental and educational support, he was also hopelessly out of touch with the times.

But none of his opponents challenged him on any such issues. Instead, for the most part, they merely argued either that they could help the country more than he could or they were discouraging about his advanced age and lack of personal sparkle as a speaker and campaigner. One of the embarrassing incidents for the Dole campaign occurred before the Georgia primary in mid-March, when an Atlanta TV station invited the senator and three of his rivals to participate in a debate but failed to include Alan Keyes, who promptly began a hunger strike in protest.

After a clash with police, the sole black Republican candidate for the presidential nomination wound up in an Atlanta prison, from which Mayor Bill Campbell quickly ordered his release, together with the abandonment of all charges. The offended Keyes called his experience a "disgrace to American democracy," but it didn't seem to affect Dole's addition of Georgia's forty-two delegates to his total.

Dole's winning streak in the primaries began in South Carolina on March 2 after he had shaken up his campaign staff following his close call in Iowa against Buchanan and his subsequent loss to that far-right TV figure in New Hampshire. In addition to his earlier victories in the Dakotas and South Carolina, through "Super Tuesday" on March 12, the Kansan won fifteen straight primaries, which took him within reach of the 996 delegates he needed in August:

March 5—Maine, Vermont, Massachusetts, Connecticut, Rhode Island, Georgia, and Colorado.

March 7—New York, a big one with 102 delegates.

March 12—Florida with 98 and Texas with 123, plus Tennessee, Oklahoma, Mississippi, Louisiana, and Oregon.

After such victories as these, Dole crashed through for a majority of the delegates on March 19, with the "Big Ten" state votes, including Illinois, 69; Ohio, 67; and Michigan, 57.

Because of the critical Republican dependence on the party's stronghold in the South, the Kansan's emphasis on his campaign below the Mason-Dixon line became of the first importance to him. And it paid off. For what the realignment of his forces did for him in South Carolina made up for his losses in New Hampshire, Delaware, and Arizona and showed him to be a credible contender once again for the top spot in the party's national ticket.

Instead of the listless, uncertain candidate he'd seemed to be in the opening phases of the competition, he emerged from South Carolina with 45 percent of the vote, or about 123,000, as compared with Buchanan's second-place finish with about 32,000, a majority of about 81,000.

As for Forbes, although he was estimated to have spent another $3 million or more on his anti-Dole ad campaigns in South Carolina, he wound up with only 13 percent, or about 15,000 votes. At that rate, the publisher's costs amounted to about $800 a vote, double what he'd figured in his previous expense per vote. It says something about the caliber of the Republican presidential contenders toward century's end that these two conservative bitter-enders were the senator's main competition—shades of Dwight David Eisenhower and Ronald Reagan, not to overlook the shuddering ghost of Theodore Roosevelt, in the party's best years since 1901!

The remaining five contenders in South Carolina—Lugar, Dornan, Keyes, Alexander, and Taylor—with their returns in the single digits, had no chance whatever of catching up with the three leaders. With dwindling funds and no hope, they were continuing in the campaign only for the exercise.

The race in Georgia was much closer for Dole, primarily because Buchanan's rural constituency apparently linked his ultraconservatism close to that of their own guiding star, Speaker Gingrich. That made Georgia a much greater scramble for Dole and, had he cared, a considerable embarrassment for Georgia's favorite Republican son, Gingrich.

As an additional slap at the Dole candidacy, it was widely reported that Georgian exit polls showed that at least 35 to 40 percent of the voters confided to polltakers that they would have appreciated a wider choice of candidates. But Dole had better luck in the exit polls on the same subjects that were taken in the five New England states and Colorado.

In New York, Dole easily put down his remaining rivals in the first contested Republican primary in the Empire State in many years. Previously, the organization of the Republican state party had frozen out all but the favored candidate, Dole in this instance, who had the support of the party's tough state leader, Senator Alfonse M. d'Amato. Forbes, to his credit, had gone to court and won a favorable decision that put him on the ballot with Dole and the alert Buchanan, always the opportunist, and followed up by getting on the New York ballot in most districts.

As might be expected under such favorable circumstances, Dole came off well with endorsements from former President Bush and the latest dropouts, Senator Lugar and former Governor Alexander, who joined the first to fade, Senator Gramm. The Bush statement, which the senator seemed to prefer, referred to him as a "great leader, a great friend with great credentials for president of the United States, mature leadership and character, and things of that sort."

Even so, Dole's campaign manager, Scott Reed, barely waited until the New York polls were closed to blast Forbes as one of the senator's two remaining rivals, the other being Buchanan. Of Forbes, Reed said bitterly, "We've moved out of the states where Steve Forbes had spent $25 million running negative ads tearing down Bob Dole. He nearly got us."

With a narrowed field, there was little to stand in the way of Dole's nomination in the remainder of the primaries. But unifying so tattered a party for the fall contest against President Clinton was something else again as long as Forbes continued to spend his millions on "hate Dole" ads and Buchanan kept threatening a last-ditch fight at the party convention against the slightest change in the antiabortion platform with its proposal for a constitutional ban on the practice, without exceptions.

Forbes, as a wealthy neophyte with scant political sense, seemed to the Republican leadership to be the easier of Dole's two remaining primary rivals to argue into withdrawal; but the publisher proved to be stubborn. What he apparently wanted to do was to spend still more money and hang on through the March 12 primaries in the South, especially in Florida and Texas, in the hope of picking up enough delegates to give him bargaining power for his widely ridiculed flat-tax program.

Immediately after the New York primary, therefore, he hired a new adviser, Jack F. Kemp, former secretary of Housing and Urban Development in the Bush administration, who was promptly warned by Dole's man, Senator d'Amato, that he'd better stay on the sidelines. Kemp acknowledged that a Republican leader had told him that he was finished.

Perhaps Kemp had afterthoughts; for within a few days, he was musing to reporters about the possibility that Forbes might eventually drop out of the contest if he could be assured of a plank favoring his flat-tax program in the party's platform. But when Forbes was asked about his adviser's tentative suggestion, he rejected the notion of making a deal. As for Buchanan, even Speaker Gingrich gave up on that extreme right-winger, saying, "The longer Pat complains, the less effect he's going to have."

Coming up to the March 12 primaries, when about two-thirds of the Republican convention delegates would have been picked, Dole gave up on pushing the two holdouts aside, referring to himself as President Dole, and announcing his mission was "to unify the Republican Party, close ranks, and face the real political target, Bill Clinton." He continued, "That's my obligation, that's my responsibility, and I'll continue doing that over the next several weeks."

Although Dole took all seven primaries that week, his latest triumphs were not without cost. A combined Associated Press/TV survey team in Tennessee reported in exit polls there that about half of the voters contacted complained that the Kansan had no new ideas — a frequent criticism among voters in the other states that climactic week. In Texas, the same survey reported that 59 percent of those contacted in exit polls opposed the party's antiabortion plan, as did 55 percent of such voters in Florida.

Another of the features of that week's voting in the southern states (Oregon voted by mail ballot) was the admission of members of the far-right Christian coalition that anywhere from two-fifths to four-fifths of those who so identified themselves had switched to Dole from "other candidates," meaning the two last holdouts, Forbes and Buchanan.

That did it for the disconsolate Forbes, who finally gave up on March 14, after admitting his first venture into national politics had cost him $30 million. In the delegate count by reason of his first-place finishes in Delaware and Arizona, he still had fewer than fifty delegates, scarcely a figure to be reckoned with at the convention. Buchanan, counting on his extremist one hundred or so delegates, including a former Ku Klux Klan chief in Louisiana, still hung on to try to make capital out of his nuisance value at the convention.

When Dole exceeded the 996 delegates he needed in the vote in the "Big Ten" states on March 19, that marked the end of the race for the party's nomination. California, Pennsylvania, and other states with late primaries merely added to his delegate count, although Buchanan popped up briefly here and there just for show.

By the time Dole returned to Washington early in April after a two-week break in the congressional session ending on Easter Sunday, he realized his troubles had redoubled. Not only had his standing in the public opinion polls dropped to two digits behind Clinton's but his friends as well as foes were saying that he couldn't for very much longer continue to be the Senate's majority leader, the captive of a conservative Congress, and still make an effective run for president. Now Dole had to take time to think about his problem.

PART TWO

Changes of Front

9   Black Hole

Almost as soon as Senator Dole clinched the Republican presidential nomination in early spring, the steam seemed to go out of the 1996 campaign. For President Clinton, being unopposed for renomination and with a clear lead in the election polls, it was business as usual at the White House.

Campaign news, therefore, seemed about to vanish down a "black hole," the theorectical end of a collapsing star, as Richard L. Berke mourned in a New York *Times Magazine* article. All he could see ahead for himself and his rivals on the presidential assignment was a dull time until Labor Day, when public interest traditionally revived in a race for the highest office in the land. That, however, was five months off.

Barring an unexpected stock market collapse, a foreign war, or some other kind of calamity, the presidential contest seemed a less than exciting source of public intelligence, at least until the formal nominating conventions of the two major parties in late summer. Perhaps additional interest would also develop in August, when, at his new Reform Party's nominating convention, H. Ross Perot would finally decide whether he would be a candidate in a repeat of his 1992 run.

But for that spring and nearly all of the summer, there seemed early on to be a scant prospect of stirring up interest in the real campaign for the presidency in the nation's daily newspapers, now cut to about 1,500 from their top of 3,600 in the 1930s and even less in the increasingly scanty periods that the TV networks set aside for news scrambled with advertising.

Once the public, through party primaries, had been given the dominant voice in choosing convention delegates, which constituted a change from party bossism, the quadrennial presidential campaign was stretched out of all proportion to either the needs or even the desires of the pub-

This chapter appeared in a somewhat different form in *Nieman Reports* (Summer 1996).

lic. Boosterism tactics of states like New Hampshire, Iowa, and Louisiana to be the first to vote had also added to the problem. And so now, unless there was some unexpected development between early spring and late fall, there seemed to be little that any challenger could do to worry a sitting president, unless that president made fatal errors of his own that alienated public support. And that was how it happened in 1996 that the black-hole theory seemed to hold up through the congressional break for Easter vacation in mid-April.

Once it was evident that the presidential fight would be Clinton versus Dole, plus a Democratic effort to regain control of Congress in November, the news media couldn't sustain public interest in politics indefinitely. Instead, television, radio, newspapers, and news magazines were all caught up at the time in the fascination of the Unabomber story. Then, too, arrangements were being made concurrently for the trial of two main suspects in the Oklahoma bomb explosion on April 19, 1995, that took so many lives. And by evil chance on April 3, 1996, Commerce Secretary Ronald Brown and more than thirty others were killed in an aircraft accident in Dubrovnik, Croatia.

Still, the pollsters, with cheerful optimism, tried to soften up the masters of the air waves and the editors with reports on public attitudes toward presidential politics; but few such accounts appeared in the dozen or so newspapers that I try to keep up with. Even fewer polls were mentioned on the major networks and on CNN. All the evidence seemed to indicate, for the time being, that the presidential campaign was in a state of suspended animation.

In early April, the Detroit *News* carried a Roper survey for the Gannett-sponsored Freedom Forum, contending that 75 percent of American voters guessed that their news media have an unspecified "negative impact" on presidential campaigning. I suppose it may have pleased some editors, especially the one who ran the poll, because most news outlets were found to be fair and unbiased.

But as an afterthought, there was also a finding that 77 percent of those polled believed that the media had too much control in defining campaign issues and that 83 percent feared that candidates too often performed more for journalists and cameras instead of defining the issues, whatever they might be.

One of a series of New York *Times*–CBS polls reported in the Dallas *Morning News* at about the same time that Clinton was ahead of Dole by a comfortable margin, even though Dole was given high marks by respondents for agreeable personal traits, leadership, and his vision for the land. That particular poll, however, also put the Republican

Party's image at a low 41 percent approval, the worst showing in the twelve-year history of the poll.

It was even more embarrassing for Dole when he addressed a fund-raiser in Des Moines in mid-April after an Iowa poll had shown that, among Iowans, he lagged 17 points behind Clinton at 53 to 36 percent. That statewide figure was larger than a national *Time*-CNN poll issued at about the same time; but not long afterward, a CNN poll put out separately rated Dole as an even bigger loser, 25 points behind Clinton.

To Iowans, Dole said, "We knew it wasn't going to be easy"; but he bravely contended that he'd be running neck and neck with Clinton by election day. Nobody took the bet.

To be fair to Dole, a large part of his trouble throughout had been the balky Republican Congress that was absorbing much of the public's blame for the two government shutdowns, the threat of a third, and the growing economic squeeze on the middle class's income. When the senator finally prodded both houses into passing a weak antiterrorist bill sought by the administration, it was regarded as a personal victory for him.

But as for a 90-cent increase in the minimum wage and a greater degree of choice for women in the case of abortions, both of them favored by a majority of the electorate, Dole remained rigidly opposed at the time—a commentary on his limits as a so-called moderate. Yet, compared to the inflexible Gingrich and his screaming young neoconservative fans, the Senate's majority leader sometimes seemed to fit, however temporarily, the Gilbert and Sullivan definition of a "little liberal or a little conservative."

Of course, there were peripheral features in the national press now and then. The Chicago *Tribune* put this fetching headline over an article by Thomas Hardy:

> IF DEMOCRAT KERREY'S HEAD SAYS
> "CLINTON," HIS HEART WHISPERS "DOLE"

The relevant support for this apparent bit of mind reading appeared in the text, as witness the following about the mental processes of the Democratic senator from Nebraska.

> Kerrey comes across as almost grudging in his new-found respect for Clinton but he is unabashed in his long-standing admiration for Dole. Millions of American voters will be similarly torn in the style vs. substance choice for President.

A rare mention of the party conventions appeared in an unflattering article in the Denver *Post* by the Pulitzer Prize–winning writer, Mike Royko. He announced that he would leave his Chicago home for a secluded north-woods cabin without a TV set before the first Democratic delegate reached the city.

To Mayor Richard Daley of Chicago, who was bringing the Democrats to the city early in August, Royko presented his compliments by expressing the hope that the mayor would "suffer through the four full days of foolish blather." He also registered his dislike for what he called "that giant multi-headed beast known as the Media."

It was quite a switch to flip through the pages of the Detroit *News* and find a piece reprinted from the Washington *Post* about Elizabeth Dole, the senator's wife, and her prospective rival in the White House, Hillary Rodham Clinton. Both were law-school graduates, Mrs. Dole from Harvard and Mrs. Clinton from Yale; both, too, had distinguished careers as practicing lawyers. The reporter wrote:

> The public views the two quite differently. Among Americans with an opinion, three times as many like Elizabeth Dole as dislike her, according to a recent poll conducted by the Washington Post. Hillary Clinton fans barely outnumber her critics and she has some of the highest disapproval ratings of any First Lady.

For a Cleveland *Plain Dealer* associate editor, Jean Dubail, the issue for Easter Sunday appeared to be an urge to deprive members of Congress of their pensions. The idea apparently originated when Poland's Lech Walesa, a Nobel Peace Prize winner, had to return to work at a shipyard as an electrician for about 650 zlotys a month, or about $260. By contrast, Dubail went on:

> Democratic Rep. Pat Schroeder of Colorado, who is heading home after 22 years in the House, could take in $4.2 million in taxpayer-supported payments over the rest of her life. Sen. William Cohen, a Maine Republican, is due $3.2 million . . . .
>
> I realize that my proposal is not without flaws but I look at it this way: If it's good enough for Lech Walesa, it ought to be good enough for Pat Schroeder and Bill Cohen.

The Miami *Herald,* in the interim between the early primaries and the fall presidential drive, also had some fresh insights on national politics. There were two front-page articles, one on the sadness of the chef at Le Mistral, a popular Washington restaurant, because lobbyists by law no longer could buy lunches there for members of Congress; the other, a companion disappointment for Senator Ben Nighthorse Campbell, who had lost temporary employment as a model for clothing for the rugged outdoors. Political editor Tom Fiedler meanwhile expressed his regrets on the editorial page that the Miami city government seemed baffled by the challenge of the Miami Heat, a basketball team, which was demanding a new arena for its home games, partly at taxpayers' expense.

April 7 was decidely an off day for presidential politics, with only an Associated Press report in the *Herald* on Clinton's policy on gays in the military passing its first court test. In the Los Angeles *Times* for the same day, there was a report of outrage in Oregon over the failure thus far of the Clinton administration to halt logging in virginal Oregonian forests.

And in a worldwide view in the newspaper's Commentary section, a writer for the World Policy Institute gave assurance that Pat Buchanan's threat to reform the Republican Party was not as frightening as it seemed, with this hopeful view: "It [Buchanan's project] is a relatively benign sideshow on a global political stage fraught with ethnic, religious and economic divisions."

But the big story in the Los Angeles *Times,* as in most newspapers of that particular time, was still the Unabomber story, plus the continued FBI standoff in Montana with the accused criminals of the Freemen gang. What had happened in Washington was relatively far from the consciousness of editors out West.

There was, however, mild interest in the Houston *Chronicle* that day with a report that congressional Republicans had made a little progress before their Easter break. A Knight-Ridder syndicate report cited Republican budget cuts, the passage of farm and telecommunications reforms, others affecting small business, and the line-item veto to the president. But one House leader lamented, "We're not getting the credit we deserve."

The big *Chronicle* story, however, was the last stand of the Texas Republican conservative Senator Phil Gramm in the November election. A *Chronicle* poll gave Gramm a big lead over his prospective Democratic opponent, Victor Morales, a high school teacher and Vietnam War veteran who was also the first minority nominee for senator in the state's history.

But as for the presidency, the black hole seemed to have swallowed news of the Clinton-Dole race long before the turmoil of the fall campaign. Either that, or the editors weren't inclined to believe that their readers were interested.

For the Nashville *Tennessean,* like the rest of the national and statewide newspapers I try to follow, the big story of necessity had to be about the Unabomber, with the presidential campaign as a distinct side issue at the time. After a fashion, the *Tennessean* did recognize the run for the White House with a Hearst special discussing the aspirants for vice-president on the Dole ticket and a New York *Times* account of how Republicans and Democrats spy on each other.

Even for the Washington *Post,* where the presidency and Congress are local news, the editorial going seemed to be difficult when it came to keeping up with the Clintons and the Doles. Like all the rest, the *Post* splurged on reader interest in the Unabomber story, beginning on page 1 and jumping to two full pages inside. It would be an extraordinary day for a presidential candidate in 1996 to get that kind of attention, except possibly the day before the election. The one political story on the first page then was the end of the Maryland assembly session, coinciding with the congressional Easter break.

Mainly, there were discussion pieces inside the *Post* on three major candidates for Senate seats in the fall election, the odd twists of financial rules for presidential campaigns, the hefty outside legal activities of the untouchable Kenneth W. Starr, the independent counsel investigating Whitewater, and—in a reprise—of three men and a budget, meaning Messrs. Clinton, Dole, and Gingrich. There was also an appeal to the Republican Congress for mercy called "The Homeless and the Heartless" that was worth rereading.

It was apparent that the *Post* wouldn't follow the general trend outside the nation's capital but would attempt, either through innovative assignments or the enterprise of its staff, to keep campaign coverage in the forefront of the news. That also appeared to be the position of the New York *Times,* among others. During the primary elections, the *Times* seemed to have been committed to running two full pages of campaign news inside, plus page-1 displays. But once Dole was certain of the Republican nomination, even the *Times*'s coverage began shrinking.

Toward mid-April, however, the *Times,* evidently unable to accept the black-hole theory of one of its correspondents, ran an exclusive detailed analysis of Senator Dole's handicapped physical condition caused by his grave World War II wounds. Dole himself had cooperated with the reporter, Katharine Q. Seelye, and was quoted in the article as saying, "It's your ability that counts, not your disability."

In his comments about the coverage of his campaign, the Kansan occasionally expressed the feeling, matter-of-fact rather than embittered, that "the press is against us."

From my standpoint, having covered or observed almost every presidential election from the era of Warren Gamaliel Harding and the Teapot Dome oil scandal, the coverage of Clinton that presidential campaign year of 1996 was, as a rule, far more critical than the attention given to his Republican rival. And that figured, given the overwhelmingly greater corporate ownership of the news media, especially in network TV; but President Clinton tried to maintain relationships with the White House correspondents, even though, at times, Mrs. Clinton was not always as forthcoming. And no wonder! They hit her harder than the president.

What Senator Dole did have reason to be concerned about was not really criticism but rather a feeling, even among some of the veteran correspondents, that reflected less public interest about Dole as a presidential contender than in the president himself. And that, too, could scarcely be avoided. Inevitably, if the president was as well established as Clinton was, the challenger usually had to demonstrate early on his credibility as a worthy opponent. And from the evidence of the polls alone, Senator Dole had yet to do so when he won out as the prospective Republican challenger in the spring of 1996.

10 Emergency!

Strangely enough, despite all the criticism that was heaped upon President and Mrs. Clinton that spring by the Republicans and their allies, it was Senator Dole's campaign that hit rock bottom. His situation as a challenger to a sitting president may in some ways have been the worst since Alfred M. Landon of Kansas had faced President Franklin Delano Roosevelt in 1936.

This time, however, instead of the panicky era of sixty years ago, when the nation was just beginning to emerge from the Great Depression, another Kansan—Bob Dole—should have derived some benefit from a record-breaking high of 5,700 in the Dow Jones Industrial Averages on the New York Stock Exchange. That he did not made the polls seem suspect, but there was no Literary Digest to blame this time. No respected polling organization in the spring of 1996 showed Dole to be anything but a loser—and by substantial margins of from 20 to 25 points.

What had happened to the laconic, seventy-two-year-old Dole, a veteran senator and a leading legislator with a distinguished World War II record, confounded the expectations of the Republican high command after he had assured himself of the party's presidential nomination. And with election day more than half a year off, all his supporters could hope for was an instant reversal of his damaged candidacy that didn't occur.

Some of the fainter-hearted conservatives in Congress, the older and less crusading types, already were suggesting *sotto voce* that the party's always substantial finances might best be applied now to maintaining control of Congress and letting Dole fend for himself. But the party's stalwarts were growling defiance; and some were even wondering, just wondering, if maybe some means might yet be found to persuade General Powell to prop up the Dole ticket.

For the party's realists, however, the only immediate solution was clear. Dole could not go on running for president while being cooped up in a deadlocked Congress as the Senate's majority leader. For while Speaker Gingrich and the conservative House majority bore the brunt of public disapproval for twice shutting down the government during the winter, it could scarcely be kept a secret that Dole, for all his excellent qualities, had also shared the blame.

Dole and his wife had already come to the same conclusion independently. And so, in mid-April, after returning from a Florida vacation during Congress's annual spring break, he and Elizabeth Hanford Dole faced up to their problem with stoical courage. Mrs. Dole, having served in the Eisenhower and Reagan administrations with distinction, was confident that her husband could make up for lost ground; and he himself was ready to make the break with Congress.

Dole, by most accounts, shared his wife's belief that his thirty-five years of outstanding service in Congress would have to end, and promptly, if he was to have even a chance of defeating a sitting president in the November election. And he, in confiding to their friends, showed no hesitation in accepting his wife's judgment; but he reported his decision initially only to his campaign director, Scott Reed, then waited a month before making public his decision.

Why the delay? There were several explanations. Perhaps he had expected a change in his favor in the polls, or he hoped for a more sucessful attempt to repair the confused state of affairs in Congress. No matter. Neither of the Doles' minds was changed about his final decision. On the afternoon of May 15, in the presence of his wife and daughter, Robin, and leaders of both parties in Congress, Senator Dole made known his decision in these terms:

> I will seek the presidency with nothing to fall back on but the judgment of the people and nowhere to go but the White House or home. . . . It is in touching the ground in moments of difficulty that I've always found my strength. I have been there before. I have done it the hard way, and I will do it the hard way once again.

Dole's surprise resignation from the Senate inevitably created a certain amount of confusion that, although nobody's fault in particular, did have a predictable result. And because the announcement of his resignation had taken the party regulars as well as the country at large by surprise, there were many blanks in his immediate schedule that had to be filled in, preferably to the candidate's advantage. The announcement also seemed to have been such a complete surprise to his campaign staff that they sometimes didn't quite arrange his schedule to fit that of a presidential contender.

The Doles' visit to their condominium in Bal Harbour, Florida, over the weekend of May 18 was a case in point. Evidently, somebody on his staff had developed the notion that Dole's appearance at a stock car racetrack in Charlotte on Saturday night, May 18, would help his campaign in North Carolina. Being agreeable to almost anything that might bring him votes just then, Dole surprised the stock car racing fans by appearing just in time to wave in greeting and to signal the drivers to start their engines.

On Sunday night, May 19, he made another surprise appearance at an anti-Castro rally in Miami, where he delivered a three-minute attack on Premier Fidel Castro and his Cuban regime. The next day, he and Mrs. Dole stopped en route to Washington at Largo, where he spoke briefly before a hastily assembled audience on his ideas about education.

What happened to him that weekend from Washington to Bal Harbour and return would have caused an uproar among candidates for the New York City Council from Sheepshead Bay, Brooklyn. But Dole's only comment was an offhand remark that, well, he couldn't be resigning every day and that the staff would now be working to pull everything together. The staff also needed time to readjust to Dole's disappointing position in the latest polls, even those that were friendly to his cause.

How long the rescheduling would take, nobody could even begin to estimate; but, undoubtedly, the candidate's affairs would begin to improve once his resignation from the Senate took effect, or so he hoped. As he once said, somewhat resignedly, while facing the prospect of strenuous political activity during the summer, "I can't quit the Senate every day." It did seem, for the time being, that the excitement over his leave taking had died down far too quickly to have any lasting effect on his chances.

If he could at least stay within reach of the fast-traveling Clinton until convention time that summer, so his advisers seemed to calculate, he still might be able to close the gap once the campaign began in earnest after Labor Day. But as even the most optimistic among his party's leaders agreed, it still would be a mighty chancy business unless there was a dramatic change in the nation's affairs.

Although embarrassed by having reached the legal limit of $37 million during his campaign for the presidential nomination with no more funds available to him just then under federal election laws, Dole now embarked on a punishing schedule of seventeen speeches before July 4 at key points around the country. And at last, these campaign trips began to attract major media coverage when fifty-eight reporters joined him on his cross-country ventures, beginning with trips to Chicago and later to California.

But despite such efforts, there was no immediate rise in his standing in the presidential polls. Nor did his critics inside his own Republican Party take a holiday. He knew he had a long way to go before he could show substantial gains on a confident president. For the time being, however, his advantage lay in his renewed hold on public attention across the land.

The black hole was covered. The drama of what his Democratic opposition called a "desperation move" seemed to have reinvigorated his candidacy. In token of his changed situation, he now traveled tieless with open shirt collar, sports jacket, and somewhat rumpled trousers, quite the opposite of his formal appearance and stilted language in the Senate. Also, he seemed to have acquired a new speech writer who was credited with enlivening his delivery.

But in his seventh decade, with almost half his life having been devoted to Congress, it was a good question whether Dole, like Dwight Eisenhower and Ronald Reagan, could now become the kind of Republican crowd pleaser that could win a tough election for the highest office in the land. It wasn't so much his age that made many wonder among the Beltway professionals; rather, he had yet to demonstrate that he cared enough about the hardships of so many wage earners and the goals of the women's movement to change his seeming indifference to the views of a substantial part of the electorate.

Would Dole, the presidential candidate, be able to change the views of Dole, the Senate majority leader, against the adoption of a 90-cent increase in the minimum wage to $5.15 an hour and moderate his intense opposition to any change in the Republican Party's antiabortion plank under any circumstances? These quesions rather than glittering generalities about the beauties of conservatism, as eulogized two centuries ago by Edmund Burke, or the current practicality of a tax cut for those who didn't need it might well be a decisive factor in judging the extent of Dole's conversion to reality as a presidential campaigner.

There was actually little difference at once between the new Dole and the old Dole, except for quick sallies within a week into Wisconsin and Florida as well as Chicago. A *Wall Street Journal*/NBC poll also appeared within twenty-four hours that demonstrated, to nobody's surprise, that Dole was now 17 points behind Clinton.

But because the senator had specified his leave taking would become effective on or before June 11, the transformation couldn't reasonably be expected to occur as quickly as friendly pollsters would have wished. And because the Chicago visit had occurred only twenty-four hours after his resignation announcement, it was evident that the candidate hadn't had sufficient time to do more than rephrase his resignation speech for the benefit of a hotel audience there. Between that speech and much handshaking among strangers, the former senator seemed to get used to the notion that he was leaving the old life within the Beltway behind him.

In Wisconsin the next day, Dole complained that President Clinton had adopted parts of Wisconsin Governor Tommy Thompson's plan for revising public welfare at the state level. "If this keeps up," the candidate said, "Bill Clinton won't have to make speeches any more. All he'll have to do is find out my stand on an issue and say, 'Me, too.'"

Those words were by no means a signal that the president and his Republican rival were anywhere near an agreement on a radical change in what the former had so often called "welfare as we know it." The disposition of welfare was still likely to become an issue to be debated on and off during the presidential campaign, except in the unlikely event of a bipartisan agreement on a more effective system of dispensing federal waivers to the states for the needy.

For the present, the White House staff provided President Clinton with an announcement that welfare recipients at the federal level had been cut by 1.3 million after his term began in 1993. Moreover, there was a routine notice that the president opposed Republican plans for revising welfare because they guaranteed insufficient care for children. And with that, the first Dole foray into the political hinterlands from the nation's capital ended not long afterward with his return.

The Clinton campaign team was already raising serious questions about Dole's right to use the funds of the Republican National Committee and the various state committees of the party for the presidential drive in the summer and fall. Of course, this was just another maneuver to add to the opposition's concern about Dole's ability to fill in the senator/former senator's time, and Dole didn't seem quite sure of what he was supposed to be doing or saying.

The Democratic argument, as reported to the Federal Election Commission, was that the Dole campaign, having accepted $12 million in federal financing, was limited under election laws to spending a total of $37 million that included $27 million directly contributed to the Kansan's cause. That fact, if the Dole campaign abided by the limitation, would allow it zero funds until it received almost $62 million in federal funds, appropriated from tax income, to finance the general election.

The problem with this allocation of mixed private contributions and tax money for the Dole campaign was that, theoretically, it left the Republican candidate without funds for the summer; and the White House crowd was determined to use the election laws to keep their opponent in a state of suspended financial animation.

The Dole campaign, however, resolved to dispose of some of its assets, at first advertised on sympathetic TV newscasts as a "political garage sale" of all manner of useful equipment, from computer terminals to office furniture, if necessary. The valuation placed on these assets was $1.2 million in late May, enough funds to keep the Dole campaign going through the summer at least in part. To which the White House at once cried "Foul!" with a contention that the value of the Dole campaign assets were "grossly overvalued."

That was just the beginning of the argument over the use of campaign funds (originally estimated by people familiar with the plans of both campaigns for TV ads and other valuable necessities at a total of several hundred millions of dollars). Of necessity, the Dole people then claimed the right, as exercised in the 1988 campaign by President Bush's Republican staff, of using the much larger funding of the Republican National Committee and various state committees as needed under activities "of benefit" to the varous parties.

That, of course, could mean almost anything, as lawyers for the Dole campaign argued; and even if the Federal Election Commission disagreed, there would then be so many court hearings on legal actions and counteractions by the concerned parties that election day would come and go before there was likely to be any final decisions, plus appeals seemingly without end.

What the Dole campaign staff actually did, anticipating such legal complications, was to pay little attention to the White House's complaints and to proceed to allocate part of their fund requirements to "benefit" the party's National Committee and other funds to various state committees. It was, as always, a highly practical application of the troublesome election laws and the necessity of obtaining the lavish funds needed to conduct TV advertising for a presidential campaign. The so-called political garage sale—limited as it was in its anticipated yield of funds—thus was held in abeyance.

If the Federal Election Commission acted against the Dole campaign for supposed misapplication of funds, the expectation was that election day would have come and gone, as was the case when there were proceedings against the Bush campaign during that president's victory in 1988. The Bush group's punishment turned out to be minimal; but because he won the election, it didn't really matter to him or to his party.

Still, if the Dole campaign took the same long-shot gamble and lost the 1996 election, the outcome before the FEC assuredly might be quite different. But then, the financing of presidential elections, especially since the advent of television, had always been a major problem in the United States; and it couldn't be disposed of with the voluntary offers of free network time just before election day to permit the candidates for president—Clinton, Dole, and any third-party qualifier—to argue their case before the public.

In the knowledge that the Democratic and Republican National Committees were each the repository of "soft money" in large sums during the current campaign, the director of Common Cause, Ann McBride, said, with good reason, "It's a scam, and everybody winks; but everybody also knows what's going on."

The scam wasn't about to change in 1996. The Senate's Republican majority filibustered to death a bill that would have forced both major parties to give a more realistic accounting of huge special funds they have always received to win elections for candidates who would "vote the ticket" as directed—that is, help favored business and special interests. Then, the most conservative Supreme Court in a generation or more voted 7–2 to reject current limits on party funds allocated to deserving candidates on the supposed ground that such gifts were made without reference to any request by the candidate.

In a dissent, Justice John Paul Stevens refused to go along with this part of the "scam," saying, "Current national expenditures by the two national parties are no less contributions to the campaigns of the respective front-runners than those that will be made in the fall." But the majority wasn't listening.

The only political organization that drew action from the Federal Election Commission in the presidential campaign that spring was the Christian Coalition, which claimed a membership of 1.7 million. Republican as well as Democratic members of the commission voted in favor of a civil suit in the federal court of the District of Columbia, alleging that the coalition merely posed as nonpartisan while actually supporting only Republican candidates in 1990, 1992, and 1994.

On that basis, the suit charged that the coalition's contributions for those years were illegal because they should have been differently reported by law. To that, for the Christian Coalition, the Reverend Pat Robertson responded by calling the suit without merit. The coalition's executive director, Ralph Reed, added his confidence that the court would rule in favor of his organization. Various liberal groups, however, commended the FEC for its four-year inquiry into the operations of the coalition following a complaint from the Democratic National Committee. No decision was expected until after election day.

11 The "New" Democrat

No matter what Bill Clinton may have thought of Newt Gingrich as one of his leading Republican critics, the president seldom hesitated in the early stages of his reelection campaign to pick up a likely vote-getting notion even from the Speaker. True, Gingrich had become decidedly unpopular to the public at large as the presumed author of the Republican government shut-down plan.

Extremists had even begun to refer to him as the male equivalent of a "Typhoid Mary," to wit, "Typhoid Newt." It followed, therefore, that friend and foe were surprised to learn that, one fine spring day, the president sent Gingrich a letter registering "strong support" for a Republican proposal for a $5,000 tax credit for parents who adopt a child and two such tax credits for two adoptions.

This, moreover, was only one part of the Republican program in Congress that caught the presidential eye so early in the campaign. As Bob Dole so often was heard to complain, Clinton had also said "me, too" to other Republican ideas and had even been anticipating a few new ones.

Was this mere accident? Hardly. Or perhaps a contrived plan to annoy Bob Dole? Not at all. What President Clinton was trying to demonstrate so early in his reelection drive was that he had become by now a "new" Democrat who, out of sheer necessity in the last years of the century, had veered from the cherished New Deal era of Franklin Roosevelt and Harry Truman.

The president and his advisers had seen clearly that this America was very far from the badly wounded nation that the New Deal had rescued from the pit of the Great Depression. Now, a more prosperous and moderately conservative America still had economic problems, mainly the frozen wage structure of the working class; but even people of moderate means were nervous about losing their hard-won gains at some future time.

After becoming president in 1993 and realizing the new issues that faced him, Clinton pinned all his hopes on a grandiose public health plan that would be conducted on the vast scale practiced by major European nations. It had been a complete failure before his first two years were over; and with it had gone whatever ideas he then had for the catch-phrase that still haunted him, "Changing welfare as we know it." The result was the 1994 election of the first Republican-dominated Congress in forty years, which proceeded to block every initiative that he attempted for much of the rest of his term.

It was during this fallow stage of his presidency, apparently, that he decided to experiment with some of the Republican ideas that attracted him, of which the adoption tax-credit proposal was but one. At that stage, he instinctively averted tackling so major an issue as changes in welfare (indeed, he had vetoed two Republican plans early on); and he seemed to give up almost entirely on health care.

But, then, both he and his Republican opposition knew quite well that they couldn't touch Social Security and Medicare in the 1996 campaign — the heritage of the past glories of programs from the New Deal and Lyndon Johnson's Great Society. Therefore, what the president had to do in approaching the reelection drive was to center his attention on smaller matters, until he was forced to deal with the large ones that would determine his future as a "new" Democrat — something more, it was to be hoped, than being a mere Demo-Republican.

In developing his role as a "new" Democrat and an open bid for moderate Republican support, Clinton had behind him a massive budget change that had halved the nation's debt, mainly through a large tax increase aimed at wealthier American families. This, more than anything else, had brought the country out of its latest recession; but much more remained to be done. Subsequently, moderate tax cuts benefited many middle-income American families; and, he also sponsored a number of measures for creating more jobs — the most successful of all his new programs.

Now, in the opening stages of his reelection campaign, what he was trying to do toward making more and better jobs available was to stress the benefits of education, research, and advanced training not only for broader employment but also for higher-paid jobs. He simply wasn't ready then to try to revive his failed health program, much less to take on the huge added risk of designing a substitute for the much-criticized welfare program.

Instead, he encouraged Senator Edward M. Kennedy of Massachusetts to seek bipartisan support for whatever health measure that appealed to a Republican Congress and to encourage the Republican leadership to produce a third congressionally approved welfare bill that he might be able to sign.

As far as the president was concerned, the stress that the Republicans placed on reemphasizing the Whitewater scandal and the Clintons' role in it had now been answered with his appeal to moderate Republicans as a "new" Democrat. And so, while Dole continued to emphasize his military sacrifices in World War II and to make disparaging references to Clinton's character, the president's reply was to promote actively and continually the kind of social issues — broader education, job advancement, and tax credits in both areas — that were bound to appeal to middle-class families, regardless of their political sympathies.

The $5,000-tax credit for all save the wealthiest families with an adopted child, the Republican concept that Clinton so heartily embraced, was exactly the kind of social development he sought to dramatize in his effort to attract bipartisan support.

"Promoting adoption is one of the most important things we can do to strengthen American families and give more children what every child in America deserves, loving parents and a healthy home," the president wrote in his letter to Speaker Gingrich. If Gingrich didn't seem to appreciate the compliment, it did make a difference to the sponsor of the adoption bill, a New York Republican, Congresswoman Susan Molinari. She responded, "President Clinton is beginning to sound like candidate Clinton again."

The president wasted no time in answering Dole's grumpy complaint about the White House's absorption with Republican ideas. Instead, Clinton followed up by unveiling an added tax credit to make a college education possible for an ever-widening mass of middle-class America.

In a speech at Princeton University, he made a number of suggestions for government help in defraying the cost of a college education; but the one that attracted the most attention was a proposal for a $1,500 tax credit for each of the first two years of a student's successful college experience. This proposal, as the White House later explained, was intended to defray the annual fees charged to students at many community colleges and their state equivalents throughout the land. (At most Ivy League and other private universities, the annual tuition fees alone now run from $30,000 to $35,000.)

The inspiration for Clinton's Princeton offer came from a successful program in Georgia that won a second term for Democratic Governor Zell Miller and the reelection of a Democratic legislature. It was from Miller's idea that the president derived the name of his project, the Hope scholarships; but the financing — which didn't cost Georgians a dime — came entirely from a state-run lottery.

The Georgia program was even larger than the more limited Clinton proposal for the nation, which was almost immediately stalled in

Congress. Under the Miller initiative, any Georgia student who maintained a B average in high school received a scholarship upon applying at any public university, college, or technical institution in the state. To those Georgia students who matriculated at a private university in the state, a $3,000 scholarship was awarded to them instead.

The figures from Governor Miller put the number of Georgia's own Hope scholars at about 124,000, for whom the profits from the lottery by law had been set aside for the 1996–1997 academic year. The program originated in 1993; and in the first four academic years, the total number of Georgia students who benefited came to nearly 200,000.

It appeared, however, that a significant number in the initial four academic years, estimated in grades of the latest freshman class at 44 percent of the total, made their B average by avoiding basic academic courses, such as English, mathematics, and science. For 1996–1997, college candidates from Georgia high schools were told they'd have to make their mark in the regular academic subjects along with everybody else.

Nevertheless, even though the Clinton program was much more modest in both cost and scope than the Georgia model, it was at least a beginning on broadening the area of college education for students in the United States during the next century. And that, too, was what the president offered to the public in his Princeton address.

Although Dole was quick to attack the new Clinton tax-credit plan as too expensive, he apparently had forgotten that during the previous winter, as the likely Republican presidential nominee, he had said, "President Clinton had an idea that was pretty good, and that was credits for two-year college students."

At Princeton, the president linked his newest proposal to make college education available to most high school graduates by recalling the enormous effect of the GI bill directly after World War II, which, he said, "helped to build the great American middle class and a great American economy." He continued, "But today, more than ever before in the history of the United States, education is the fault line, the great Continental Divide between those who will prosper and those who will not in the new economy."

Emphasizing that the new jobs in today's market require greater skills, the president pointed out that fifteen years ago a worker with a college education made 38 percent more than a high school graduate—a ratio that he said had increased since to 73 percent. He went on, "Our goal must be to make the thirteenth and fourteenth years of education as universal to all Americans as the first twelve years are today.... Now, we want to expand work study, so that a million students can work their way through college by the year 2000."

President Clinton looked forward to the next few years when, he predicted, education at most community colleges across the land would be free for all students who can keep up their grades. "And," he went on, "the very few states that have tuition above the amount that we can afford to credit, I would challenge those states to close the gap. We are going to take care of most of the states; the rest of them should help us the last little way."

The tax credit plan, he forecast, would eventually offer free tuition and training "to every adult willing to work for it" with the result, he hoped, that nobody would ever need again "to be stuck in a dead-end job or in unemployment."

The president offered no apologies for his enthusiastic predictions of a nation full of cheerful, dedicated, and highly educated workers. All he seemed interested in was selling his rosy point of view to what would be, by and large, a doubting public. He concluded earnestly, "This plan will work because it will go to people who by definition are willing to work for it."

There was much more to Clinton's campaign salesmanship to attract more middle-class people to his vision for an expansive future, a point of view he apparently counted on to attract more moderate Republicans to his standard on election day, if not before. Under the auspices of the Department of Housing and Urban Development, he also set a new goal of 8 million new homeowners, or 67.5 percent of all American households, by the year 2000. In 1995, a ten-year record had already been set in his first administration, he said, by people who owned their own homes — a total of more than 65 percent.

He now proposed to exceed that figure, saying, "I want to have 8 million more average Americans able to say two of the most beautiful words in the English language: 'Welcome home,' by the year 2000."

Since his 1992 election, the president recalled that he had directed a 25-percent reduction in the up-front mortgage insurance premiums of the Federal Housing Administration. To that, he now added a second 11-percent cut. Together, these moves, so he calculated, saved the average holder of an FHA mortgage toward century's end up to $1,000 in closing costs. At that time, the average FHA mortgage was put at $80,000.

By contrast, the president then recalled that he had contracted for the purchase of his own first home at $20,500, with a monthly mortgage payment of $174 — his inducement when he asked Hillary to marry him in 1976 while they were both teaching law at the University of Arkansas in Fayetteville. Knowing something of academic salaries at the time, north and south, I am sure that such modest pay for college teaching as the purchase price of the house would indicate was not confined to Fayetteville, Arkansas.

Since then, a cut in home-buying expense had been a part of the president's larger program of addressing the most urgent needs of families with children among the middle- and lower-income workers. Still another White House conference was held in which President Clinton asked TV executives to provide at least three hours a week of programming for children to vary the steady tube entertainment diet of violence, sex, and more violence. At that stage in the presidential campaign, Clinton's lead over Dole in the polls still registered in double digits without change, a boost for the strategy of the "new" Democrat who was appealing to moderate Republicans.

Despite its early failure, President Clinton had never given up on his health program; and so he supported Senator Kennedy's effort to revive the proposal through a bipartisan sponsorship with Senator Nancy Kassebaum of Kansas. The coauthors had dropped almost all major provisions from the original bill, leaving only the right of workers to take their health insurance with them if they changed jobs, with a guarantee that no one would be denied such insurance, despite a preexisting condition damaging to health.

Had the Republican leadership accepted Senator Kassebaum's participation in this small remainder of the failed Clinton health program, the bill could easily have sailed through Congress. But Bob Dole, before his resignation, had insisted on including in it a provision for a tax-free "Medical Savings Account," which Senator Kennedy at once labeled as a "poison pill." As Kennedy viewed it, Dole's Medical Savings Account would benefit only well-to-do people who were able to deposit funds tax-free in these accounts and, as long as they were healthy, would be allowed to withdraw money for purposes other than insurance if they wanted to do so.

Still, this had been Dole's condition for offering the amended bill for passage in the Senate, and Speaker Gingrich supported him in the House. The Republican leaders argued that those well-off with medical savings, being more cost-conscious than lesser folk, would tend to hold down medical expenses for the government.

At one point, the Republicans did suggest a possible compromise — a test that would be made of the effectiveness of these savings accounts on the establishment of portable health insurance. But compromise then remained a long way off. Senator Kennedy, for one, appealed directly to Dole to come to terms with minimal health insurance legislation, saying, "If Senator Dole is serious, it is difficult to believe that he cannot make it happen." But Senator Kassebaum, who was then serving her last term in the upper house, still couldn't persuade her leaders to support the modified bill.

What Dole seemed to be more interested in at the time was a Dole-Gingrich "Defend America Act." Like President Reagan's tremendous investment in the armed forces during his administration, this proposal was intended to produce an instant burst of millions of new jobs, defense contracts for eager industrialists, and a sudden revival of renewed prosperity across the country. By contrast, the middling surviving portion of Clinton's all-inclusive health program sank out of consideration.

The nonpartisan Congressional Budget Office saw no merit in the proposed new defense bonanza, however. It estimated the cost at anywhere from $30 to $60 billion and up — prohibitively expensive even for the masters of the Pentagon. The final blow to the Dole-Gingrich defense program was delivered by the chairman of the Joint Chiefs of Staff, General John M. Shalikashvili, who warned that the project, if put into effect, would violate all arms-control treaties bearing the approval of the United States.

More amendments meanwhile had so overburdened the once-simplified bipartisan effort to enact a limited health insurance measure that it was stalled indefinitely in Congress. Such was the status of President Clinton's efforts, as a "new" Democrat, to attract more of middle-class America to his cause in his enlarged reelection campaign.

This, after all, was still gridlock in action for Congress under Republican domination; and the One hundred-fourth session was producing little legislation of consequence as a result. What President Clinton would have to do, if he expected any progress whatever toward improvements in the nation's health, minimum wage, and welfare reform legislation, was to wait patiently toward the end of the session before trying to force any compromise legislation through the Senate and the House. Until then, he would have to temporize by continuing to adapt the Republican program in Congress to his own advantage.

12 Dole Quits the Senate

Nothing semed to go quite right for Bob Dole that June except for his sentimental farewell to Congress. The likely Republican opponent to President Clinton's reelection still had been unable to put much of a dent in the president's two-digit lead in the opinion polls. Nor was there any change in his weakness among women voters, a flaw directly attributable to his fidelity to his party's position against abortion.

Having failed to persuade General Colin L. Powell to join his ticket as vice-president, the Republican front-runner now was experimenting with the idea of asking a leading prochoice advocate of influence and prominence to be his second-in-command. But one of the outstanding prospects, Governor Christine Todd Whitman of New Jersey, had also deliberately removed herself from consideration before being asked.

Worst of all, in his mild effort to insert a statement of tolerance for the proabortion views of a substantial number, though still a minority, of the party's leaders and delegates, he was risking an open split with the hard-line religious right at the Republican National Convention in August. It was in such circumstances that he said farewell to his Senate colleagues on June 11 after thirty-five years in Congress, including eleven years as the Republican leader in the Senate.

Almost tearfully, he concluded his last speech, lasting a bit more than a half an hour, to bipartisan applause:

> So the Bible tells us to everything there is a season, and I think my season in the Senate is about to come to an end. But the new season before me makes this moment far less the closing of one chapter than the opening of another . . . . And like everybody here, I'm an optimist. I believe our best tomorrows are yet to be lived.

Across the continent in Los Angeles, where President Clinton was appearing at a Democratic fund-raiser, he signaled a temporary truce with his rival that day by calling upon a partisan crowd for applause, then telephoned the retiring Kansas senator to wish him well.

The Senate's Democrats also joined in the cheers for Dole's leave taking, although they didn't go as far as some of their Republican colleagues, who cried, "Dole in ninety-six!" The temporary presiding officer in the Senate at the time of the seventy-two-year-old Dole's last bow was the ninety-three-year-old Republican Strom Thurmond of South Carolina, who was seeking reelection for a six-year term in the fall.

Symbolizing the change in his status upon leaving the Senate that afternoon, former Senator Dole stopped off at his presidential campaign headquarters in preparation for the last four and one-half months of his effort to unseat President Clinton. If his chances at that moment of upward change in a long and productive life seemed slim, he took no notice of it.

After all, this was a day for him to cherish in memory for as long as he lived. His successor as majority leader, Trent Lott of Mississippi, would take over the next day, as would his Kansas replacement, Sheila Frahm, the state's lieutenant governor, who had been chosen by the governor to serve out Dole's term.

Lott joined his fellow southern conservative, Speaker Gingrich, and thereby continued Republican rule of Congress—a significant change in the generation that had passed since two Texas Democrats had dominated Congress—Lyndon Johnson in the Senate and Sam Rayburn in the House. Thus the South was supposed to be Republican territory for this election; but President Clinton wasn't conceding any section, much less any state, to the opposition. He was campaigning to win the largest states south of the Mason-Dixon line—Texas with thirty-six electoral votes and Florida with twenty-six—as well as some others, particularly Arkansas and Tennessee.

Former Senator Dole's efforts to mollify opponents of the party's rigidly conservative position against abortion apparently had done little so far to make him more acceptable to the majority of American voters, especially women voters, who still favored freedom of choice by a large margin in current polls. He was also up against a severe limitation of funds, caused by overspending during his primary campaign, pending the formality of the party convention's vote approving him as the Republican challenger.

The controversy over abortion, however, was infinitely more dangerous both to Dole and to the party itself. After stumping the country, the Kansan knew perfectly well that the party's rigid decision against abortion and his own acceptance of the position accounted for part of the distance he had fallen behind the president in every poll of consequence. It therefore followed that he would have to make an attempt, sooner rather than later, to bridge that gap, without doing violation to his or the party's stand against abortion.

It was then that Dole came up with the notion, first used by Ronald Reagan in 1980, of a statement of tolerance for opposing points of view. But although Reagan had put a semidisclaimer in the preamble to the party platform so that it referred to abortion and other sources of disagreement among the delegates, Dole wanted it hinged deliberately to the section on abortion because so many distinguished Republicans championed freedom of choice, including at least four governors, who probably wouldn't have won their posts in their respective state houses without holding that position.

And so it happened that a kind of Gilbertian argument developed then between Dole, who wanted abortion rights' people singled out for tolerance, and mainly the Christian far right, who did not. Now the Kansan wasn't the most patient of people, and this was a situation in which he could easily be provoked. Ultimately, he exploded. In a televised interview in Kansas City, Missouri, he singled out Gary Bauer, one of the most adamant prolifers and the president of the antiabortion Family Research Council, saying:

> What's the difference if it [the statement on tolerance] is in the preamble or the platform? I mean, this is a moral issue. I don't know where Gary Bauer's been all his life, but I've always known we had prochoice Republicans and prolife Republicans. I think Gary Bauer's tolerant. If he's not tolerant, he ought to say so. . . . I mean, I think he looks for reasons to put out press releases.

The somewhat amazed Bauer commented, "I just don't think this is a Gary Bauer–Bob Dole issue. I think it's about whether the Republican Party will be unambiguously prolife. This is one of the most profound issues facing this country."

It remained to be seen whether the Republican National Convention could be put in the peculiar position of tearing itself apart over a statement of tolerance for opposing views on abortion and its placement either in the preamble of the platform, directly in the plank that repeated the party's usual all-out position against abortion, or elsewhere.

There was no question, however, that the party's structure itself would be decisively weakened if far-right factions like the Family Research Council and the Christian Coalition could dominate its proceedings and a relatively minor figure like Pat Buchanan could realistically threaten the head of the party's presidential ticket. The August convention, therefore, was likely to be decisive in more ways than merely approving Bob Dole's right to its presidential nomination on the basis of the majority delegates who had been chosen to confirm him.

Just before leaving Congress to campaign full time against President Clinton, Dole had complained, "We don't dare put out our speeches in advance bacause he grabs them and gives the speech." Like so much of the sound-bite morality on both sides that generally distracted public attention in the overly long presidential contest, there was a grain or two of truth in Dole's latest complaint against the president. The fast-moving Clinton campaign organization, ever anxious to beat the opposition in the early evening TV news across the country, usually was able to achieve so limited an objective—a dubious advantage so long before election day.

However exaggerated Dole's complaint may have been, he proceeded in his informal remarks before a Republican crowd in Nashville to call the president a plagiarist, then cited presidential support for Republican views for nighttime curfews for school children, approval of tax credits for adoptions, and partial repeal of the gasoline tax. This was a sample of the kind of sound-bite campaigning that filtered past mass public consciousness without any great reaction of the type that accompanied a shift in abortion, Medicare, or Social Security on either side, to name a few of the major issues.

Once he was free of his congressional obligations, Dole of course tried to make a few points here and there with local and regional issues while still using a general sound-bite technique. In Kentucky tobacco country, for example, he attacked the Food and Drug Administration's prospective claim to regulate the use and sale of cigarettes. He said:

> I don't think the FDA has the authority to do what they want to do. In fact, if they should claim jurisdiction and find that cigarettes are a drug, then in effect you're banning cigarettes and the production of tobacco so it's going to affect the lives of a lot of people.

Then there was another sound bite on the way to Baton Rouge, Louisiana, by paddle boat, where he picked up the president's denial of harmful intent in the use of FBI files, deriding the White House's claim that it was an "innocent mistake." "They make more innocent mistakes in this outfit than anybody I've ever known. If we had made this many mistakes in World War II, we wouldn't be here today. I believe America deserves better. And I'm better."

Then, in Toledo, Ohio, he developed another sound bite against the

Clinton proposal for a tax credit to cover the first two years of college costs, the first year for all students, and the second year for those with a B average. Before a business crowd, the former senator warned, "There are always some phrases you should be skeptical of. The check is in the mail. I'll start my diet in the morning. Let's do lunch sometime. And how about this one? 'I'm Bill Clinton. I'm running for reelection, and I'm going to cut your taxes.'"

Dole even tossed off a sound bite to try to benefit the Republican-controlled Congress, saying, "They say we're too business-oriented. But we want you to make a profit. We want to reduce some of the regulations. We want to reduce your capital gains rate." (All that, and no mention of a balanced budget!)

On his first day of freedom from Congress, there were even occasional sound bites for the reporters on his aircraft at the start of an eight-city swing through the South and the Midwest. At one point, he said, "My father told me you can only sweep a walk and empty the garbage so many times a day in retirement. I called the office this morning, and I got a recording. Said nobody's here." He paused, then went on, "I knew I wasn't there. That chapter in my life is over and another's opened."

The technique was pure Dole. Unlike the often painful last few days of his Senate leadership, when some of his time was spent skipping through scripts that had been carefully prepared for him, he seemed much more relaxed amid almost continually changing scenes while he was out in the heartland of America.

He also seemed to have altered his original notion of campaigning tieless, with open-collared shirt and slacks. Now he was dressed as usual in a business suit, plus matching shirt and tie, an outfit that seemed more pleasing to at least one important bystander, Elizabeth Dole.

Except for the internal arguments about tolerance for opposing points of view on the party's steadfast antiabortion position and Clinton's troubles in the FBI file blitz, the Dole who was tossing off sound bites while campaigning free of links to Congress seemed infinitely more relaxed than the stiff-necked, irritable Dole who had antagonized so many with whom he dealt, including some in his own party.

The road-company portrait of Dole, at least during the outset of his travels, didn't square with the image he portrayed to a Democratic polltaker, Stanley B. Greenberg, who called him "Dour, negative, and dour." Such grimness, Greenberg went on, was the likely Republican candidate's worst fault, then added, "That might have been appropriate for 1968, but I don't think it's for now. I think people would like politics to be more uplifting."

Whether an uplifting, sound-bite Dole would last very long was a good question. The Republican National Convention would be his sternest test.

As for President Clinton, meanwhile, he was doing what all sitting presidents have done in modern times when seeking reelection — using the White House as the kind of "bully pulpit" it had been for Theodore Roosevelt, updated with a newspaper and magazine coverage and the inevitable TV sound bites for the evening news. What had hurt him, to some extent, was the FBI file hunt.

If not all sitting presidents for much of this century have been re-elected through this involuted method of campaigning — Messrs. Ford, Carter, and Bush were among the most recent failures — the practice did seem to retain considerable merit through such winners as FDR, Eisenhower, and Reagan. But there were sterner tests for Clinton's reelection yet to come.

13 A One-Two Punch for Clinton

Just when everything seemed to be going beautifully for President Clinton's reelection campaign late that spring, he ran into a stiff one-two punch that he hadn't expected and had to scramble for a somewhat qualified recovery. Two Clinton partners in the ill-fated Whitewater land deal and the current governor of Arkansas were convicted on criminal charges growing out of a special prosecutor's investigation. Even though the president and the first lady were not accused of any crime and his part in the trial was limited to brief taped testimony for the defense, the case was supposed to have accounted for a slight drop in his standing in polls concerning his reelection.

The second punch, which seemed to catch the Clinton White House completely by surprise, led directly to the president's public apology for the misuse of almost one thousand FBI files, including those of prominent Republicans. He called the incident a "completely honest bureaucratic snafu," saw to it that one responsible White House official resigned, and maintained that he and the FBI would make sure there never would be a recurrence of the file misuse.

Nevertheless, this being a presidential election year, friend and foe were on edge. Bob Dole, being the likely Republican nominee for president, remarked that the incident "smells to high heaven"; and FBI Director Louis J. Freeh expressed his outrage in his own inquiry.

But for all the furor, the president's lead in the polls remained substantially within two digits over Senator Dole because jurors in the Whitewater-related trial said that they hadn't considered presidential testimony to be an important factor; and the matter of the FBI files was so complicated that it probably was difficult for an average citizen to determine fault, if any, at the presidential level.

The whole business was more symbolic of the unprepared and untested Clinton administration soon after it replaced the twelve-year Reagan/Bush administration, when the new, untried, forty-six-year-old president had to make lame excuses as he shakily grasped for the reins of government. There was no evidence then of criminal misconduct; nor, for that matter, was any uncovered in the two unrelated incidents at the start of the 1996 presidential campaign.

As for the matter of an examination of so many FBI files by Anthony Marceca, a civilian employee of the army at the Pentagon who, at the time, was on temporary duty at the White and who, in his testimony before a congressional inquiry took the Fifth Amendment, his conduct, in the expression of White House Chief of Staff Leon E. Panetta, was "completely inexcusable."

In any event, both incidents shook the complacency of the Clinton White House and served to remind the president, if ever he had needed it, that running for reelection in a self-governing democracy of 263 million people was serious business.

Even after three years, Whitewater continued to haunt both the Clintons as an issue from which they couldn't seem to separate themselves either in the first federal court trial in Arkansas conducted by the special prosecutor, Kenneth W. Starr, or subsequent prosecutions. Starr himself had faced criticism because of his continued outside private business interests while serving as special prosecutor. But like Dole's ally in Congress, New York's Senator Alfonse d'Amato, who had to face ethical questions, Starr still had not been able to produce evidence of wrongdoing on the part of the president and the first lady.

What the special prosecutor was able to accomplish in his first trial, however, was a finding of criminal liability against the two Clinton partners in Whitewater, James B. McDougal, who ran the failed Madison Guaranty Savings and Loan in Litle Rock, and his former wife, Susan. With the current governor of Arkansas, Jim Guy Tucker, they were accused of misusing $3 million in federally backed loans in the Madison Guaranty bankruptcy case that had been an outgrowth of the Whitewater land inquiry. The case moved to appeal, as a result of which Tucker resigned as Arkansas's governor.

Clinton's involvement in the trial had been limited to his testimony for the defense, taken in a taped deposition made under prosecution questioning at the White House and played before the jurors in Arkansas. As James McDougal had testified, the president, while governor of Arkansas, had seemed to pay scant attention to his Whitewater investment and knew little about the problems that led to the failure of Madison Guaranty. As for Hillary Rodham Clinton, she had continually maintained that her part in the Whitewater investment had been even sketchier in her brief role as counsel for Madison Guaranty just before it filed for bankruptcy. Both Clintons said that they had lost $100,000 on the investment, instead of making the gains that the inquiry implied.

Subsequently, when the special counsel on the Whitewater matter tried two Arkansas bankers in Little Rock on related charges, both were acquitted on four felony counts, deadlocked on seven others, and won a federal judge's finding of mistrial on the latter. What pleased the White House in particular was that a friend of the president's, Bruce R. Lindsey, a deputy counsel for his office, had been involved in one of the felony acquittals and had even been named as an "unindicted co-conspirator."

The verdict was a stiff return punch for Kenneth Starr, an ardent Republican who had worked for two years to seek convictions against the two owners of the Perry County Bank, Herby Branscum Jr. and Robert M. Hill, on a number of charges, the chief one being that they plotted to conceal big cash withdrawals from the bank for Bill Clinton's 1990 drive for Arkansas governor.

The White House announced that the president was "happy to learn the news" of the acquittals and added, "Today's not guilty verdicts . . . confirm what we always knew: Bruce Lindsey acted properly." Otherwise, the verdict, issued on August 1, made up in part for the findings of guilt on May 28 against the president's friends. One other part of Whitewater in which the Clintons figured was the payment of $2,910 in back taxes and interest having to do with their failed land deal in the 1980s.

Senator Dole was more interested in the White House's misuse of FBI files, saying it reminded him of Watergate. To which R. W. Apple Jr. of the New York *Times* responded, "Watergate it is not. There is no evidence here, as there was in the Nixon era, of a premeditated attempt to subvert the democratic process and the operation of government agencies for narrow partisan gain."*

Louis J. Freeh, director of the FBI, concluded on the basis of his own investigation that his bureau, in providing the White House with so many files, including that of former Secretary of State James A. Baker III, had been guilty of "egregious violations of privacy" and explained, "The prior system of providing files to the White House relied on good faith and honor. Unfortunately, the FBI and I were victimized. I promise the American people that it will not happen again."

The first move in that inquiry by Special Prosecutor Starr was to examine Anthony Marceca, the civilian army investigator who, while on temporary duty at the White House, had obtained the mainly Republican FBI records. Craig Livingstone, the chief of the White House

---

* New York *Times*, June 16, 1996, E-1.

security office, had requested Marceca's services because of what he called an overload of White House clearance required in 1993 for the then new Clinton administration.

Both Marceca and Livingstone had worked on previous Democratic presidential campaigns and knew the security business procedures, including the matter of obtaining private FBI files on prominent Republicans and others allegedly for security clearance purposes. As for the list of whose files were to be required, their story was that they had worked from what turned out to be an outdated Secret Service list, and so some prominent Republicans who had already left government service were included.

The problem with these explanations was that Secret Service witnesses denied they had ever seen so outdated a list of names for investigation for clearances. But when Marceca was asked why he had examined the file of former Secretary of State James A. Baker III, he replied calmly, "It was not a part of my job to determine who should and who shouldn't be on the Secret Service White House list."

That was not the only problem with the FBI files, however. The number at first included about three hundred names; it grew to more than four hundred; and eventually, upon further examination of Marceca's list of files that were requested from the FBI, the investigation determined that more than nine hundred FBI files had been requested for examination and an undetermined number of them still were locked up in the White House vaults. To complete the puzzle offered by the numbers of files unaccounted for by any list whatever, the special prosecutor sealed the vault in the White House, where the files were kept, to preserve evidence for his inquiry.

At that point, Marceca had testified that only three low-level employees' files had been set aside for inquiry before giving them clearances. As if all that hadn't been enough of an embarrassment for the White House, Congressman William F. Clinger Jr. (R, Pennsylvania), who had made the original disclosure of the White House requests for FBI files, pitched in with a public hearing of his own investigative committee. Clinger's interest had been aroused originally because one of the requested FBI files obtained by Marceca and Livingstone was that of Billy R. Dale, the discharged chief of the White House travel office, whose record had been scrutinized seven months after he left his White House job. He had been tried and acquitted of misusing travel-office funds.

When White House officials then contended that they had had no particular interest in Dale and the travel office, Congressman Clinger said that the file of another discharged travel-office worker, Barney Brasseux, had also been sent to the White House, although his name was not on the supposedly outdated Secret Service list used to requisition the files. While this back-and-forth continued in a congressional hearing and at the special prosecutor's office, Craig Livingstone was first placed on leave from his job as head of White House security and then, as the inconsistencies grew, he suddenly resigned while he was under congressional investigation. At about the same time, his temporary civilian agent from army service in the Pentagon, Marceca, took the Fifth Amendment, which protects witnesses from self-incrimination.

In his own testimony, Livingstone had conceded that he had not adequately performed his sworn duties in the security office; but he denied participating in what Congressman Clinger called a "campaign rooting around for dirt."

The witness explained, "Neither I nor, to my knowledge, anyone else in the White House participated in any kind of a smear campaign or an effort to compile an enemies list as some have alleged." His mistakes, he insisted, had been innocent errors of procedure, not a determined, conniving scheme.

Democratic members of the Clinger committee meanwhile did their best to try to avert pinning a scapegoat's role on the angry and now helpless Livingstone. They alleged that the Republicans were turning the inquiry into a "witch-hunt" that would make victims of employees who were trying to do their jobs under difficulty.

But nothing helped the frustrated security chief. At one point just before the hearing closed, he protested that he had been described before the committee as a "beefy former bar bouncer" and a "henchman" who allegedly engaged in misconduct despite twenty years' government service, concluding, "These are false and unfair caricatures."

In concluding that day's hearing, Chairman Clinger said, "Whether or not these events turn out to be a blunder due to the colossal incompetence of those the president put in charge of highly sensitive matters or whether it veered into something more serious or even criminal, the casualness with which this White House has approached many areas of security provided a climate for either of these troubling alternatives." Marceca's decision to invoke his Fifth Amendment right to remain silent probably halted similar scenes before Senator Orrin Hatch's Judiciary Committee in the upper house.

Marceca had already testified before the Clinger committee in the House that he had obtained the FBI files out of error through the use of the outdated Secret Service files. During the Judiciary Committee's hearing, a Secret Service agent, Arnold Cole, said that Livingstone had confessed to him privately that the use of the outdated list was "our fault," that an accurate list had been available "but I don't know what happened."

Neither for that matter did anybody else. The unofficial committee for getting out from under, always swollen in membership in such cases, seemed to be in continual session for as long as the controversy lasted, which was quite a few weeks. But when it was all over, President Clinton's lead in the polls was still in substantial double-digit figures. It was not through any fault of Dole's that he still had failed to show any appreciable gain in the polls, despite the Clinton administration's troubles with Whitewater and the FBI files. The prospective Republican rival to President Clinton had been diligent throughout in discussing the FBI files scandal, going to the length in a Saturday morning radio address of accusing the Clinton administration of "a pattern of ethical arrogance." He concluded, "The Clinton administration came into office vowing to set a new ethical standard. Unfortunately, the standard they have set cannot be defended."

When the FBI scandal began developing into a Republican campaign issue, President Clinton by ironic circumstance was arguing the cause of better crime prevention before a college audience at the University of Nevada at Las Vegas during a western fund-raising tour. In a discussion of the crime prevention aspect of the current anticrime law, he said, "We simply cannot jail our way out of America's crime problem. We are going to have to invest more money in crime prevention. It's amazing to me how much some of these community programs can do on a modest budget."

But once he returned to the White House, he found that the FBI files had become a Republican campaign issue in which he had been obliged to intervene several times, once when he was entertaining distinguished foreign visitors. In an apologetic aside to inquisitive reporters, he said that the improper examination of the FBI files was "really an honest bureaucratic mess-up."

Even so, by that time, the FBI director had accused the White House of victimizing him and his agency; and what had at first been thought of by the president as a "bureaucratic snafu" now had become a minor *cause célèbre*. For better or worse, the president would have to tough it out for as long as his rating in the campaign didn't take a nose dive.

14 Guns in June

Despite concern about scandal and the economy, the greatest danger to President Clinton's reelection was all-out war in the Middle East; and lamentably, it was possible that June. The president knew it. Bob Dole suspected it. But worst of all, the leaders of the outlaw states around the Arab crescent were restless — from Libya to Iraq and Iran — where anti-Americanism had been mounting ever since the election of a new and defiant American-educated prime minister of Israel, Benjamin Netanyahu.

An Arab summit of twenty-one nations had already been called in Cairo, Egypt being one of the few Arab states to have made peace with Israel since its creation in 1948 by the United Nations. And Netanyahu had only emphasized the platform on which he had been narrowly elected; that is, security for Israelis first and peace second. Viewing the threatening scene from the White House, all President Clinton could do at first to try to restrain the combatants was to invite Prime Minister Netanyahu to the White House for a conference and to send Secretary of State Warren Christopher back to the Middle East to take soundings at the chief trouble spots, first of all Jerusalem. And in time, if a conflict could be averted before American troops in the Persian Gulf area were endangered, the president of Egypt, Hosni Mubarak, would also be asked to Washington for a state visit as a conciliatory approach to the far more hostile Arab leaders who had been given the American designation of outlaws.

The safety of an American contingent of about five thousand Air Force personnel and their dependents in Dhahran, Saudi Arabia, was particularly vital in this extremity. They were virtual hostages to ensure the continued flow of Saudi oil, estimated to be one-third of the total required annually in the United States to keep industries and automobiles in operation. Like everything else in the Middle East, this American mission could not be simply explained as a contractual relationship between the royal Saudi rulers and the Treasury of the United States as authorized by Congress. For the powerful resurgence of a fundamentalist Muslim orthodoxy was spreading alarm far beyond the Arab crescent to outlying Muslim states from Indonesia and Pakistan in Asia to Algeria and Morocco in Northwestern Africa. And so the once-powerful Saudi kings had now also become targets of the Muslim revolutionary leaders centered, of all places, in London.

The scene from the White House, therefore, was disorderly in the extreme — and even more difficult to explain in terms of Arab opposition to Israel and the negotiations with the Palestine Liberation Organization. The aim here was still to set up a separate state of Palestine on the Israeli-held West Bank of the Jordan River and the Gaza Strip on the eastern Mediterranean, bordering on Egypt. Although that was just a part of the whole trouble, if any part could provide the spark that would set the entire Muslim world aflame, it was the issue of a Palestinian state.

There had been a time when President Clinton, newly established in the White House in 1993, had been cheerfully optimistic about a durable peace that he proposed to bring into being in the Middle East. That was when he had only recently emerged from the rudimentary gamesmanship of being Arkansas's three-term governor to become the chief executive of a great nation. And while presiding over the signing of an Israeli-Palestinian Peace Accord on the White House lawn that year, he had seemed quite comfortable — even secure — as a potential peacemaker. But now, three years later, while campaigning for a second term, he wasn't at all certain of a favorable outcome for his first major diplomatic initiative in a disorderly and lawless world.

Even in the relatively small area of foreign policy that embraced Israeli and PLO signatories to their White House agreement, about the size of a state like Maryland, there had been fearful complications. Only the previous November, Yitzhak Rabin, the Israeli prime minister at the 1993 ceremonial meeting with Yasir Arafat at the White House, had been assassinated by a right-wing Israeli zealot. His successor, the seventy-three-year-old Shimon Peres, who had been backed by both Clinton and his predecessor, George Bush, had suddenly fallen from power that June in a razor-thin election result favoring the forty-six-year-old Netanyahu, the leader of the conservative Likud Party.

Netanyahu, a veteran of five years of Israeli army service, had campaigned on his security slogan for all his fellow Israelis with open contempt for Peres's policy of trading Israeli land, including a part of Jerusalem, for a never-very-credible Arab guarantee of peace. Just before the Israeli election and probably the reason for the change of a few votes that gave Netanyahu victory, was the invasion of Israel by four

Arab suicide bombers, who had blown themselves up and taken sixty-three Israelis with them. Such deeds as these had turned the electorate against the idealistic peace concepts of the Labor Party and sent the elderly Peres into retirement.

Peace without security, as Netanyahu put the case, had been worthless; and Yasir Arafat and his Palestine guards had also been the losers. Nevertheless, soon after assuming office and before the completion of his cabinet, the new Israeli leader had made a routine offer to his Arab neighbors of a peace conference without preconditions. The reply of President Hafez al-Assad of Syria, who badly wanted the return of the Israeli-occupied Golan Heights in a southern part of Lebanon, was extreme skepticism that peace could be preserved. The organization of the Arab summit followed.

Netanyahu, who had lived in the United States on and off since his fourteenth birthday and held a master's degree in business from the Massachusetts Institute of Technology, had welcomed President Clinton's bid to the White House. He told his followers that the United States was still a part of the peace process. But as a former Israeli soldier whose oldest brother, Jonathan, had died defending their country, it was inevitable that he would place his confidence in the ability of the Israeli army to defend the land.

That was the tough, realistic manner of the latest Israeli leader, who had warned his fellow citizens, "When they [the Arabs] see a weak government like Peres's, they demand everything, they get everything, and they demand more." To those who criticized him during his campaign as being more American than Israeli, he responded, "I come from a Jewish Zionist family with roots in this country, Israel, for more than a century."

Netanyahu was born in Israel October 14, 1949, to an immigrant Zionist family headed by his grandfather, who had settled in Palestine, then under British control, from Eastern Europe in 1920. When his father came to the United States to teach after the future prime minister turned fourteen, the youngster finished high school before returning to Israel for his military service, emulating both his brothers. Following his military service, he came back to the United States to conclude his education at MIT. He gave up his first American job at the age of twenty-seven to return to Israel when he heard that his brother Jonathan had been killed while on military duty. It happened entirely by chance that the Americanized Israeli attracted the attention of Moshe Arens, then the Israeli ambassador to the United States, who became in effect his diplomatic and political mentor in the years yet to come.

From Washington, he advanced to chief of the Israeli delegation at the United Nations, an invaluable listening post in international affairs, where he also was inducted into the art of making something out of very little on the Sunday morning American TV talk shows. It paid off. For after that, upon becoming active in Israeli politics, he advanced to the leadership of the conservative Likud Party and became the spokesman of the opposition to the Peres land-for-peace program in negotiations with the Palestinians. But in so doing, he also aroused the enmity of David Levy, who became a lifelong rival and an opponent within his own cabinet as his first foreign minister after he succeeded Peres.

Despite the sense of amity that had developed between President Clinton and the new Israeli prime minister immediately after the results of the election became known, a triangular misunderstanding developed with Secretary Christopher and others in the State Department who were trying to downplay a report that Netanyahu would build more Jewish settlements on the West Bank instead of reducing them, as specified in the agreement with the PLO. When the secretary was embarrassed as Arab leaders put this interpretation on his own well-meant suggestion of "adapting our [United States] policy to the situation as it develops," he explained publicly in Geneva that all he was trying to do was to keep his option open. He concluded thereafter that there seemed to have been a change in Israeli policy but left it to Prime Minister Netanyahu to decide how to proceed.

Amid such complications as these and the difficulties of forming a cabinet that included David Levy and would stand up under challenge by Labor in the Knesset (the Israeli parliament), the prime minister was thoroughly occupied and couldn't have departed immediately for Washington, even if he'd wanted to do so.

Thus only four days after the new Israeli cabinet was sworn in and began operating, the first Arab summit in six years convened in Cairo, with president Mubarak calling for peace but warning Israel in vague but carefully chosen words, "If any party allows itself to choose what to negotiate or what not, then this means that the other parties have the same right, which thus reverts the peace process to the zero point — or totally destroys it."

The twenty other potentates who joined him at the Arab summit weren't as considerate in drafting their response to Israel's new regime after two days of discussion. What they demanded was an immediate Israeli withdrawal from all occupied Arab lands, which was quite a challenge in itself. Also, while this was being done, they wanted the independent state of Palestine established around the remains of Israel, with East Jerusalem as its capital. And, if Israel refused, the communiqué went on, then the Arab leaders would have to reconsider their position so that, as they put it, "the Israeli government will bear sole and full responsibility for the situation."

To that, Netanyahu replied at once, "One-sided demands that harm security are not reconcilable with peace talks. In order for the process to continue successfully and fruitfully, such demands must be stopped." Two days later, all hell broke loose in Saudi Arabia. An entirely different attack, apparently conducted by other Muslim fundamentalists, began the second offensive in seven months against the Saudi regime and its American military protectors. A huge bomb tore the front off a military housing complex in Dhahran, killing nineteen American servicemen and injuring more than four hundred other persons. A communiqué, issued later by the bombers, demanded the immediate removal of American forces "from our holy Saudi soil."

This is how violence dominated the American position in the Middle East in the closing years of the century in a once peaceful area while threats of renewed warfare were being made elsewhere at a different location and for different reasons, so far as could be determined.

The Dhahran explosion apparently had been linked to a bomb attack the previous November that resulted in the deaths of five American civilians in Riyadh, the capital of the Saudi monarchs. In retaliation, four Saudi citizens were arrested, forced to confess, and were publicly beheaded as a warning to others by the Saudi regime. The Muslim fundamentalist rebels responsible for the bombing were unrepentant and unafraid. In a message telephoned to the American embassy at Riyadh, an unidentified caller pledged revenge. After that, an Arabic-language newspaper in London reported that it had received another message that more violence would follow until all American and other foreign troops were expelled.

Meanwhile in the United States, greater suspicion was attached to the outlaw states of Iran and Iraq in retaliation for the Persian Gulf War directed by President Bush to liberate Kuwait, which had been seized by Iraq at the end of 1990 and was liberated by American and allied forces in early 1991. Still, while the investigation of the November bombing was under way, two terrorists put a gasoline truck filled with explosives in position beside a fence barely 30 feet from the American military complex in Dhahran on the night of June 25, then escaped after one man was seen apparently lighting the fuse, then jumping into a waiting automobile driven by a colleague, and escaping just before the blast erupted.

Neither the Saudi government nor the United States moved to withdraw the 20,000 troops in the Gulf area generally. They now became an added defense against interruption in the oil traffic between the two nations, but there was also no doubt that the protection of the Saudi regime itself was vital to American interests in both bombings. The renewal of tensions between Israel and the Arabs elsewhere in the Middle East was serious enough during the early stages of president Clinton's reelection campaign, but the two Saudi bombings and the probability of more attacks became even more important because American military forces were now directly involved.

During Prime Minister Netanyahu's visit to the United States on July 9–11, neither President Clinton nor other American leaders seemed to have swayed him from his commitment to his people that their security must precede peace with the Arabs. He justified his suspension of peace with the Palestinians by calling on them to carry out their share of the agreements with Israel, beginning with the Oslo Accords, and the Clinton-sponsored Rose Garden compact of 1993.

Although he seemed to be under mild pressure at the White House to give ground, the Israeli visitor set no time for the resumption of peace talks. Nor did he offer to open Israel's borders again to the desperately jobless Arabs in the Gaza Strip and the West Bank who had previously enjoyed steady employment in the Jewish state. The most he conceded was that he would be the judge of when it would be safe to let transitory Arabs into his country again.

The prime minister emphasized throughout that his immediate responsibility was to carry out the two pledges he made during his campaign: to maintain Israel's security against new attacks from Hamas, Hezbollah, and other anti-Jewish Arab military organizations and to restore Jerusalem as the 3,000-year-old capital of the Jewish state. In defending his ambition for Jerusalem's undivided restoration as Israel's ruling center, he said that he expected the Palestinians to vacate their office and small staff there as a part of the Oslo Accords.

On the more immediate matter of Arab expectations that Israeli armed forces would begin vacating the main cities on the West Bank as a preliminary to reducing Jewish settlements there, he gave no indication when such downsizing could be expected. Indeed, as it was later learned, Israel, at the time, was actually increasing the number of Jewish settlements in some areas that had been designated at first as part of the new Palestinian state. As a result, and this was stressed during the news conference that followed for both the president and his guest, there was now no timetable for the development of the Palestinian state, although that did not mean that the project had been abandoned. The inference seemed to be that the new Israeli leader wanted to restart negotiations on the basis of his own ideas of what kind of peace would provide Israel with the tightest security. The two conditions appeared to him to be indistinguishable.

Despite President Clinton's disappointment in not being able to renew the process of Israel's swapping land for peace in the Peres mode, there was no suggestion that the United States might reduce, much less cancel, the investment this and previous administrations had made through loans, grants, and other forms of economic assistance to Israel and its firmest partners in working toward a broad Middle East peace, Egypt and Jordan. For that matter, Netanyahu once again expressed his gratitude to the United States for its military and economic support and announced that he hoped, with the growth of the Israeli economy, to reduce substantially his country's dependence on the annual American aid package. But as for military assistance, neither the president nor his guest suggested that any change was contemplated. In view of the Muslim attacks on American armed forces in Saudi Arabia before Netanyahu's visit, emphasis on both Saudi and Israeli security could not very well be reduced. In essence, therefore, the prime minister, through his visit to the White House, had stressed his response to the Arab summit's demands by insisting that Israel's security came first and was nonnegotiable.

During Netanyahu's visit to Capitol Hill on July 10, the day after the meeting with the president, both the Republicans and the Democrats appeared to accept his position that reciprocal acceptance of the Israeli-Palestinian agreements would have to be the basis for any future resumption of negotiations. And if the prime minister was obviously prepared for an indefinite delay in the proceedings, that put the next move up to the Palestinians and their Arab supporters. Despite that, he was so well received by Congress with five minutes of sustained applause at the outset that he remarked wistfully, "If I could only get the Knesset to vote like this!"

The highlight of his congressional appearance was his declaration on Jerusalem, "There will never be a redivision of Jerusalem. We will not drive out anyone, nor will we be driven out of any street of our capital." And for the benefit of those who might think him too harsh, he added, "Governments that pursue peace at any price pay a very high price, indeed, and do not achieve peace. And those governments that pursue peace prudently and stand on their security and their vital interests, they're the ones that ultimately attain this peace."

Netanyahu's American visit concluded next day in New York City with a reassuring meeting with Bob Dole, who helped him by proposing that American ties with Israel should be strengthened under such mounting pressures from its enemies, not weakened. Once again, whenever the prime minister was pressed by other dignitaries to give ground, he refused and once said sharply, "We keep commitments, you keep commitments. We insist that the deal be kept on both sides. It is reciprocity."

During a subsequent visit to President Clinton by President Mubarak of Egypt, both were questioned repeatedly at a news conference about how Israel could be brought back to the conference table. The Egyptian leader, who had also been given reassurance of continued American support, talked somewhat aimlessly about the problem until the president, probably out of sheer sympathy over his visitor's discomfort, explained to the reporters, "There are some things we can do and some things we can't do. You see, there's been a change with the election of a different government in Israel, and they have to have time to figure out their position."

But time was also a problem for the United States and its armed forces in Saudi Arabia, at least until election day. For different reasons throughout the Arab crescent from Libya to Iran and Iraq, changes were likely to be more violent. The message of the guns of June could not be mistaken. All parties to peace had been put on warning.

15 State of the Campaign

President Clinton tried to make the best of what seemed like a sluggish American economy in much of that reelection campaign year. He *did* have some dramatic upward movement for which he could claim credit from a public that realized, despite a number of heartening statistics, that the gap between rich and poor in America was still widening. Most financial authorities agreed that it had been at least twenty years since there had been a realistic rise in the income of many of the nation's wage earners.

Even so, the President cited—in his own interest—an unemployment rate of 4.3 percent of the total work force that spring as the lowest in six years, which was followed during the summer with a loss of only one-tenth of a point. He also stressed a low inflation rate of a bit more than 2 percent for the same period, together with a rise in the nation's gross domestic product at an annual rate of 4.2 percent.

But he had to take a hit from a University of Michigan survey that demonstrated how far apart the nation's rich and poor really had drifted. The university figures showed the upper 10 percent of American families owned 66.8 percent of the country's wealth in late 1994, and the poorest 10 percent could show only debt, averaging $7,075.

It was, so the university survey reported, the largest gap between the classes since World War II, but Clinton took no notice of it. He said, "Our strategy is working. The economy is growing, and our nation is moving in the right direction." But his likely Republican opponent, Bob Dole, accused him instead of "reigning over the first recovery since World War II to leave the American worker behind."

The president doggedly argued his view of a prospering America with a flurry of statistics, such as a small rise (eight-tenths of 1 percent) in hourly wage rates in early summer, atop his feat of cutting the nation's budget deficit in half. He also cited a 3.7 percent rise in personal consumption.

The Federal Reserve agreed with the White House's view, as was shown when the summer passed without a rise in the interest rate. The stock market boom in Wall Street, which had cooled somewhat in the spring with a sharp drop from its high of more than 5,700 in the Dow Jones Industrial Averages, had long since turned around with substantial gains in the averages with the approach of the national political party conventions in August.

But the sticking point for the economy was still the continued failure of an otherwise prosperous nation to improve the position of the poorest families, many of them blacks and Hispanics, and to relieve the hardships of the children of one-parent families, most of them living on welfare grants and food stamps because of the refusal of fathers to provide for them.

What the president tried to do for the least favored workers, particularly when the great corporate downsizing movement seemed to be at its peak with massive discharges of old employees, was to plead with the Republican-controlled Congress to pass his proposed wage-increase program from $4.25 an hour to $5.15. (It amounted to a rise of $1,800 a year, from $8,500 to $10,300, which was still far below the government-designated poverty level.)

Even before leaving the Senate, however, Dole had argued against the minimum-wage boost unless some of the smallest businesses were made exempt, plus a "Medical Savings Account," which was nontaxable and could be included for families that saved against the prospect of damaging accidents or ill health. The wage increase, as a result, was stalled in Congresss for the time being.

What Dole and the Republican high command countered with, hoping to offset the president's advantage in the opinion polls, was to float rumors that the former senator intended to propose massive tax cuts as the centerpiece of his campaign. The argument he made was that it had helped Ronald Reagan, so why not Dole?

To that, even when the tax cut was still in the rumor stage, the Democrats countered that the Republicans were hoping for a financial miracle if they counted on the growing economy, all by itself, to make up for the many billions that the government would again sink in debt to finance so generous a tax cut.

President Clinton argued that, if Dole were elected, any such tax cut would, in the end, send the national deficit soaring once again. But Dole, still sinking in the polls, decided on his tax-cutting campaign proposal as the best way he could get himself back in the presidential race. The approximate time for making public a detailed plan was just before the Republican National Convention in San Diego.

President Clinton was still leading Dole as his presumptive Republican challenger by 20 or more points at that juncture, despite the White House's bad breaks in Whitewater and the embarrassing matter of FBI files, among other benefits for the Republican cause. Despite Dole's continual criticism of every aspect of the Democratic administration, together with the support of the Republican-controlled Congress, nothing had seemed to make a difference in the President's superior standing in the polls.

The most discouraging part of the Dole effort for his Republican supporters appeared to be the ineffective manner of the former Kansas senator's campaigning — his tendency to stray from or entirely disregard the advance texts that were prepared for his speeches and his dour, sometimes snappish, posture so often when he addressed public issues or answered reporters' questions.

The total effect, even for those who sometimes were inclined to favor his cause, was a mixture of wonder and shock that so distinguished a leader of Congress for thrity-five years should continually make so poor an impression on a substantial part of the American public. And all this had occurred long before H. Ross Perot and his Reform Party had given serious indications of entering the race.

A Washington *Post* poll at the onset of summer gave President Clinton a figure of 55 percent as an approval rating against only 35 percent for Dole in a two-way presidential race. And only a few days later, a New York *Times* poll gave Clinton an approval rating of 54 percent, with Dole still tagging along at 20 points lower.

Not even usually favorable polls in the *Wall Street Journal,* with the largest circulation of a daily newspaper in the nation, could produce a consistent lead for the presumed Republican challenger to the president. The only excuse the Republican high command was able to offer was that Dole, through no fault of his own, had been tied up far too long by his duties as the majority leader of the Senate and that things would change once he could devote himself solely to his presidential race.

Even so, the change in the Republican standard-bearer was a long time coming; and he became involved meanwhile in a bitter dispute over the total ban on abortion in the party's platform, as championed by the Republican right and its Christian Coalition allies. The presumptive candidate's best efforts to leave room for moderates who supported women's right of choice seemed only to create still enlarged difficulties for him, even after he was willing to settle for a mere statement of tolerance for opposing views.

On the continuing problem of job losses through corporate downsizing, the best Dole could do was to protest the education of illegal immigrants, mostly children, at taxpayers' expense. The assumption presumably was that the illegals, from teenagers up, were a threat to American full employment.

True or not, the White House responded quite seriously that Dole in 1982 had voted against a proposal to permit states to drop paid education for illegal immigrants. To that, Governor Pete Wilson of California added that his state had been paying $2.6 billion annually to support about 150,000 illegal aliens and that their education cost $1.8 billion of that total.

Dole and the Republicans weren't as careful of Clinton's feelings, however, when they renewed their attack on him for failing to go to Vietnam for military service. His prospective opponent also took another crack at him by saying that the nation couldn't afford "would be statesmen still suffering from post-Vietnam syndrome."

In their advertising commercials meanwhile, both sides opened their war chests early to make damaging personal attacks affecting both major candidates as early as May. The "character" issue was regularly used against the president to the point of suggesting infidelity, laziness, and lack of discretion in his official duties. Nor was the first lady spared in the these vehement TV displays.

The Republican TV ad campaign, in particular, was so overstressed and so unbelievable that it seemed to have little effect in the period immediately before the national conventions. There was, for example, a rather childish plea to the TV audience to "tell the president to stop wasting money," the nature unspecified and the amounts left to the imagination. Nor did the Democrats make much better use of their clients' contributions.

These early TV-ad wars were, in brief, a carnival of insults that had the same general effect as two children sticking out their tongues at each other. To the Republican presentations, the Democrats replied in kind by accusing Congress of blocking progress—a discredit to the leadership of both major parties.

It could scarcely be imagined that this sorry exhibition of political gamesmanship could have the slightest effect on the outcome of the election. It was predictable that, up to the time of the conventions, the summer's polls would show not a bit of difference in Clinton's lengthening advantage over Dole. And it wasn't all Dole's fault by any means.

Had the Republicans been alert to their responsibilities as the opposition party, President Clinton's administration could have been in big trouble when Valujet Airlines was termed "safe" soon after one of its DC-9s crashed in the Florida Everglades on May 11 and all 110 people aboard died. The officials involved were Transportation Secretary Federico F. Peña and Chief of the Federal Aviation Administration David R. Hinson.

But less than one month later, the FAA concluded that the first judgment was wrong and grounded the airline, pending rigorous inspection and changes in its operation. Trying to explain the reversal, Secretary Peña said, "The FAA is no longer confident of the airline's ability to operate at the required levels of safety."

The FAA had disclosed that the Valujet management and a contractor, Sabretech, had blamed each other for putting some potentially dangerous devices, known as oxygen generators, in the baggage compartment of the crashed aircraft that probers suspected as the cause of a fatal fire that directly preceded the crash.

The FAA inquiry also disclosed that, for at least one year before the Everglades accident, Valujet's DC-9s had flown their commercial routes with large passenger loads, even though defective parts in the aircraft had been subject to neither repeated inspection nor repairs. The inquiry, according to the FAA, also revealed that one plane had flown with a hole in an engine cowl and another with a hydraulic fluid leak in the pressure gauge. After being hit by lightning, still another aircraft was reported to have been put back in service without sufficient inspection.

As a result of these and other flaws, there were management shifts, and Valujet agreed to pay the FAA $2 million for the inquiry expenses in return for the agency's pledge to seek no civil penalty, except possibly for security breaches if any were found. But throughout, apparently, there was no major move by the Republican opposition to inquire into the administration's anxiety to promote cheap travel as safe travel, despite the Everglades crash.

The same reluctance to move into another area of public interest, a congressionally approved ban in 1994 on nineteen different kinds of assault weapons, also seemed to hurt Dole's standing. But the enormous public support given the gun-control measure when it was approved by a Democratic-controlled Congress had also added to President Clinton's standing in the polls.

In the early stages of his reelection campaign thereafter, the president vowed to veto any attempt to repeal the assault weapons prohibition when he addressed the National Association for the Advancement of Colored People. In due course, because Dole was known to have his doubts about the weapons ban, the NAACP also asked the Republican challenger to speak before its membership on the subject; but surprisingly, he rejected the invitation.

It was a strange turn of affairs, for what the prospective Republican presidential nominee was doing was to affront the oldest civil rights organization in America, its 3,000 convention delegates, its 1.2 million membership, and its new president, Kweisi Mfume, a former member of the House of Representatives.

Meanwhile, Dole seemed to have had second thoughts about opposing the ban on assault weapons. In a relatively brief talk on crime problems at the Virginia State Police offices in Richmond, he repeated his criticism that the new law was ineffective, but added, "We've got to move beyond banning assault weapons; and instead of endlessly debating which guns to ban, we ought to be emphasizing what works."

Still, he wouldn't appear before the NAACP to discuss "what works" and excused his nonappearance by saying that there were "conflicts on timing." But at last, he admitted that he had feared "being set up," as he called it, by "a leading liberal Democrat," President Mfume.

Worse still, Dole also conceded a certain amount of concern about "not being well-received," President Mfume was not amused and alleged that it was he, and not Candidate Dole, who was being set up. Eventually, Dole tried to paper over the fault by saying that he would try to arrange to meet the NAACP.

The likely Republican nominee also tried criticizing President Clinton's foreign policy, what there was of it. In Philadelphia in June, Dole accused Clinton of having done little or nothing to support an ailing President Boris N. Yeltsin in Moscow against a strong Communist challenger and said, "It's time to take our foreign policy out of the hands of an administration engaged in the dreamy pursuit of an international order, that cherishes romantic illusions about a former adversary."

Yeltsin's reelection, stopping cold a Communist return to power, disposed of that issue. Next, while approving Clinton's contribution of American troops to a UN peace-keeping mission in Bosnia-Herzegovina, Dole criticized the White House for not providing a plan to remove the American contingent from its dangerous mission when the time came.

As he put it, "After sort of haphazardly getting America into Bosnia, President Clinton now has no idea how to get Americans out or how to accomplish the mission they went to fulfill." What Dole proposed was to provide the Bosnian Muslims with enough arms to defend themselves against the victorious Bosnian Serbs in their continuing civil war.

In Dole's Philadelphia address, as in two others on foreign affairs that July, it became evident that his differences with President Clinton on Russia, Bosnia, China, Cuba, and the Middle East were confined to degree rather than substance.

Although that wouldn't eliminate foreign problems as an issue in the presidential campaign, it did demonstrate that the basic interests of the United States outside its borders would not change substantially by reason of political differences. It followed that Dole could not possibly hope for a change in his current low standing in the polls by reason of anything he said or did in the area of foreign policy.

Thus the state of the Republican campaign at the onset of summer was consistently low. President Clinton's lead over Dole in the opinion polls remained in double digits, with no perceptible change in sight as convention time approached.

PART THREE

Purposes and Principles

16 Big Tobacco

Until Bob Dole threw a temper tantrum before NBC-TV's cameras, his appearance on the *Today* show had seemed like a pleasant interlude that early summer's morning of July 2. But then, as members of his Republican campaign staff were well aware, you never could tell when the moody Republican challenger to President Clinton would change his script, forget his lines, or otherwise mess up some of his carefully planned appearances.

In this scheduled book-promotion session being broadcast, the former senator and his wife, Elizabeth, had been expected to talk mainly about the reissue of their autobiography, *Unlimited Partners,* on the face of it an unlikely source of controversy. But the news business and Dole being what they are, the host of *Today,* a mild little woman named Katie Couric, tentatively brought up the subject of tobacco's addictiveness.

Why tobacco? Well, it seemed that the Clinton White House had been critical of Dole's relationship with the tobacco industry, and so the Republican's response seemed called for; besides, Katie had a point.

So did Dole, who responded on tobacco's addictiveness, "I'm not certain whether it's addictive. It is to some people. I had a lot of trouble stopping. Some people say it's addictive. It's harmful. People shouldn't smoke. Children shouldn't smoke."

But when the interviewer referred to criticism of Dole's views by former Surgeon General C. Everett Koop, the Kansan's irritated response was to agree with another surgeon that Koop had been "brainwashed." What the former surgeon general had said was that the former senator had either been giving "blind support to the tobacco industry" or was ignorant of the plague of nicotine addiction.

Although Mrs. Dole anxiously attempted to return the interview to the subject of the autobiography, Dole himself was wound up by this time and probed suspiciously at Ms. Couric's motives in bringing up tobacco addiction. She explained, without showing tension or strain, that she was merely offering him a chance to respond to criticism of his position on tobacco as a questionably addictive drug.

That was when the presidential candidate flared, "You can't respond because the media have already made up their mind. I've said I don't know whether it's addictive. I'm not a doctor. I'm not a scientist. People shouldn't smoke." He reverted later to Dr. Koop's criticism, saying "He [Koop] watched the liberal media and probably got carried away."

When President Clinton was informed of the back-and-forth between his presumptive opponent and the host of the *Today* show, he commented in Chicago, where he was addressing an audience of senior citizens, "I've been amazed at the debate that's been injected into the national campaign on this issue. I notice that Senator Dole questioned the other day whether or not tobacco was really addictive for everybody."

Then, in defense of Dr. Koop, the president added, "I believe Dr. Koop knows more about the dangers of tobacco than the so-called liberal media or Senator Dole." The president predicted that Medicaid would pay at least $10 million to registered patients to compensate for the treatment for sickness arising from excessive smoking of cigarettes, cigars, and pipe tobacco.

The National Broadcasting Company, the *Today* show, and Ms. Couric came in for criticism from the Dole campaign for the rough exchange about the ills of smoking and the candidate's failure to recognize the seriousness of the tobacco industry's position. Still, NBC insisted, Ms. Couric's questions had been fairly put before a huge national audience.

Of course, the Clinton camp was pleased. It had been trying for weeks to promote the campaign for regulation of tobacco as an addictive, contrary to Dole's much-publicized doubts.

Only a little more than one month later, on August 9, in Jacksonville, Florida, a state circuit court took a decisive part in the controversy by awarding $750,000 in damages to a male patient suffering from lung cancer after he had smoked cigarettes for forty-four years.

The verdict against the Brown & Williamson Tobacco Corporation, although it was only the second of its kind against tobacco interests in many years and the company served notice of an appeal, sent stocks tumbling on the New York Stock Exchange. The Clinton campaign, anxious to capitalize on the issue, had created a 7-foot "Butt Man" cigarette soon after the NBC dustup over Dole's argument. In response, the Republicans put out a "Joint Man," a parody on Clinton's admission he'd once smoked pot. Despite these silly-season objects, however, Big Tobacco at last had real cause for concern because countless other lawsuits were pending.

Although Dole and the Republicans suffered a certain amount of public disapproval over the candidate's ill-judged doubts about the spread of tobacco-related illnesses, the Democrats were not without fault.

As the Center for Responsible Politics and other public-service organizations were quick to suggest, the Democratic National Committee and others in responsible party posts had also accepted tobacco money in election years, even though they continually claimed in solemn postures of virtue that the gifts didn't influence them.

Their position evidently was that those weak-kneed Republicans couldn't resist doing Big Tobacco's bidding. All that the available government records showed in this regard was that the Republicans usually got more money from Big Tobacco and its allies than the Democrats, although the latter's share still amounted to much more money than an average citizen could earn, even in a lucky year.

From 1995 until early 1996, leading up to the presidential campaign, the reports regularly issued by government agencies showed that the Republican National Committee alone received $2.1 million from tobacco interests, and the Democratic National Committee received $78,000.

That, however, was just for starters and did not include a complete accounting in a presidential campaign, where all indications early on pointed to total costs by all concerned of several hundred million dollars. Just what proportion of the total Big Tobacco dispensed in the expectation of favorable treatment and how much both parties spent to try to gain the votes of tobacco farmers and their communities in tobacco-growing states like Virginia, the Carolinas, and Kentucky may never be determined to everybody's satisfaction.

But the political and industrial problem presented by an industry that was fighting for self-preservation was scarcely as simple as the two options available to the consumer—to smoke and face the chance of severe illness or death in years yet to come or to quit while still in good health.

Depending on how deeply an organization or an individual was committed to accepting Big Tobacco's largesse, the problem for political organizations was phrased in various ways. As President Clinton once put the case, "What I seek to highlight is the difference in our policies. When you see a pattern of contributions and then a dramatic difference in the policies, it is the policies and their impact on the American people that I am concerned about."

In the opinion of the citizens' organization Common Cause and its president, Ann McBride, that concern would have been greatly diminished if the tobacco money had been returned to its source. As Ms.

McBride said, "The Democrats have correctly criticized Dole for the huge amounts of political money that have come from tobacco interests, and for his position on nicotine. But the Democrats should not only not take tobacco money in the future. They should give back all the tobacco money they have taken in this election."

That, of course, didn't happen in this election and wasn't likely to happen in future elections, the costs of running for public office being what they are and the additional expenses of TV time mounting ever higher per candidate. The eventual result, as Common Cause put it in commenting on the responsibility of both the Republican and the Democratic National Committees, was to contribute annually to 400,000 tobacco-related deaths in this country.

Common Cause figures for the last decade showed that Republican organizations accepted $7 million, and that Democratic groups accepted $2.6 million from tobacco interests—contributions that also included gifts to members of both houses of Congress.

For major recipients of gifts from Big Tobacco from 1986 through 1995, again according to Common Cause, the largest contributions to Republicans in the lower house were to Thomas Bliley of Virginia, $123,976; Jim Bunning of Kentucky, $72,450; and Howard Coble of North Carolina, $61,892.

The largest contributions to House Democrats for the same period, according to Common Cause, were to Charlie Rose of North Carolina, $104,800; Lewis Payne of Virginia, $92,899; and Rick Boucher of Virginia, $75,350.

Compilations by Common Cause of major Republican recipients of Big Tobacco money in the Senate for the same period included Jesse Helms of North Carolina, $77,000; Mitch McConnell of Kentucky, $67,500; and Daniel Coats of Indiana, $58,500. Their Democratic counterparts included Wendell Ford of Kentucky, $76,057; Ernest Hollings of South Carolina, $52,796; and Charles Robb of Virginia, $41,000.

During the decade from 1986 to 1995, Common Cause reported also that Big Tobacco gave $2.3 million to Republican House candidates and $2.1 million to Democrats; in the Senate, the totals were $1.2 million for Republicans and $607,000 for Democrats.

None of this money included "soft money" gifts that corporate America is allowed to make to political committes—a practice upheld by the Supreme Court on the eve of the 1996 presidential campaign. To that extent, at least, there was legal approval for the way that Big Tobacco and other large industrial organizations went about distributing their largesse.

Accordingly, it was a practice that deeply concerned millions of citizens still affected by the smoking habit and many more children of the next generation who, if major social changes were not made, would be as victimized by smoking as their elders had been in the twentieth century.

Regardless of Big Tobacco's financial contributions to the Democratic National Committe and to leading Democrats in Congress, the Clinton campaign proceeded in eary July to use commercial TV ads assailing Dole and other Republicans for the same practices, except that the latter received larger sums than their rivals in the opposing party.

After portraying children smoking cigarettes and using Dole's doubts about tobacco addiction in the televised commentary, the Clinton venture into this issue demanded, "Bob Dole or Bill Clinton, who's really protecting our children?"

The Dole campaign organization responded, "For Bill Clinton, distortion is habit-forming. Bob Dole has never supported tobacco ads that target kids."

Nevertheless, the Democrats' campaign hit hard at the efforts of Dole and those of about two dozen other senators to attack the Food and Drug Administration's endeavors to restrict advertising intended to attract children to smoking. Dole's people, however, were quick to argue that he had joined in the president's appeal to tobacco companies to keep cigarette billboard advertising at a considerable distance from schools.

The Republican candidate never did change his basic position, which was to doubt the addictive power of tobacco; and at the time, the Democrats never did take an outright position against accepting Big Tobacco money in their reelection campaign.

Neither side, for that matter, ever considered the usual attraction of the confirmed child cigarette smoker to the next available addictive so often glamorized by their elders, hard liquor, and beyond that the lure of the dope peddler for big-time self-destruction.

Yet, as the condition of society in the most crowded and least policed sections of large cities in America so often demonstrated, there seemed to be no limit to childish addiction to destructive substances once the cycle was permitted to take hold on an individual. Indeed, that was the most dismal part of an age when self-destruction reached appalling depths.

Grady Carter, the sixty-six-year-old plaintiff who won a $750,000 verdict for his tobacco-induced lung cancer, was one of the very fortunate few who managed to punish Big Tobacco for promoting life-threatening excesses among its products. He had originally asked for at least $1.5 million from Brown & Williamson, the maker of Lucky Strikes, the brand he smoked for forty-four years.

The Florida circuit court jury in Jacksonville, who had found in his favor, took two days after receiving the case to reach their verdict. What the jurors decided in effect was that the company had been at fault in offering the public a product that was defectively dangerous and that it had been negligent in failing to warn the public of its life-threatening potential in smoking it. The company served notice of appeal directly after the verdict was announced.

As for Carter, a retired air controller whose cancer was in remission at the time, he commented, "Sombody needed to take these people on. A lot of people are dying of lung cancer."

The plaintiff had started smoking Lucky Strikes in 1946 and testified that, although he had tried to quit, he always lit up again to satisfy his noxious habit until 1972. Then, for the next nineteen years, he changed to other brands of cigarettes until 1991, when he had to quit for good because doctors found that he had contracted lung cancer.

In a subsequent operation, Carter lost his left lung and was in remission for the time being. He then filed his lawsuit against Brown & Williamson. During the trial, company lawyers argued that the company couldn't be held liable because the plaintiff knew perfectly well that smoking was dangerous, yet he persisted in continuing to smoke.

The reason that he quit, they continued, was not that he suddenly became aware of the danger of smoking but that he started coughing blood. The company climaxed its plea to be free of responsibility with the statement that it had been the plaintiff's right to smoke as well as his right to quit, and that the company had had nothing to do with either decision.

The legal gimmick didn't work in Carter's case, although that and other arguments of similar nature had been used for years by cigarette makers to turn back a host of lawsuits.

As a result, it was not until 1988 that a plaintiff won the first award from a tobacco company in a legal action. The victor was the family of a smoking victim in New Jersey, Rose Cipollone, who won a $400,000 award but never got a cent of it because the verdict was overturned on appeal and dropped four years later.

In another case in 1990, a Mississippi jury found that another veteran smoker, Nathan Horton, had died of cigarette poisoning but gave his survivors no money. The finding here was that both the smoker and the American Tobacco Company, the defendant, had been equally liable.

It followed that in the Carter case in Florida, the current and future plaintiffs against cigarette poisoning and the companies involved would be vitally concerned with the finding of an appeals court in the case. In nineteen previous cases, no company making cigarettes has paid monetary damages to any plaintiff so far.

But as mentioned earlier, in resultant activity on the New York Stock Exchange after the Carter case verdict in July and well on into late summer and fall, the shares of large cigarette companies were losing ground. That situation was particularly true of the two big ones, Philip Morris and RJR Nabisco, which led a spectacular drop in mid-August more than one month after the Carter verdict.

Brown & Williamson, which bought Lucky Strikes from American Brands in 1994, declined only moderately at that time. The market, so the wise ones of Wall Street guessed, appeared to be looking for more bad news for Big Tobacco.

17 Clinton and Russia

As more than one American president has discovered, picking winners in foreign elections is a tricky business and sometimes not worth the effort when an American favorite loses. But when an American-supported foreign candidate wins, particularly on the eve of the Fourth of July, that is a proper cause for celebration.

For Independence Day 1996, while most other American fathers were setting off firecrackers and sparklers for the kids, President Clinton released a bald eagle to a flight for freedom over Maryland and hailed the reelection of the ailing Boris N. Yeltsin as Russia's president. Yeltsin had defeated Gennadi A. Zyuganov, who was leading an attempted Communist Party comeback, by an impressive 14 percent of the vote on July 3.

As far as another recent election was concerned, it was, in a way, a comeback for Clinton because he'd also gone through the embarrassment of welcoming the new Israeli prime minister, Benjamin Netanyahu, who had narrowly defeated the Clinton-backed, seventy-three-year-old Shimon Peres, the former occupant of the post.

And so the American president could scarcely be faulted for dusting off every time-honored Fourth of July oratorical cliché as it applied to the outcome of the Russian election. "The Russian people," he said, "have turned their backs on tyranny. They are turning the corner towards freedom. They and their leaders have cleared another important hurdle in building a new and enduring democracy. As we celebrate our freedom and independence, we applaud them for their freedom and independence as well."

But for all the American's patriotic flourishes, both he and his beneficiary, Yeltsin, knew quite well that Russian democracy was fragile; that the Communists were still the best organized—if not the strongest—political element in the former Soviet Union; and that Zyuganov would have to be dealt with on his own terms, although not now.

In his usual sour manner, Bob Dole, as the likely Republican challenger to President Clinton's reelection, made the point that Russia had a long way to go before a democratic system, Russian style, became a secure principle of government in Moscow. As he remarked, "Democracy is not built on any one individual or even any one election."

What properly bothered the United States government at that juncture was the concern emphasized by U.S. Ambassador Thomas Pickering over Yeltsin's health. Referring to the Russian leader's failure to campaign during the last few days before the election, Pickering expressed the pious American hope that Yeltsin would have a strong cabinet of reformers who could carry on the really hard work of government no matter what happened next.

There were other Americans who were also not greatly confident about Russia's slow advancement toward responsibility and self-rule among the family of nations. If Yeltsin proved unable to govern by reason of bad health, for example, the direction of his cabinet became a proper matter of foreign concern, especially among those whom Washington seemed to be encouraging to trade with Russia and even invest in Russia's future.

It was likely then that a new member of Yeltsin's cabinet, General Aleksandr Lebed, could become a center of influence as the government's security adviser, especially if Yeltsin's health took a critical turn. As the candidate with the strongest support of the Russian military establishment, Lebed had finished third to Yeltsin and Zyuganov in the preliminary voting that led to the July 3 election runoff. Most people familiar with politics in the sprawling Russian nation also credited Yeltsin's immediate engagement of Lebed as the crucial factor in his victory over the Communist machine.

But just what role Lebed would take, considering his reputation as a career militarist in the Red Army, became a matter of the most immediate concern to others in the Yeltsin cabinet, particularly the leading figure, Prime Minister Viktor S. Chernomyrdin.

There was little doubt among experienced observers of the Russian scene that a disabled Yeltsin almost certainly could create a power struggle between Chernomyrdin and Lebed. Chernomyrdin was a survivor of the Soviet era who seemed to have adjusted to Yeltsin's anti-Soviet policies with vigor, so much so that he had won grudging if guarded trust from Western diplomats. His post-Soviet career had begun in the regime of Mikhail Gorbachev as chief of natural gas operations, after which he jumped into the Yeltsin camp and became prime minister in 1992.

Lebed, a veteran Red Army paratrooper and the head of the Russian Fourteenth Army stationed in Moldova, had lost his command over his opposition to the Chechen War that had begun on Russia's southwest flank in December 1994. He had argued that it wasn't worth the ultimate cost in blood and treasure, and he turned out to be eminently correct. The tiny province, with its Muslim-dominated freedom fighters, had become Russia's Vietnam.

The war had begun well enough for Yeltsin in December 1994, with the Red Army's capture of the rebels' capital, Grozny, within three months; but the Russian troops couldn't hold it. The rebel guerrillas swarmed all over them and were finally able to recapture the town.

At just about that time in 1996, Yeltsin had made his deal with Lebed to win military support in the runoff election and promptly sent his new ally to negotiate a truce with the Chechen rebels. Fortunately for Yeltsin, the truce held during the election.

Meanwhile, in a preelection sensation that strengthened Lebed's position, the ailing president had fired his security chief, General Aleksandr V. Korzhakob; General Mikhail Barsukov; and Deputy Prime Minister Oleg Soskovets. As it developed, Yeltsin had taken a calculated gamble on the military vote through this maneuver; and he evidently succeeded, as the election results demonstrated. But by that time, he was back in his dacha outside Moscow, admitting to a cold and laryngitis, as the rumors of his heart trouble mounted around the Kremlin.

He was nonetheless able to discuss common interests with President Clinton, who telephoned him with congratulations for the "Comeback Kid"—a title that the American had coined for himself in a previous tight election. The immediate result was to arrange a trip to the Kremlin by Vice-President Al Gore as a new American emissary whose duty it had become to check on Yeltsin's health and the strength of the Communists in Parliament after the election.

But strangely, when President Yeltsin was able to arrange for a celebration of his electoral victory for TV and film crews, he seemed to make it a point to invite Prime Minister Chernomyrdin and Mayor Yuri M. Luzhkov of Moscow, but not General Lebed, who meanwhile had temporarily taken charge of the office vacated by an unpopular defense minister, Pavel S. Grachev.

If, however, this was a gesture intended to limit Lebed to a secondary role, as most Moscow politicians surmised, it didn't last very long. For soon after the election there was a sudden renewal of the Chechen War, after which Moscow itself was attacked with two huge bomb blasts that were attributed to Chechen spies who had infiltrated the Russian capital. As far as that was concerned, therefore, the election had settled nothing beyond renewing a faltering president's uncertain hold on the highest office in the land.

But as for the speculation in Washington that the election had settled the fate of communism in Russia for good, a theory advanced by the Soviet expert Deputy Secretary of State Strobe Talbott, the shock effect of the Moscow bombings in themselves seriously undercut the pretensions of the Yeltsin government to be able to maintain order after his return to power.

It also became apparent as weeks passed without any sign that Yeltsin was well enough to take charge in the Kremlin that his illness was far more severe than his government was willing to admit. Before long, more reports began circulating in the Russian capital that the president would have to undergo heart surgery, possibly by foreign experts rather than Russians, who might be reluctant to undertake such responsibility.

The name of Dr. Michael E. DeBakey of Baylor University, a renowned American heart surgeon, was prominently mentioned by Russian specialists as a likely consultant if not the chief of an American-Russian operating team.

It also became known, in the peculiar way that news of government circulates in Moscow, that the president was no longer making decisions for his government but was leaving them to Prime Minister Chernomyrdin. Relatively little was now being heard of General Lebed, although he was still technically the prersident's security adviser.

That is how matters stood in Moscow until much greater concern was created in Washington and other European capitals by the televised figure of a trembling and distinctly unhealthy-looking Yeltsin being sworn in on August 9, 1996, as Russia's first democratically elected president.

After being twice hospitalized in the previous year for heart ailments, it was obvious that he was not in shape then to carry out the oath of office that he had undertaken that day. The Communists were already calling on him to resign because he was unfit to hold office.

That day, the only speech that the president made after his inauguration was at a Kremlin luncheon before about 1,000 guests, who toasted him with champagne glasses aloft, to which he responded wearily with a toast of his own and these remarks in less than a minute. "Popular support gives me the right to act firmly and decisively. It is progress that has distinguished Russia during the current decade, and these four years will finally determine the outlook for a new Russia."

It was not long after Yeltsin departed once again for the hunting lodge outside Moscow, where he had been staying with only a few trusted retainers, that the world learned that he would have to risk a heart operation if he ever meant to return actively to the head of government.

All pretense was finally dropped, so that the Russian people, the last to be let in on his real condition, would have no doubt about who from then on was running their government.

Through a decree signed in September by the ailing president, Prime Minister Chernomyrdin was also given final authority over the control of Russia's still large and awesomely powerful nuclear arsenal along with the day-to-day decisions of government. The decree would come into effect, so the government announced, at a time shortly before the proposed heart operation and would be revoked at a time to be determined thereafter.

And so it now became definite that the prime minister, in immediately assuming all other presidential functions of government, would have his finger on the so-called nuclear button that included "powers to control the strategic nuclear forces and tactical nuclear weapons" through computerized communications that would order the Russian general staff to start firing.

All that was heard from General Lebed, the security adviser, was a public warning, presumably to the prime minister, that many among the military were growing restless because, so he said, they had not been paid for weeks. Under the circumstances, the confusion in official Moscow was understandable; but for official Washington, always concerned about a threatened Communist return to power, the news was unsettling.

The new Russia would clearly have to await the outcome of Yeltsin's heart operation, for none could then say when it would happen or even if he could survive it in any condition to govern a vast country wasted by seventy-three years of Communist rule. For the United States and the Clinton administration, which was then in the midst of the president's own reelection campaign, the uncertainty about government in Russia was unsettling news, indeed. Whatever gains America and the West may have derived from the end of a Communist regime in Moscow were once again very much at risk.

When Dr. DeBakey arrived in Moscow late in the summer and examined President Yeltsin, he pronounced the patient fit for the heart bypass operation, provided there were six to eight weeks of hospital rest beforehand. Despite Yeltsin's reputation as a two-fisted drinker, the visiting American specialist found the patient's heart, lungs, and kidneys in good shape for someone sixty-five years old who seemed to have treated his body with benign neglect.

Dr. DeBakey explained that he saw no more appreciable risk in the operation than would be the case with any other elderly patient with severe heart problems. With President Yeltsin's approval, the decision was then made to schedule the operation sometime around the end of the year at Moscow's Central Clinical Hospital by an all-Russian team, headed by the chief surgeon, Dr. Renat S. Akchurin, who had trained under Dr. DeBakey at Baylor's College of Medicine in Houston.

Dr. DeBakey vouched for the Russian team by saying, "They're right on the ball and the tests and facilities they are using are the most advanced and they really know what they are doing."

In an effort to leave nothing to chance, so far as possible, the American specialist also made arrangements for all members of the operating team to visit Houston for demonstrations of the latest techniques in the always difficult heart bypass surgery.

What still seemed to bother both the Russian specialists and their American mentor, despite the elaborate advance arrangements, was bouts of past internal bleeding that had made it necessary for Yeltsin to have daily transfusions of limited quantities of blood to combat anemia. Although the internal bleeding had stopped by the time of Dr. DeBakey's preoperative examination, the cause still remained undetermined, and that situation was understandably bothersome.

Still, the American specialist agreed with his Russian counterparts that there remained a blockage in the right coronary artery leading to the heart that would have to be made up for somehow by the patient's regular flow of blood to the left coronary artery, at least until the time set for the operation, which was now held in abeyance.

Further efforts were made, therefore, to try to find the cause of the blockage so as to resume the normal blood flow; but this investigation did not interfere with the favorable prognosis for the operation itself.

President Yeltsin was of course duly informed of these events at the Central Clinical Hospital, where he was now sequestered; and he took them well, according to those close to him. But thereafter, he wasn't likely to be lying abed all the time awaiting his date under the surgeon's knife. In addition to the regular tests of his arteries, blood flow, and the like, his schedule called for a strict diet, no alcohol whatever, and regular exercise of a limited nature.

But in between all else, even though Prime Minister Chernomyrdin was running the country by decree, there were some decisions that still had to be made by Yeltsin—one of the most critical of which had to do with the assignment of the always touchy security adviser, General Lebed. With the ascension of Chernomyrdin, it was to be expected among the gossipy Kremlin crowd that Lebed's role in the government machine would deteriorate; and that is what happened.

The general began fussing whenever he felt that he was being ignored. The ultimate outrage came early in October, when Yuri M. Baturin, a security operative who had been displaced, was suddenly given leadership of a critical military commission.

This appointment was one that Lebed had particulary opposed; and so he pushed his way into the Central Clinical Hospital for a bedside protest directly to President Yeltsin and threatened to quit. In response, Yeltsin told him that he couldn't very well continue to pick fights with those around him, urged him to stay on, and then announced the whole confused business over Moscow TV.

The only satisfaction for Lebed came with President Yeltsin's broadcast gratitude for the general's part in reaching agreement with the Chechen rebels to halt their conflict. To the Communists in Parliament who were biding their time for still another attempt to regain power, Yeltsin also had a word of caution. "I said before the elections and repeat now — don't rush to change the portraits."

The reaction of the White House was pretty much that held by ordinary Muscovites — a sick Russian anti-Communist leader facing heart bypass surgery was still preferable to a Communist return to power. But for the moment, the steadiness of a surgeon's knife would play a part in the next page in Russia's tumultuous history.

18 Perot Redux

When Ross Perot bankrolled his Reform Party and claimed one million members in a typical whirl of Perotean confusion just before the onset of the 1996 presidential campaign, it was a foregone conclusion that he would try to make his influence felt before election day. Among the fearful Dole Republicans and the hopeful Clinton Democrats who pondered their chances in a three-way race, the first question that the Texas billionaire asked was, "Will Perot run himself or send in a substitute?"

In the enigmatic manner that so often aroused conflicting emotions in the American body politic, Perot's response came with tantalizing delay. Then, early that election year, after months of feints and threats, the surprise recipient of almost 19 million votes in 1992 announced that he would try his luck again.

The decision came directly after a different voice was heard within the newly organized Reform Party, that of former Governor Richard D. Lamm of Colorado, a conservative Democrat who announced his candidacy for the party's presidential nomination with a defiant flourish. Lamm's move created still more confusion in the camp of the party's founder and financial patron, Perot; and their major-party rivals looked on with a mixture of skepticism and wonderment.

Lamm, an elderly veteran of three terms in the Colorado state house, had been helpful in organizing the new party and had aroused a modest amount of interest with a speech extolling conservative values before the party's membership in California. For the record, at least, he seemed not to have asked for Perot's counsel and advice, much less his permission, to seek the party's highest honor under the very nose of its founder.

The first reaction to the Lamm announcement from the ever-critical newspaper press included a mild notation of his decision on a less-than-prominent area of page 1 and a few snarling "So what?" editorials. But mostly, the consensus appeared to be that a Lamm candidacy would make little difference in the eventual outcome of a straight Clinton/Dole match.

To the Republicans, who had figured to lose some of their much-needed on-the-fence constituency to a second Perot candidacy, the Lamm announcement brought at least temporary relief. As early as March, after Bob Dole had been within reach of a primary election victory for the Republican presidential nomination, he had appealed to Perot to stay out of the race, arguing, "I should say to Ross, 'We *are* the Reform Party. If you want Reform, it is the Republican Party.'"

Allowing for a general public understanding of the Dolean message despite the dubious syntax, the Republicans had a brief respite from concern that another strong third-party contender would draw more votes from Dole than from Clinton, their biggest fear. There had been no response whatever meanwhile from the Perot headquarters in Dallas.

But on July 10, after the Lamm announcement, Perot appeared on CNN's *Larry King Live*, beginning at 9:00 P.M. EDT, with what seemed like a restful view of the Lamm candidacy for the Reform presidential nomination and said, "If anybody should do this, I should do it."

That declaration evidently wasn't forceful enough from a presidential candidate to suit the finicky AP and the morning newspapers in the eastern time zone for their first editions. Either that or Perot himself didn't make enough of a fuss to suit his critics when he seemed to back into another declared run for the presidency.

In any event, there were no wails from the Republicans, no cheers from the Democrats, and no extra contributions to the Reform Party's coffers from sources other than Perot himself. What happened next? A more determined Perot arranged to appear on *Good Morning, America*, the early talk show of the leading network, ABC, on July 11.

This time, in his own circumferential manner, he tried a slightly more elaborate declaration of his intentions in a conversation with a somewhat sleepy-eyed talk-show host, saying, "Whatever it takes to leave a better country for our children and grandchildren, if anybody should do it [run for president], I should do it. And I will do it, and I'm in a unique position to do it."

The ABC host, like his CNN predecessor, still wasn't quite sure how far Perot really meant to go and cautiously sought to pin him down, asking deferentially why he didn't make a formal declaration of his candidacy for the presidency of the United States in 1996. That did it. Perot simply observed he'd already done it — once on CNN and again just then on ABC — and so former Governor Lamm now had to contend with the founder of the Reform Party, unless there was still more to the script in this developing political melodrama on the air. And with Perot, one never really knew what had been planned in advance and what had been improvised to fit the occasion.

What it looked like that morning directly after Perot's declaration was a scrap within the Reform Party for the presidential nomination between Perot, the former Republican, and Lamm, the former Democrat. Alternatively, the skeptics also began whispering that it was possible to settle this seeming contest, once Perot emerged as the likely winner, by offering Lamm the vice-presidential nomination. But that, of course, was getting ahead of the story, ever-advisable in a situation where Perot could take charge.

Otherwise, the reaction to the Perot candidacy was predictable. The fears of the Republicans had been realized, although Dole himself had held out hope to the last that the little Texan might be persuaded to remain on the sidelines. On the morning of Perot's announcement, the presumed Republican nominee had said on a radio program, "I'd hoped that Perot wouldn't run, that it would be a two-man race." But as it turned out, the Republican's luck continued indifferent.

As for Lamm, he wasn't particularly surprised when he learned that he had acquired a distinguished rival for the Reform presidential nomination. Now, he concluded for public consumption that the only way for him to go was, as he put it, "to beat Perot in his own party." That would take quite a bit of doing. To suit words to action, he argued that half the people he'd consulted in the Reform Party were against having Perot as their presidential candidate. True or not, it made for more headlines and still more TV interviews.

As had been known well in advance, Perot had arranged for a suspenseful showdown—or so he hoped. On the opening day of the Reform Party's convention, August 11, in Long Beach, California, the names of all declared candidates for the party's presidential nomination would be announced, after which mail ballots would be issued to all members—all this on the day before the Republican convention in San Diego to confirm Dole's presidential nomination.

Then, immediately before the Democratic convention in Chicago, August 18, the Reform Party would reconvene at Valley Forge, Pennsylvania, to receive and authenticate the winning candidates for a president and vice-president—presumably Perot and his choice for a running mate.

Quite naturally, all this pleased the Clinton Democrats, for a leading current poll showed the standings as follows: Clinton, 51 percent; Dole, 31 percent; and Perot, 13 percent. It was no great feat of memory for Democrats to recall that Perot had polled 18.9 percent of the actual vote for president in 1992; and so the current ratio clearly favored President Clinton's reelection for as long as he remained healthy, stayed out of trouble, and benefited from a strong economy with low unemployment and low inflationary pressures.

As a result, a leading Democratic commentator took the cheerful view, referring to the Perot candidacy, "The more this fall is about substantive ideas important to America's future, the better. We haven't heard much of this from the Republican side." To which the Republican National Chairman, Haley Barbour, added glumly, "A vote for Perot is a vote for Clinton."

For Dole, possessed of monumental troubles not entirely of his own making, it was back to *Larry King Live* on CNN and a public confessional on the night of July 15, this time with Mrs. Dole's attractive presence and support. King's first question, as would have been the pitch of any other professional newsman in such a situation, was to ask Dole how he felt about the Perot candidacy. "How do you think I feel?" was the dour response.

It wasn't particularly satisfying to the glum Republican presidential candidate to examine the record, either. By unlucky chance that same night, CNBC released a poll that supported the former senator's contention that, this time, Perot would draw equally from both major parties. CNBC gave this standing: Clinton, 50 percent; Dole, 25 percent; and Perot, 13 percent. The estimated 25-point Clinton lead given by CNBC was bad enough, but the estimated reduction of the Dole figure to only 12 points more than Perot's was a danger signal that not even a Republican pollster could wave aside.

Yes, it was still three and one-half months until election day. And, yes, the costly and massive Republican advertising campaign for Dole was bound to bring him some advantage; how much, no one could say. But the very idea that a Republican presidential candidate might finish third in a three-man race was chilling in itself. That hadn't happened in eighty-four years, not since the 1912 victory of Governor Woodrow Wilson, a Democrat; with the Bull Moose Party's candidate, former President Theodore Roosevelt, second; and with Republican President William Howard Taft, seeking reelection, a distant third.

Now Perot, no matter how enthusiastic his partisans may have been, was no Teddy Roosevelt, the hero of the cavalry charge up Cuba's San Juan Hill in the Spanish-American War; and Woodrow Wilson, by background and training a university professor, towered above Bill Clinton as a historical figure. This president had called on Congress on

April 2, 1917, to declare war against the Germany of Kaiser Wilhelm II in these well-remembered words, "The world must be made safe for democracy." It should have given pause, also, to those who believed it incredible toward century's end that Dole, after thirty-five years in Congress, might that next election day emulate the third-place finish in 1912 of William Howard Taft, twenty-seventh president of the United States and tenth chief justice of the United States.

But these were the political risks in that next-to-last presidential election of the twentieth century, and they could not be ignored. It was in this manner that the presidential field settled down for the rest of that summer, to be followed by the crux of the campaign that began after Labor Day with whatever inducements the major parties traditionally reserve for the electorate during the fall.

But for the sixteen days of the Olympic Games in Atlanta, beginning July 19, when the attention of much of the nation would be on world-class sports competition rather than politics, there was bound to be a lull in the presidential contest. Amid preparations for the conventions in August, the Clinton and Dole camps had a last chance to review strategic plans for the fall windup and to assess the importance of the Perot threat.

The Republican problem of creating far greater support for Bob Dole, which was difficult enough for the two-man race of springtime, had now been compounded by Perot's decision to make another run for the White House. It was clear enough that the talkative and ever-ambitious financier couldn't win against two major-party contenders, but he had already demonstrated that he might be able to wound Dole's candidacy. And the former senator was well aware of his dangerous position long before summer's end.

It was a good question how any presidential contender's staff could operate in so seemingly impossible a situation, made worse by Dole's own temper tantrums and his frequent opposition to the counsel that was offered him by competent professionals. For a part of that unhappy summer, reporters covering Dole headquarters were mildly surprised by what appeared at first to be off-the-record complaints by dissatisfied staff people against the candidate's behavior. The breach between Dole and at least a part of his staff became so noticeable after a time that there was open discussion, at first in the printed press, of dissension at the candidate's headquarters.

Almost as a matter of course, what followed was a processional in which critical staff people dropped out or were shoved out, depending on how swiftly changes occurred, and new advisers were brought in to replace those whose advice had more often than not been rejected by the candidate. Even so, reports of unidentified criticism of Dole's candidacy by some among his own staff continued to appear. Accordingly, the impression grew, particularly after Perot declared himself a candidate, that Dole needed a big break of an unspecified nature to get back in the race after Labor Day.

But as mid-July came and went without any major improvement in Dole's standing in the polls, the only possible move left for the Republican high command was to stiffen their attack on the president so as to relieve the pressure on Dole and hope for a turn of events that might make the Kansan a more attractive candidate to the average voter. The bottom line was the opinion, frequently published or heard among even friendly commentators on the almighty tube, that the Republican candidate would have to present the public with a more forceful explanation of what he hoped to accomplish as president instead of emphasizing the negative approach of continual criticism and complaint against the administration's shortcomings.

Even those supposedly in Dole's confidence couldn't offer any explanation for his sometimes erratic behavior on the campaign trail, which seemed to be a factor in his reduced standing in the polls. As one of his associates said when asked why the candidate sometimes seemed to resent the well-meant advice that was given to him, "Dole is going to be Dole no matter what happens."

Those who had critically observed Perot's return to the presidential race also had cause to wonder why he often showed such animus toward both major parties, especially the Republicans. True, he no longer referred to his strange 1992 charges that, in some obscure way, the Republicans at one time even threatened to intervene in his daughter's wedding. Instead, he now usually campaigned openly against both major-party candidates on the issues, particularly those that affected family values.

His was a gradiose view, put forward on the spur of the moment, that he wanted to leave a better country to his children and grandchildren. But, his critics were quick to demand, in what way was this to be done within his view? Through what means and at what cost? He could very well fail to elaborate on his dream, as he did in 1992, and still draw a whopping third-party vote. But this time, despite his early standing in the polls, his critics seemed to agree that it would not be so easy for him to win votes through his Reform Party unless he markedly improved its presence on more statewide ballots. There were only a few, mainly paid adherents on the roster of the Reform Party, who were willing to predict that he might win a third or more of the total vote this time.

Even in the imaginary vistas of mid-July, a never-never land in presidential politics, so tremendous a turnout for a new party and a politically untried candidate would have amounted to a monumental swing of public opinion, such as the change that reelected Harry Truman over Thomas E. Dewey in 1948.

Despite all the difficulties Dole's candidacy continued to encounter that summer, the Clinton headquarters was then in no mood to claim a forthcoming Democratic return to control of Congress after the Republican sweep of 1994. The president's lead in the polls was gratifying, to be sure; but there was no telling just how deeply public resentment of congressional gridlock, plus two government shutdowns, would affect both the House and the Senate. It was one thing for Democrats to point with satisfaction to Speaker Newt Gingrich's unpopularity and the assault that was being made against his freshmen allies in the House; it was quite another to envision a Democratic return to power in Congress.

As for President Clinton himself, he was his own best advertisement in stressing his administration's accomplishments and resisting the temptation to tear into the Republican opposition as well as the new threat posed by the reviving Perot campaign. Speaking to the National Governors' Conference in Puerto Rico on nationwide TV on July 16, however, the president made the somewhat risky claim of great economic progress during his administration. At the time, he had seemed reasonably safe in announcing a 60 percent reduction in the national debt during his administration, a record low unemployment rate, and a satisfactory growth of more than 10 million new jobs. "We have the strongest economy in a generation," he said.

But as the billionaire Perot could have told him, being wiser in the ways of Wall Street, such claims—however well based—were decidedly risky in the midst of what appeared then to be a sluggish economic recovery. That same day, during the Ides of July, the New York Stock Exchange registered a 161-point plunge in the Dow Jones averages, the worst day's drop in five years. And the next day, the Dow was down 212 points by midday, then gained 219 points, and managed a slight increase at the closing bell.

Was it the end of the great bull market of mid-1990? Wall Street (and probably President Clinton's advisers also) were shivering when Chairman Alan Greenspan of the Federal Reserve rushed to the rescue on July 18. Testifying before Congress, he confirmed the favorable state of the economy. The bulls took heart, boosting the averages to 5,376; and by early August, the Dow was back in the 5,700 range and within striking distance of the high of 5,778 set on May 22 of that year.

Even so, there were relatively few professionals who believed the market would take off again toward a new high before election day, despite the billions of dollars in new money that eager investors throughout the land were still pouring into mutual funds and other favorite investments like IBM, Microsoft, and other leading technology stocks. One highly regarded strategist, Byron R. Wien, of the famous firm of Morgan, Stanley & Co., even went so far as to predict a 1,000-point drop in this spectacular bull market.

It didn't turn out that way. On Friday, September 13, 1996, the market wiped out a brief midsummer turndown and surged to a record all-time high of 5,838.52 on the Dow Jones Industrial Averages. When long-term interest rates thudded below 7 percent to 6.95 for bonds, that part of the market pushed ahead, too. And as for the broader 500-stock Standard & Poor's index, that also hit a record-breaking 680.54.

Wien, the Morgan, Stanley expert, still stuck to his forecast of a 1,000-point drop but seemed uncomfortable when he was quoted after the new all-time record. "This has not turned out as I thought." For the White House, the message of the day was, "It's still the economy, stupid."

19 The War on Terror, I

President Clinton ordered emergency security measures for the nation that summer when an explosion wrecked a Paris-bound Trans World Airlines plane, with the loss of all 230 aboard, and a fatal bomb blast tore through Atlanta's Olympic Village. This is how the war on terror hit America in mid-July that year:

At home, the president by executive decree called for tighter inspection of the nation's air routes, airports, and suspicious travelers—moves that effectively limited the public's freedom of movement after the two fatal incidents. Abroad, the president also won congressional support for acts intended to punish Libya and Iran for supporting terrorism and directed closer scrutiny of moves being made by the old enemy in the Persian Gulf War, Saddam Hussein's Iraq.

Having sponsored an antiterrorist law in 1995 and broadened his assault on drug smuggling and crime in general, the president was in no mood at the time to defer such emergency security measures while Congress solemnly debated what could and could not be done.

Well in advance of inquiries, the president's emergency measures were accepted without public protest. Many a traveler, waiting in line for an outbound flight, agreed it would be better to be safe than sorry. As for the Atlanta bomb scare, surging crowds quickly demonstrated the nation's response to the president's summons never to give in to terrorists. Indeed, former Senator Dole, who had collaborated with the White House in pushing the antiterrorist act through Congress, echoed Clinton's summons to the public never to let terrorism shape their lives.

The first broadened rules issued by the White House led immediately to more forceful and detailed personal and baggage examinations and demands on some passengers for personal identification. The purpose, as continual explanations were offered, was to be certain that every piece of luggage that went on an aircraft also had a registered ticket holder aboard for security.

Quite naturally, that ended many a last-minute race to airports that customarily had been considered a privilege by professional travelers in the United States because delays were now inevitable in the more detailed examinations of people and inspections of luggage and carry-on items. What was happening to Americans belatedly had long since been accepted without complaint by European travelers and particularly those in the Middle East. In Israel and surrounding Arab states, for example, it was not unusual for ticketed passengers to be searched to the skin in cases of doubt of their intentions.

There was, of course, a price to be paid for the American move toward greater security for air travel. As the president reminded audiences in his TV appearances to explain his effort at greater safety along the nation's air routes, there was likely to be a modest increase in fares because of the heightened pressures on the aviation industry to order and install new and expensive machines for detecting bombs or other suspicious materials in air baggage and containers used by commercial interests.

In assigning to Vice-President Gore the responsibility for developing a long-range plan for greater air travel security, President Clinton had also called attention to expensive experimental devices for detecting plastic and other types of new explosive materials. Two of these baggage scanners with sensitive electronic feelers, priced at about $1 million each, were already undergoing tests at airports in San Francisco and Atlanta, the president said. From other sources, it also became known from authorities familiar with such devices that there was still no guarantee that they were foolproof and that they could, under all circumstances, flash an alarm against suspicious cargo intended for air transportation.

Almost as important, in estimating costs for the future of American air travel, the public learned that it would take one hundred or more such machines, when perfected, to service major airports throughout the nation — in itself a costly undertaking. Security for air travel, therefore, could scarcely be guaranteed for all domestic flights, let alone abroad, for the balance of this century and perhaps for some years well into the next one.

There was one other major factor in assessing the problems of insuring greater safety even for domestic flights — the constitutional right of every American, at home, at work, or aloft, to remain free of unwarranted government interference. This aspect of the security problem became known when the leaders of the Republican Congress, Speaker Gingrich in the House and Senator Trent Lott of Mississippi, who had succeeded Dole as majority leader of the Senate, reluctantly volunteered to try again to give the president two borderline methods for checking on terrorist suspects in an open society.

Both proposals had originally been included in Clinton's omnibus anticrime bill in 1995 but had been dropped in the final version. The first was an attempt to give the government the right to tap telephone lines of suspected terrorists, subject to application for a court order. The second, just as controversial, was to provide for the use of tracer materials mixed with black powder or smokeless powder as a means of trying to track suspects after a terror bombing.

To the president's disappointment, Congress once again refused to adopt either measure. Both the libertarian American Civil Liberties Union and the conservative gun-control lobby, for opposite reasons, rejected both measures. The ACLU charged that the proposals infringed on civil rights, and the gun lobby alleged interference with the right of people to own guns and use them as desired.

The president expressed his regret, saying, "I'm disappointed. More importantly, the American people are disappointed that the job was not done."

What Congress did give the White House was a new weapon against terrorist states by authorizing the president to penalize foreign companies that are big traders with financial interests in such countries. That in turn brought calamitous warnings from France and Germany when both protested that their private firms had heavy investments in the affairs of Libya and Iran and would be badly hurt. Iran at once fired back that the new American weapon wouldn't do it any harm and envisioned myriad appeals against the American action to the World Trade Organization, the United Nations, and other international bodies. Another problem with such antiterrorist trade legislation, first used against Cuba, was that its complications were bound to make it difficult to enforce.

In his campaign mode, however, President Clinton refused to be swayed. To America's allies who continued to criticize the new law, he said in a statement from the White House, "You cannot do business with the countries that practice commerce with you by day while funding or protecting the terrorists who kill you and your innocent civilians by night. That is wrong. I hope and expect that our allies will come around to accepting this fundamental truth."

The war on terrorism had been escalating in the United States since December 21, 1988, when Pan Am flight 103 perished in a bomb attack over Lockerbie, Scotland, with the loss of 270 lives—a crime that was charged to two intelligence operatives whom Libya had sheltered and refused to yield despite American demands for extraditing them and bringing them to the United States for trial.

As late as the summer of 1996, a Libyan representative to the United Nations was quoted on CNN as saying that Libya had a law against such extraditions. To which Washington responded that the next Congress, the One hundred fifth, if not the current One hundred fourth, would be asked to counter with a newer, stiffer proposal for extraditing criminals from abroad. That, in any event, accounted for the depth of President Clinton's feeling against Libya.

As for Iran, there had been a long history of terorist attacks involving Americans abroad following the overthrow of the shah in 1979–1980. But the first major crime of an Iranian on American soil resulted in several trials, the first in 1993 resulting in the conviction of a blind sheik, Abdel Rahman, and three other Iranians for the fatal bombing of the World Trade Center in New York City. Still another Iranian, Ramzi Ahmed Yousef, accused of being the mastermind in the World Trade Center blast, received a trial of more than four months in federal court in New York City, which explored his worldwide terrorist ventures elsewhere as well.

The blind sheik and his followers were sentenced to life in prison, but that didn't stop the sheik from making still more threats from his prison cell. Yousef and others were also convicted.

It was no foreign outlaw but two Americans, Timothy McVeigh and Terry Nichols, who were accused in the terrorist bombing of the Oklahoma City Federal Building on April 19, 1995, killing 169 people. It was a shock to the home front, which until then had paid little heed to homegrown hate groups. McVeigh was convicted.

There had also been a tendency among Nice Nelly diplomats to ignore the fundamentalist uprising of fanatical Muslims against the royal rulers of Saudi Arabia, despite the American troops sent there for added protection for the Saudi leaders. That mistake, too, ended in tragedy — a terrorist bombing of an American military installation in Dhahran on June 25, 1996, that killed nineteen American servicemen and injured four hundred others, including their dependents and foreign personnel.

After that, Defense Secretary William J. Perry warned Congress that a known terrorist group and a foreign power had been involved — mainly Iran and terrorists who did Iran's bidding from Saudi Arabia to Libya. Secretary Perry also testified, "We have to be prepared for a chemical weapons attack, a biological weapons attack, bombs even larger than the 3,000-pound category used at Dhahran. Bombs in the 10,000- to 20,000-pound category also could be used against us."

All that moved the Saudi government to cooperate with the United States in shifting American troops there from Dhahran to a safer outpost in a more remote part of the Arabian peninsula.

But then came the most frightening blast of all, the fatal explosion of July 17, 1996, that tore Trans World Airlines flight 800 apart shortly after takeoff for Paris from New York City, killing all 230 aboard. During an exhausting salvage operation in the depths of the Atlantic Ocean 10 miles off Long Island's east end, more than 90 percent of the damaged aircraft and all except fewer than 20 bodies were recovered by deep-sea divers working from U.S. Navy salvage vessels without determining the cause of the fatal explosion—attributed variously by the authorities to a bomb planted in the aircraft, a missile shot from the ocean surface aboard a boat, or a mechanical malfunction. Although most investigators suspected malfunction, proof continued to be elusive, even after months of salvage work.

Nor was there much progress in the related Atlanta bombing when a guard who called attention to a bomb package on July 27 was cleared by the authorities as a suspect when weeks went by without enough evidence to arrest him, after which he threatened civil suits.

By that time, too, the Iran/Libyan boycotts weren't working well, and Foreign Minister Lamberto Dini of Italy forecast failure.

Far more important in European terms was the status of German, French, and other suppliers of oil industry technology to the two states the president had outlawed. The Europeans worried that the American war on terrorism eventually would drive up oil prices, which seemed to be the bottom line of much of European thinking. President Clinton commented, "Fascism and Communism may be dead or discredited, but the forces of destruction live on."

Some of the broad legal measures enacted to help fight against terror also turned out to be useful in the president's enlarged struggle to control the spread of crime and drug trafficking. In the antiterrorist law that he pushed through Congress, there was a provision that limited the ancient writ of habeas corpus, one of the primary guarantees of a free people, by allowing federal courts to review constitutional aspects of criminal trials in state courts. In the same statute, the federal government was also given authority to deport legal aliens and to bar financial aid to foreign terrorist groups like the anti-Israel Arab organizations Hamas and Hezbollah.

Most important of all, the president won an expanded death penalty for the government that covered at least fifty offenses. But such broadened power also brought the White House a great deal of criticism from libertarian groups. Moreover, the June 1996 issue of the *Harvard Law Review* warned that the new authority vested in the president and the federal government might be aceptable in today's world for fighting crime and terror, but it also set a dangerous precedent.

An editorial in the *Harvard Law Review* said:

> The majority may be able to accept broad, vaguely defined law enforcement powers when the minority's constitutional rights are at

stake. But the tools used against "them" today can easily be turned against "us" tomorrow. For this reason, the Constitution strikes the balance in favor of free speech, free association and privacy rights, even when other societal interests may be hampered as a result.

Nevertheless, in operating against crime, the president insisted on the use of the government's broadened authority even after the American Civil Liberties Union expressed its doubts, questioning whether "Constitutional principles matter to this President in a criminal justice context." To that, some of the White House's defenders argued that there had to be a better balance between the defense of individual rights and the protection of the public as a whole against criminal offenses.

The same arguments carried over into other aspects of President Clinton's program against crime and terror. The National Rifle Association, the tough lobbying group that usually could turn a Republican Congress its way, bitterly objected to the president's successful drive to outlaw many types of semiautomatic weapons but couldn't defeat his program. The president also sponsored the enactment of a waiting period for the purchase of any handgun while the applicant's background was investigated, the substance of the Brady bill.

A Clinton campaign ploy in his 1992 election, the creation of a new 100,000 force of police to be distributed across the land wherever needed also became useful in the federal government's anticrime program when Congress funded it. Attorney General Janet Reno said after the COPS legislation took effect, "It is one of the most important initiatives I have seen in law enforcement since my first summer job in the sheriff's office in 1956."

The Clinton administration, however, was by no means as successful in limiting the inflow of habit-forming drugs, despite the creation of a special command force under former General Barry R. McCaffrey and a $15 billion budget. Unlike the war against terror, the war on drugs was still a losing proposition for the administration, and the Republican opposition in this presidential election year jumped on the failure with scorn and derision. A Republican spokesman attacked the Clinton administration's record on antidrug enforcement as an "abysmal failure."

At the president's suggestion, the drug war—unlike the attack on terrorism—seemed to have shifted to greater emphasis on preventing addiction among young people and a much wider program of public education. There was nothing exciting about this, as had been the case in the war against terrorism; but there seemed to be little else for the time being that the White House could do. Also, in General McCaffrey's judgment, this was the course that eventually would have to be taken to create a drug-free America.

It also developed, in the anticrime offensive as well as in the war against terror, that the Clinton administration was following the lead of the Bush presidency in building more prisons to confine a vastly enlarged criminal population. In the middle of the ninth decade, more than 1 million people were behind bars in America, all but about 80,000 in state prisons, with no end in sight.

Whatever the success of the war on terror, it would be a long time before any significant progress was made in the broader conflict against crime in general. Declines in the federal uniform crime reports, particularly in violent crimes, had been registered only in single digits in recent years; but the overall total of those serving more than one year in jail was still staggering.

President Clinton often tried to stress the importance of education for the rising generation—the building of more schools rather than more jails—but greater public support of the American program as a whole was also needed. The principles that united the nation against outburst of foreign terror would also have to be invoked somehow in years yet to come to bring together a society that was so often divided against itself.

20 "Of the People, by the People . . ."

"Shame! Shame! Shame!" chanted the protesters in the Senate gallery that historic August 1 as the One hundred fourth Congress was undoing sixty-one merciful years of America's aid to families with dependent children. There were only ten who shouted, and so guards removed them without trouble.

Had the issue been one of importance to more powerful interest groups, such as the Christian Coalition or the National Rifle Association, the opposition would have been formidable. But who was there to care for a million or so children, many of them in families headed by a single mother? They were the most helpless of the nearly 13 million people on public welfare and the additional 26 million on food stamps.

Nevertheless, the Senate was about to complete action that day on welfare reform and rush off for a month's vacation; for this was how government of the people, by the people but not necessarily for all the people operated in the third century of the world's oldest democracy.

One of the last of the old-fashioned liberals, Senator Daniel Patrick Moynihan of New York, a Democrat and a Roman Catholic, had reminded his colleagues among the Republican majority on the Senate floor that day of the opposition to ending welfare by such eminent conservatives as the Roman Catholic bishops, saying. "They [the bishops] admittedly have an easier task with matters of this sort. When principles are at issue, they simply look them up. Too many liberals, alas, simply make them up."

The senator's jibe could have been taken as a reference to President Clinton, who had been agonizing in the White House for days over whether to veto this Republican welfare reform measure when it reached his desk, as he had done to others twice before. In the decision-making process, he had divided his personal staff and his closest advisers — the very heart of the Democratic Party he was leading into another election day. Also, changing "welfare as we know it," his phrase, had now been turned into a campaign issue; and he feared alienating the great American center vote, so crucial to his reelection.

But of equal importance, as a "new" Democrat, he couldn't very well dismiss out of hand a campaign pledge in 1992 that had helped bring him the presidency. Moreover, with the aid of Dick Morris, the former Republican adviser who had helped him take over so many Republican proposals and make them his own, he had brought his party back from the dismal swamp of defeat in the 1994 congressional elections. Could so promising a trend now be abandoned?

Such reasoning as this may have accounted finally for the president's decision the day before, and a startling one it was, that he would sign this new Republican welfare reform bill if Congress passed it and sent it to him. To say that the crucial pro-welfare people closest to him were shocked is putting it mildly.

The president justified his decision in this way:

> I will sign this bill first and foremost because the current system is broken; second, because Congress has made many of the changes I sought; and third, because even though serious problems remain in the non-welfare reform provisions of the bill, this is the one best chance we will have in a long time to complete the work of ending welfare as we know it, by moving people from welfare to work, demanding responsibility, and doing better by children.

But the president still couldn't sell his damaged package to liberal Democrats that day, July 31, when the House of Representatives hustled the disputed measure to a vote while at least one of its dismayed Democratic opponents, Representative John Lewis of Georgia cried:

> Where is the compassion? Where is the sense of decency? Where is the heart of this Congress? This bill is mean. It is base. It is downright low down. What does it profit a great nation to conquer the world only to lose its soul?

To that, the chairman of the House Budget Committee, Representative John R. Kasich of Ohio, responded frostily, "People are not entitled to anything but opportunity. You can't be on welfare for generations."

The House vote was an overwhelming 328–101 in favor, and the Senate was expected to follow the next day. But just before the necessary step, Senator Moynihan let his emotions get the better of him in a savage final commentary:

> This bill is not welfare reform, but welfare repeal. It is the first step in dismantling the social contract that has been in place in the United States since at least the 1930s. Do not doubt that Social Security itself — which is to say, insured retirement benefits — will be next.

The bitterness of the veteran liberal senator from New York, however, did not halt the drive of the Republican-led Congress to approve a welfare reform package to which the president had agreed.

The Republican response came from Moynihan's Republican colleague in New York, Senator Alfonse M. d'Amato, who credited his own party with the outcome over Democratic objections. After that, the Senate completed action on the bill; but the president, beset by protests within his own White House staff, deferred signing it, presumably to let passions cool.

Despite the imperfections of the measure, principally the withholding of aid to many needy children, there was justification for the widespread public nervousness about what many called the "busted system" of public welfare and those who cheated it. The chief complaint was that the system had been wrenched out of control by too many people who either misused welfare or didn't need it and were taking the money and food stamps illegally without being caught.

In some cities across the land, there was public knowledge of an open but illegal trade in food stamps at discounts of up to half their actual dollar value. And as for welfare grants, ineligible unmarried men and women were also alleged to have collected welfare checks illegally without being called to account. True or not, these charges were at the base of public suspicions about welfare.

Such situations as these had outraged otherwise liberal-minded people, including some minorities, so that conservatives in both major parties had little difficulty in finally passing a welfare act more to President Clinton's specifications. Even so, giving states the federal block grants didn't resolve the problem of finding jobs for welfare recipients for which private business and industry would pay, locating people to care for small children while their unmarried mothers sought work, and many another remaining problem.

The welfare act, called "Aid to Families with Dependent Children," had been part of President Franklin D. Roosevelt's path-breaking Social Security Act in this country in 1935. Under the reform measure, that responsibility along with food stamps and other provisions for the relief of human misery were passed along to the states with the block grants that vastly reduced the sums available to counties, cities, towns, and villages with their own problems even in a time of relatively high employment across the nation. One of the most criticized changes was the end of the federal guarantee for cash assistance to poor children.

Other major provisions for welfare reform were:

1. The states were now responsible to see that the head of every family on welfare, including single mothers, would be obliged to find work within two years or lose all benefits for the family.

2. Unless adults found regular jobs after receiving welfare for a set period, states would have the option of forcing them to perform community services. In any case, lifetime welfare benefits would be limited to five years, although 20 percent of the families involved could be declared exempt in cases of hardship.

3. In the case of unmarried teenage parents, payments could be made by states and cities only if an unmarried mother under eighteen remained in school and lived with an adult. (Senator Moynihan was authority for the estimate that half of all births in New York City were illegitimate at the time of the reform act's passage.)

4. Food-stamp spending by the states would be cut by about $24 billion over six years, with at least $3 billion being saved by denying stamps to legal immigrants. Unemployed childless workers would have only limited food-stamp privileges.

5. Legal immigrants were barred from almost all federal social services and welfare benefits, and noncitizens at once would be denied benefits, even if they had been receiving such aid. The guarantee of food stamps for poor people was otherwise preserved, and the states and their subdivisions were held responsible for providing funds and personnel for day care for children of working parents, married or not.

Once again, just how all this was to be done when the burden was passed on to the states became a problem not only for the fifty governors but also for the welfare clients who now would have to depend on entirely new sources for their means of survival. In the criticism that arose over the many changes that also put less money at the disposal of the state sources than had been the federal government's due, President Clinton replied by saying:

> Not so very long ago at the beginning of this very Congress, some wanted to put poor children in orphanages and take away all help from mothers simply because they were poor, young, and unmarried.

Still, the merits of the changed reform package continued to create doubt among the president's own cabinet. Some remained doubtful that the states would be able to make the welfare system work any better than the one the Republican Congress dismantled. The image of a few desperate protesters shouting "Shame! Shame! Shame!" from the Senate gallery was thereby impressed on the history of public welfare in the richest country in the world.

Once the gridlock between a Democratic White House and a Republican Congress broke before the legislators left the Beltway for their August break, President Clinton also managed to obtain passage of a number of his cherished beneficial projects other than welfare reform, although these, too, for the most part, bore Republican alterations of consequence.

The most important of these was the minimum-wage increase, the first in six years, from $4.25 to $5.15. That amounted to a $1,800 boost in the annual minimum wage to $10,300, still below the poverty line in the government's statistics. Even so, in the congressional version as approved by the Republican majority, this was divided into two stages, with 50 cents being added on October 1, 1996, and an additional 40 cents on September 1, 1997, for the more than 10 million Americans in that category.

But for the benefit of small businesses that might be inclined to lay off a worker or two rather than grant the increase, the Republicans inserted provisions in the wage bill for $21 billion in tax benefits for affected businesses over a ten-year period. What these amounted to was a succession of faster write-offs for new equipment as well as a $5,000 tax credit when couples adopt a child.

For the packet of benefits mainly engineered for the Democrats by Senator Kennedy, the majority Republicans contributed more than the necessary votes in the House and Senate to make the bill law.

The president was obliged to settle for much less in the ambitious European-style health program that he introduced shortly after assuming office in 1993. Following that failure, Senator Kennedy once again came to the rescue by forming a nonpartisan alliance with Senator Nancy Kassebaum, a Republican senator from Kansas, for a more modest approach to the problem. What finally was passed by Congress in August three years later was a health insurance bill, the first in ten years, which gave workers the right to take their insurance from one job to another, once it was issued to them. Of equal importance was a provision that barred exclusions from insurance based on preexisting health conditions.

There was a struggle over the bill, however, when the Republicans insisted on adding a proposal that Bob Dole had made while a senator to allow beneficiaries to open what he called medical savings accounts, free of taxes, in which money could be set aside to meet future health bills. The Democrats protested in vain that these were merely tax shelters for the well-to-do who could use the money for any purpose, not merely medical bills.

What finally settled the argument was a last-minute agreement, once again made possible by Senator Kennedy, in which a limited number of medical savings accounts would be permitted as a test of their usefulness. And on that basis, Congress finally gave the president a modest return on the grandiose health scheme that had failed.

The Senate majority leader, Trent Lott, wasn't as successful in proposing still another amendment to the health bill, this one to give a patent to the American Home Products Company for an antiarthritis drug. Although the senator said that he only wanted to maintain competition in the field because a rival, the Monsanto Company, had already won a patent for its own drug, the deal fell through because of Democratic objections.

Another attempt that failed, this one to oblige insurance companies to accept mental health coverage on the same basis as physical health, touched off charges from Democrats that the extension had been killed as a favor to the insurance interests, something the Republicans denied. It was that kind of contentious windup before the August vacation break.

One of the few important measures that required neither argument nor horse trading was a bipartisan agreement to improve the quality of the nation's drinking water. Curiously, the majority's opposition to extending environmental standards had delayed consideration of the clean-water proposal for two years. But, faced with so little to show for the record of the One hundred-fourth Congress beyond sheer necessities, the Republican leadership called up the water legislation so that members of Congress who were seeking reelection would have something special to demonstrate their interest in improving home standards to the voters. President Clinton was enthusiastic when he signed the water measure, calling it a boon for American families.

What the new law did was to revise and improve federal drinking water standards, an obligation to be met by local suppliers whenever contaminants are found in water that is specifically used for drinking. It also pledged federal assistance to states and cities to improve municipal water supplies. Before a gathering of city and state officials at the White House, President Clinton called the measure a product of bipartisan cooperation — a rarity in this Congress. He said:

> The legislation represents a real triumph because it demonstrates what we can achieve here in Washington and in our country when we turn away from partisanship and embrace shared values.

In the last days of this Congress, there was relief as well for the members of black churches in the South that had been burned or mutilated by hate groups over almost a decade. To add to the work that was already being done by sympathetic private religious organizations that had begun rebuilding some of the damaged structures, President Clinton approved a $12 million appropriation to investigate, identify the culprits, and punish them, thereby warning others that such crimes would not be tolerated in the United States. The funds for enforcement were given to the Bureau of Alcohol, Tobacco, and Firearms with a mandate to conduct a broad inquiry into many church fires, mostly those damaging or destroying black churches in the South.

That marked the virtual end of the one hundred-fourth session of Congress, the first with Republican leadership in forty years, under a president who moderated his Democratic heritage by sponsoring some proposals that had originated with Republicans.

If this made Bill Clinton a "new" Democrat, as he defined himself at midterm, there wasn't much that the old-fashioned liberals like Senator Moynihan could do about it. The Left, for all practical purposes in this administration, was dead, with the president plainly bent on seeking a center position. Even so, there was no place for the Left-leaning liberals to go except to remain on the president's side.

This was how government of the people, by the people worked toward the end of President Clinton's fourth year in the White House; and if not all the people were pleased with the outcome, they would have to bide their time and hope for something better.

21 Dole's Rescue Operation

Something had to be done—and quickly. Three months before election day, Bob Dole was still too far behind President Clinton in the opinion polls, despite slight although indefinite gains.

There was also no way of seeking an alternative Republican nominee for president because the Kansan had won the primary elections, the role of the party's national convention was merely to validate the verdict of the voters, and nobody was within shouting distance of him. The only other candidate with more than one hundred pledged delegates from the primaries, Pat Buchanan, had already been warned by Dole as the front runner to shape up or get lost. This convention, Dole was determined, would not be dominated by divisive forces.

Still, despite all the power and wealth that the Republican establishment had thrown behind the Dole candidacy, there seemed now to be scant hope for a resurgence, except if he could come up with a once-in-a-lifetime jump-start issue that would turn the campaign around. That and an articulate, younger vice-presidential candidate, Dole and the party leaders agreed, were the necessary ingredients for a rescue operation. But finding a Veep could wait.

Now, the problem was to define that all-important new issue that would give the public a jolt and the back-of-the-hand to Clinton. So all kinds of gimmicks were reviewed that might serve to give the Dole campaign a bounce in the polls and thrust him back in contention when the party convention in San Diego officially made him the Republican presidential nominee.

Eventually, Dole himself came up with the most striking—and at the same time the most risky—proposition: a major tax break for everybody. Actually, the proposal had come from a defeated primary rival, Malcolm Stevenson Forbes Jr., the chairman, editor, and CEO of the prestigious *Forbes* financial magazine. What Steve Forbes had produced during his losing effort was the notion of a 17 percent flat tax on all incomes across the board and the end of the federal income tax system as it now exists.

Even though Forbes's idea hadn't caught on—he'd won only a few primary election delegates before bowing out of the race—Dole had thought enough of the magazine editor and his pet notion to talk to him about his flat-tax proposal and how he'd planned to make it work for a skeptical public.

Not only that, but the Kansan also seemed to find a surprising affinity for a one-time rival and critic of his, Jack F. Kemp, a sixty-one-year-old former New York congressman from Buffalo and a one-time quarterback for the San Diego Chargers in the National Football League. For Kemp, as events turned out, had also been impressed with Steve Forbes's flat-tax plan and had joined in discussions of it with Dole.

Now not everybody in the Republican establishment leaped at the Dole-Forbes-Kemp theory that a grand slam tax break of stupendous proportions was the way to revive the sagging presidential campaign. Some viewed it only as a diversion from the most serious split within the Republican ranks—the fight led by the champions of women's groups against the party platform plank calling for a constitutional amendment to end all abortions in America without exception.

This, many believed quite sincerely, was one of the principal reasons for Dole's poor showing to date against President Clinton and the probability of worse to come if H. Ross Perot really meant to spend his money to get his Reform Party on the ballot in all fifty states.

Nothing, however, could be done just yet about Perot and the Reform Party. But the proabortion forces—those who deeply believed in the right of a woman to choose whether she wished to have a child—were threatening a convention-floor fight to soften or otherwise revise the antiabortion platform plank.

This was not only a matter of principle; as the polls demonstrated very clearly, the nation's prospective women voters were aligned against the Dole candidacy by more than two to one, a major reason for Clinton's dominance in the polls as a prochoice candidate.

Even Dole conceded that the abortion controversy would have to be resolved somehow to bring about an agreement between the pro- and antiabortion factions, or there would be no sense in putting forward a big tax plan. This was not a case of either/or. Such prochoice Republican leaders as Governor Pete Wilson of California, Governor William Weld of Massachusetts, and Governor Christine Todd Whitman of New Jersey were a formidable force in themselves against the dominance of the Reverend Pat Robertson and his Christian Coalition at the convention. And of course the religious right would insist on maintaining the antiabortion plank as written.

But now there was no time to lose with the opening of the convention on August 12 less than two weeks away. And so, while behind-the-scenes efforts were made to avert an abortion floor fight, the tax plan that had been hammered out in haste through the combined efforts of Messrs. Dole, Forbes, Kemp, and their advisers was made public in a flurry of TV oratory.

It promised a $548 billion savings to taxpayers through what was in the main a 15 percent across-the-board reduction in personal income taxes plus a reduction by half of capital gains taxes. Under Dole's terms, the operation would start in 1997, when he hoped to be in the White House, and be completed over three years.

The Republican challenger wasn't prepared to say how this tax bonanza for the public would be paid for, except to predict that the new revenue generated by the program would, in effect, help it pay for itself—something that was seized upon at once by his opponents as proof that the new initiative would not work.

President Clinton told a California audience immediately after Dole issued his detailed proposal in Chicago on August 5:

> You'll hear a lot of talk between now and November about tax cuts and how much we should have and whether we can afford them. I say to you that it will not be popular, but I will not advocate any cuts in taxes in this election that cannot be paid for in our attempts to balance the budget.

To that, the president's chief of staff at the White House, Leon E. Panetta, added, "He [Dole] is saying that part of this is going to be paid for by growth in the economy, which again is the kind of supply-side voodoo that did not work in the 1980s."

In the broad economic plan entitled "Restoring the American Dream: The Dole Plan for Economic Growth," the presidential candidate made it clear that he did not go so far as to favor the 17 percent flat tax proposed by Forbes, although the editor was with him at the formal announcement. But like Forbes, Dole proposed the restructuring of the Internal Revenue Service.

To make certain that all taxpayers understood that they would benefit under the proposed new tax schedules, Dole issued these anticipated lower new rates in his plan for those paying respectively 15, 28, 31, 36, and 39 percent:

His proposed revised rates were respectively 12.75, 23.8, 26.35, 30.6, and 33.66 percent. About 90 million taxpayers would be affected, the candidate's experts said. For about 40 million lower- and middle-income taxpayers, however, what he wanted IRS to do was to use automatic withholding payments for taxes due, instead of filing long and complicated forms.

Complementing the new tax-cutting venture, the Kansan also made it clear that he hoped to obtain the repeal of the 1993 tax increase created by the Clinton administration that affected top-level Social Security benefits. He also endorsed another Republican financial objective, a $500 tax credit for each child in a family.

This long-shot initiative by the Republican campaign organization was not undertaken without much soul-searching and doubt by all the principals at a conference before deciding that the attempt would have to be made. Significantly, it was Dole who gave the final go ahead for the big tax cut, a supply-side procedure that he had consistently opposed during his thirty-five years in Congress. In so doing, he deviated from his standard remedy for all government undertakings to bolster the economy — debt reduction and budget balancing. That, finally, was how he began his rescue operation.

In the search for a suitable vice-presidential runing mate, the other part of the Republican program to improve Dole's chances in the fall campaign against President Clinton's reelection, what the party's elders hoped for was a younger, more articulate present or former government officeholder with a reputation as a crowd pleaser and the vitality to take some of the burden of campaigning off a presidential candidate who had just turned seventy-three.

The prescription was not easy to fill; and there was no assurance, once the most attractive possibility had been decided upon, that he would be able to make a significant contribution to the campaign. After all, voters cast their ballots for presidents, not vice-presidents.

Dole knew right off, as did his closest associates, that the search for a suitable running mate would not be easy. The first choice of nearly everybody in the circle around the candidate had been General Colin L. Powell, the former chairman of the Joint Chiefs of Staff; but he had not been interested. Several others who might have been considered also bowed out. Whatever suggestions came from the Republican campaign high command also came to naught; and so both the search and the decision were at last left to Dole himself.

As he said, upon considering the field, it dawned on him after a while that Jack Kemp, who had supported Steve Forbes in the primary campaign, might be the most suitable of the choices that were left to him. Kemp was, first of all, enthusiastic and likable, a first-rate speaker, and certainly an asset in California, which had long been considered Democratic territory, but where he had been of immense assistance as housing secretary in the Bush cabinet.

The most serious objection to him had been on economic grounds because he was a supply-sider, a believer in cutting taxes, at a time when Dole was still a budget balancer; but the Kansan's change of heart eliminated that problem. And while Kemp was far from a youth at sixty-one, his reputation as a former Buffalo Bills quarterback gave him a breezy air of vigor that made up for his years, the gray hair, and eyeglasses.

True, Dole and Kemp had had political differences other than their original disagreement on economic nostrums and other issues. On affirmative-action programs, Kemp was all for them and Dole wanted them cut out.

Dole also sought to check or even halt immigration; but Kemp liked the notion of the Statue of Liberty still holding out the torch to the persecuted as well as the hopeful and adventurous from abroad. Atop all that, Kemp had backed the wrong candidate in the primaries; but that, like the rest of their differences, was now history.

It seemed to please Dole to keep his intimates as well as his enemies guessing at his choice for vice-president, even after he had determined on Kemp, made sure that he would accept the designation if offered, and even set a time for notifying his man. It all turned out well, however. The two met on August 10 in Dole's hometown, Russell, Kansas, and traveled together to the Republican National Convention in San Diego that opened two days later.

If there was now any tension between them, it seemed to be mainly over Kemp's take-charge enthusiasm; but as he later admitted, Dole had led him aside early on and told him a story about a president who had to remind an overly demonstrative vice-president, "I'm the quarterback." On TV long afterward, Kemp repeated the story with a big grin and added, "Bob, you're the quarterback and I'm the blocker and we're going all the way."

There remained the problem of the threatened floor fight over the abortion issue that must have been bothersome to the newly formed Republican executive team, even though they both were lustily attacking the Clinton administration at every turn the weekend before the opening of the convention. What Dole tried initially was to attach a conciliatory phrase indicating tolerance for opposing points of view to the part of the platform demanding fealty to the antiabortion faith. But the conservatives and religionists would have none of it. The chance of an explosive floor fight spluttered again.

What to do? Dole and his associates then sought to compromise by offering the proabortionists space at the end of the platform, in an appendix, to state their position along with those of delegates opposing other parts of the basic Republican document. But even though the word *tolerance* disappeared from the text entirely, the doubters' appendixes seemed to resolve that most delicate of issues.

The lineup of speakers for the four days then had to be reexamined by the convention's movers and shakers to make certain that no extreme views would disturb middle- and upper-class complacency during the meeting. What happened then was that major proabortion party leaders like Governors Wilson of California, Weld of Massachusetts, Pataki of New York, and a few others either were offered spots on the program outside prime time or denied outright any chance to make their views heard.

The procedure was scarcely new in Republican annals. It had been tried with success in the starry Reagan era and with partial success in a few others. But in this one, which was planned more as a national carnival on TV than a political epiphany, there would be four tightly scripted days that shut out any people or ideas that might create disorder.

Even demonstrators outside the convention hall, with the assistance of heavy policing provided by San Diego, would be kept at a distance and even forced to draw lots for the order in which they would be given permission to speak. For the long hairs and the romantics who undressed to get attention, the ultimate guarantee of peace and quiet was the threat of arrest and jail until the convention was over.

Once Dole was satisfied with these arrangements, he apparently felt sufficiently confident to proceed as he saw fit by quietly reminding all concerned that he still had to fight a long and difficult campaign against a sitting president and couldn't stand entirely on ceremony. What he proceeded to do, in some of his rather chaotic news conferences before the convention opened, was to dismiss the party platform with its contrived appendix as a matter of no concern to him, so much so that he emphasized several times that he hadn't even read it. To be sure that the point wasn't ignored, he added that he didn't feel bound by his party's statement of its deathless principles.

Whether or not that extraordinary position was taken seriously by a press corps less interested in the dullness of harmony than in the excitement of threatened conflict, the prospective presidential nominee then proceeded to pick an entirely different kind of keynote speaker to add to the roster of the illustrious who had already been announced.

The newcomer, so it was revealed just before the convention opened, would be Representative Susan Molinari of New York. She was young, handsome, a prochoicer of passionate conviction, and in effect a prototype of the vast panoply of femininity determined on progress toward equal rights with men rather than regression to confinement to the kitchen, nursery, the bathroom, and the bed. As such, it was apparent that Dole was gambling that Ms. Molinari would attract a certain number of the women of her generation who were impatient with any in the party who were unable to abide the thought of feminine choice in anything of vital importance in their lives. She would serve, therefore, as a counterpart in his campaign to Dole's choice for vice-president, Kemp, both of them being his notion of the pattern of future leadership for the party.

Just how all this would work out when it was ground through the cameras, microphones, and computer/cyberspace technology of some 10,000 reporters and other media representatives at the convention remained a disturbing question for the more thoughtful of those among the Republican leadership. But this was how the primary voters' choice of Dole as their presidential candidate had affected the party convention and the $40 million TV show it was about to present to a self-governing nation of 265 million people that late summer of 1996.

Now, the orchestra was striking up the Republican theme, "The Stars and Stripes Forever." The applause, the cheers, and the dismayed cries of protest were already being heard throughout the land. And on the small screens in many millions of homes, the Republican Party began to plead its cause for a return to power in the White House.

22 Show Time in San Diego

There may never be another national political convention quite like the one in San Diego at which Bob Dole's nomination for president was confirmed by the Republican delegates.

In his acceptance speech on the concluding night, the tough old veteran of thirty-five years in Congress called himself "the most optimistic man in America," and he had to be after surviving a four-day televised spectacle that was featured mainly by mandated dullness.

The reason for the unadmitted censorship was to avoid any outward appearance of conflict in the party's effort to unseat President Clinton, so much so that the very word *abortion*—a major source of party differences—was used only here and there. To nobody's surprise, the viewing audience outside the San Diego Convention Center was called decidedly smaller than in 1992.

Among the victims of the party's passion for conformity during the convention were major figures such as governors, members of Congress, and others who either were denied prime time for their five-minute appearances or were entirely barred from the podium.

And in one celebrated encounter, which was televised, one of the rebels at the rowdy 1992 Houston convention, Pat Buchanan, mused plaintively to a reporter four years later, "How long d'ya think it would take for them to tackle me if I tried to get to the podium?" That, too, was show time at San Diego.

To reassure both the presidential nominee and all others concerned, the vice-presidential nominee, Jack Kemp, obligingly reversed his own long-held liberal views on abortion, affirmative action, and immigration so that they conformed to those of Dole's. The position was publicly announced, apparently because there seemed to have been some concern about Kemp's lively reputation as somebody who was likely to bound off the reservation now and then. In this Republican campaign, such conduct would have been called awkward, if not thoroughly reprehensible.

Anyway, Kemp and his chief drew cheers and prolonged applause for their acceptance speeches that last night and were rewarded with the grant of $62.8 million in the federal government's campaign spending, a badly needed gift because, as Dole said, the party had been "running on empty."

The opening hours of the convention on August 12 invoked the treasured memory in film of Ronald Reagan and his White House, the Valhalla of the party in the late twentieth century. For so familiar a theme, there was no need for the party's leaders to worry about dissent, although the faithful even then were prepared to move in against troublemakers.

The most appealing moments of this emotional scene came with the personal appearance of a tearful Nancy Reagan, who introduced the film of her husband, stricken with Alzheimer's. And after that, General Colin L. Powell won attention with his plea for compassion, welfare, and health reform and "better ways to take care of Americans in need than the exhausted programs of the past." He placed his faith for the future in greater economic growth that he believed would bring better jobs, wages, and living standards.

Having been a Republican for less than one year, the former chairman of the Joint Chiefs of Staff said:

> I became a Republican because I truly believe the federal government has become too large and too intrusive in our lives. We can no longer afford solutions to our problems that result in more entitlements, higher taxes to pay for them, more bureaucracy to run them, and fewer results to show for them.

Apparently out of sympathy for Dole's problem in accepting, then disavowing a platform containing an unworkable proposal for a constitutional amendment banning abortion, the general sidestepped the issue but endorsed the candidate for his strength, maturity, and integrity, and added, "He is a man who can bring trust back to government and bring Americans together again."

If the fifty-nine-year-old general had any particular interest in running for or seeking high office in th immediate future, he didn't show it and suggested his participation in the Dole campaign would be limited.

That his interest was aroused, however, was evident in the care with which he prepared and delivered his speech and the somewhat old-fashioned manner in which at times he flailed the air with emphatic gestures. If the performance amounted to anything at all politically, it might have been an attempt to test the waters for the future, perhaps

2000, perhaps not at all. But he gave the impression that he wasn't just along for the ride.

Dole's much more damaging experience with the end product of the Platform Committee that opening day of the convention was likely to have a direct effect on his fall campaign, the decisive phase of this presidential election.

For even if the very word *liberal* seemed to offend tender Republican ears, a large part of the electorate was still deeply interested in affirmative action; sensible immigration policies; and, above all, nondiscrimination against little children, some of the no-nos of this platform. Like the abortion plank, discriminatory policies could create many adverse votes.

The Republican platform also raised other civil rights problems by denying government benefits to illegal aliens, refusing citizenship to children born to foreign parents, and seeking to limit American membership in international trade organizations.

Even so, before a half-filled delegates' section in the convention hall early on the opening morning of the convention, the platform was rushed through to approval without discussion and, indeed, without even a mention of such controversial proposals as those affecting abortion, immigration, affirmative action, and other limitations.

This was the result of a collaboration within the Republican Party of the religious right and the Buchanan super right, a conservative alliance that ran counter to every humane principle backed by many people outside the convention hall.

To have agreed to such limitations would have done irreparable harm to the Dole campaign at the outset, which is why he continued to disavow the platform, repeated that he hadn't even read it, and proceeded to set his own policies without regard to it.

Apparently, the candidate's purpose was to dissociate himself mainly from the abortion controversy. Anyway, this seemed to indicate that other platform debates were also out.

But three dissenters on official abortion policy, Governors Wilson of California and Weld of Massachusetts and Senator Olympia Snowe of Maine, announced before TV cameras on the floor of the convention hall that they not only opposed the abortion plank but also predicted that four years hence they would be among the majority of an entirely different set of delegates' leaders.

Later, Ralph Reed, the chairman of the Christian Coalition, the loudest of the evangelicals if not the most influential, also announced before the TV cameras on the floor of the convention hall that the Republican Party was still a "prolife party," which was true enough, even if the presidential candidate didn't want to go quite that far on the abortion issue.

Apparently, this was the way the Republican high command had decided to permit discussion of platform positions so that delegates could indicate their opposition publicly when they couldn't do it from the podium. It didn't seem to be a very open way to be running a great American political party, but that was how it had been arranged during that particular convention.

It was under such circumstances that Messrs. Dole and Kemp arrived from Russell, Kansas, to take their places in the convention hall and await their approval as the party's candidates for president and vice-president. What they and their wives witnessed from then on was a party-ordained effort to entertain the electorate with platitudes of conformity while trying by all means to avoid the damaging uproar of the 1992 Houston convention.

On the second day, there were more speeches, including one by Speaker Gingrich; but the main purpose was centered on a many-sided attack on President Clinton, personal and political as always, plus the attractive presence of the convention keynoter, Representative Susan Molinari of New York. Ms. Molinari, Dole's personal choice, was picked because she was representative of the majority of the women who opposed his candidacy in the polls; but, curiously, she wasn't allowed in her scripted text to say that she was prochoice and argue her cause.

Evidently, the authors of the San Diego TV show hoped that the feminine audience on the home front might guess that the speaker's policies opposed those of the convention and probably her candidate's, too. What she did say briefly but with punch was to use as many anti-Clinton lines as she could in her relatively short remarks. "This speech," she said, "is like a Bill Clinton promise. It won't last long, and it will sound like a Republican."

That was also the case with another effort by Senator Kay Bailey Hutchison of Texas, who went after President Clinton with more vigor, although neither speaker seemed to arouse the audience to fighting pitch. That, presumably, would be the role reserved to Dole and Jack Kemp in their respective acceptance speeches on the fourth and concluding night of the convention.

The show was still proceeding according to script; and the assembled news media representatives, now variously estimated from 6,000 to 12,000 in number, were beginning to get itchy. Nothing was happening, a complete freeze in the news business, beyond tailored speeches, "The Stars and Stripes Forever," "The Star-Spangled Banner," and assorted musical interludes that included such highly regarded performers as a twelve-year-old African American boy soprano with a beautiful voice; a wavery Caucasian woman soprano with a reputation as a specialist in religious recordings; and a collection of hard-working members of a drum and bugle corps.

Moreover, the Republican specialists who were contributing so heavily to TV political advertising in their own interests were also beginning to mutter that they weren't getting enough free TV time. The TV broadcasters were beginning to repeat themselves while interviewing the same people on the same subjects to keep from falling into a void. And some of the print specialists—independent columnists, editorial writers, and the like—were pulling out for home before Dole's acceptance speech.

This awkward situation became public property on the air, as may be imagined, even if it wasn't really supposed to be part of the script. But there wasn't very much that could be produced for a whammo effect on the third day of the convention, at which the team of Dole and Kemp became the official Republican nominees for president and vice-president respectively.

If, by that time, there had even been dissension in the ranks, the news representatives hadn't heard about it. There had been rumors of a walkout by hard-boiled antiabortioners when Representative Molinari began speaking; but what actually happened was limited to a relatively few people abandoning up-front seats, which were promptly occupied by eager, less-privileged citizens in the rear who couldn't even see the podium because of obstacles.

Just about the only semicritical reporting that had emerged before an undemonstrative public by that time was an analysis of the composition of the Republican delegates, nearly 2,000 strong, that had been conducted by several news organizations, including NBC News and the New York *Times*–CBS News.

Whether this convention was intended to be show business or not, what seemed bothersome generally were the demographics and the wealth of the delegates as compared with the electorate in general. This was, after all, an elite organization even if it did have a political function to formalize a voters' decision on nominations for the two top executive offices in the nation.

And yet, 70 percent of all the delegates called themselves conservatives, as compared with only 11 percent among all voters and 50 percent among Republicans. As for wealth, 47 delegates had family incomes of more than $75,000 annually, with almost 1 in 5 a millionaire, whereas only 11 percent of voters have incomes of more than $75,000 and only 17 percent of Republicans do as well.

The disparity was even greater in the demographics of the two largest racial units in the country, white and black. Among the delegates, 91 percent were white, 3 percent black, and the rest scattered (the head count of the black delegates varied from 48 to 55 in separate counts), whereas the percentage among all voters was 84 percent white and 11 percent black.

Within the Republican Party itself, the ratio was even more extreme, 95 to 2 percent. The gender gap, too, made the party seem to have not done very well in recognizing the responsibility of women. Among delegates, the ratio was 64 to 36 percent, as against 53 to 47 percent among Republicans; and among all voters, the ratio favored women by 54 to 46 percent.

That being the general sitaution, it is not to be wondered at that the delegates seemed to be almost in a class by themselves, as compared with even the Republican Party, let alone the electorate at large. But this is the way that the party was organized in 1996, and these were the delegates who had accepted and ratified the decision of the Republican primary voters to make Dole their presidential candidate. That night, climaxing these four anxious days over fear of controversy, the convention would hear the big speech of Dole's career.

In the hours leading up to Dole's appearance before the convention, there had been heartening reports of gains in the polls that were to the Kansan's advantage. But he knew perfectly well that such conventions as this one nearly always produce a bulge in voter surveys for the favored candidate, that Clinton would have his own bulge the week following the Democratic National Convention, and the most credible figures might not appear until after Labor Day.

What must have interested the newly anointed presidential nominee even more were the reports of a CBS poll that showed that not all voters were convinced that the offer of a big tax cut, the basis for Dole's hope of gaining on Clinton, could be taken at face value. The poll said that there was a certain amount of skepticism abroad in the electorate about his tax proposal, that nearly half in one survey doubted there'd be any increase, and about 30 percent even expected taxes to increase.

Clearly, if Dole meant to be president, he would have to make a greater effort that night to prove to the electorate that he meant what he said. In the day leading up to his own appearance before the convention, he had been heartened by Elizabeth Dole's performance when she wandered around the floor of the convention on impulse and had spent hours of the previous evening talking to people. And that day, too, she was still circulating with pleasing scenes on TV. At one point, she told a group of young voters, "You're going to hear a speech you'll always remember today."

Kemp by this time was already well into his own acceptance speech for the vice-presidential nomination, in which he charged that the Clinton administration was reducing the growth of economic recovery to the slowest pace of any in this century and "stifling the genius of the American people." The former housing secretary, conscious of the criticism in opposing media for changing his position on social issues, concluded that, whatever happened, he'd be following Dole's leadership "all the way."

Dole then began formally with the acceptance of the convention's presidential nomination, stirring a roar of approval and proceeding directly into his theme: "I am profoundly moved by your confidence and trust, and I look forward to leading you into the next century."

There was a folksy interlude, a recollection of his early years in Kansas, his love of family, the declarations of a plain-spoken man in facing his future.

"I do not need the presidency to refresh my soul," he said. In a fling at those who thought him too old, he replied, "Age has its advantages." And to Hillary Rodham Clinton's concern for children in her book *It Takes a Village,* he responded without naming her, "It does not take a village to raise a child. It takes a family."

This developed into a speech about values — family values, personal values, national values — the rock on which America was founded. He said, "I am here to say to America, do not abandon the great traditions that stretch to the dawn of our history; do not topple the pillars of those beliefs — God, family, honor, duty, country — that have brought us through time and time again."

There was no question of the candidate's sincerity; but even as he spoke, the moneyed interests seeking congressional favors — Big Tobacco and the like — were entertaining the acceding powers in Congress under a new rule permitting such largesse. And at least two networks, ABC and NBC, were broadcasting the details with illustrations.

That, however, was outside the hall while Dole was speaking. Answering criticism that he was too harsh, too unfeeling about ordinary people, he responded:

> If I am too combative, it is for love of country. It is to uphold a standard I was born and bred to defend. And to those who believe that I live and breathe compromise, I say that, in politics, honorable compromise is no sin, it is what protects us from absolutism and intolerance.

Now and then in his 40-minute address, Dole would descend from such high-flown oratory to the mundane; and it was always a bit of a shock to see the practical politician peeping out from behind the fancy literary phrases prompted by his speechwriter, as, for instance, this principled attack on the Clinton administration, coupled with one of his own pet peeves: "For too long, we have had a leadership that has been unwilling to risk the truth, to speak without calculation, to sacrifice itself."

Then, a few paragraphs removed, there was this about the Teachers Union, which had backed Clinton so vigorously in 1992 and had thereby earned Dole's enmity: "When I am president, I will disregard your political power for the sake of the children, the schools, and the nation."

He repeated the substance of his 15-percent-across-the-board income-tax-reduction package. And once again, without saying where the money would come from, he pledged to have Congress pass a budget-balancing amendment, followed by his own balanced budget as president in 2002.

"Jack Kemp and I," he said, "will restore the promise of America and get the economy moving again; and we'll do so without leaving anybody behind."

To that remark, he added his own vision of the Republican Party as the means of making the American Dream a reality for all: "The Republican Party is broad and inclusive. It represents many streams of opinion and many points of view. But if there is anyone who has mistakenly attached himself to the party in the belief that we are not open to citizens of every race and religion, then let me remind you:

> Tonight this hall belongs to the party of Lincoln; and the exits, which are clearly marked, are for you to walk out of as I stand here and hold this ground — without compromise.

He repeated the Republican contention that it bases itself on the Constitution that mandates equal protection under the law which, he declared, "is not code language for racism." He pledged his administration to oppose racism, saying there should be no favoritism by race, "no expectation of judgment other than it be even-handed. We cannot guarantee the outcome, but we shall guarantee the opportunity."

He promised an expanded education program, a strong military, a foreign policy that would be of greater benefit to the nation. But for his conclusion, the last four paragraphs over which he himself had worked much longer than his speechwriter, Mark Helprin, a novelist and a *Wall Street Journal* writer, Dole seemed to be trying to grasp for some higher value for the nation that only he could fulfill. The conclusion of the Dole address, therefore, deserves the kind of attention that he gave it in stating his philosophy of government:

> My friends, a presidential campaign is more than a contest of candidates, more than a clash of opposing philosophies. It is a mirror held up to America. It is a measurement of who we are, where we come

from, where we are going. For as much inspiration as we may draw from a glorious past, we recognize America preeminently as a country of tomorrow. For we were placed here for a purpose by a higher power. Every soldier in uniform, every school child who recites the Pledge of Allegiance, every citizen who places her hand on her heart when the flag goes by, recognizes and responds to our American destiny.

Optimism is in our blood. I know this as few others can. There was once a time when I doubted the future. But I learned that obstacles can be overcome, and I have unlimited confidence in the wisdom of our people and our country.

Tonight, I stand before you tested by adversity, made sensitive by hardship, a fighter by principle, and *the most optimistic man in America*. For my life has taught me that America is a land without limits.

With my feet on the ground and my heart filled with hope, I put my faith in you and in the God who loves us all. I am convinced that America's best days are yet to come. May God bless you all. And may God bless America.

Whatever one may think of Dole's presidential chances, what he tried to do that night was more fitting for the end of a national convention than the suppression of the rights of opposing delegates to speak. That, too, was show time in San Diego.

23 The Hapless Warrior

When Ross Perot returned to the presidential wars in 1996, it was with renewed scorn for the monied interests' domination of his rivals' two-party system. He called it a "little snake," and he vowed to kill it.

This time, unlike his first campaign in 1992, the hapless warrior had his own bought-and-paid-for vehicle, the Reform Party; but he assured his 1,500 cheering followers that, if elected, he would be their servant, not their master. However the cliché might be interpreted, it was at least a pleasant thought.

Still, it was obvious that the gutsy little billionaire's election as president was as unlikely this time as it had been in 1992. And so the importance attached to his candidacy now was to try to figure how many votes he might take from his far more powerful foes, President Clinton and former Senator Dole.

The Republicans, after all, had been Perot's main victims in 1992, when a majority of his almost 20 percent of the total vote blocked President Bush's reelection and Clinton was thereby boosted into the White House. As a result and for the time being, the Democrats were the least worried by Perot's renewed candidacy in its opening stages.

How much this altogether rare excursion into political philanthropy would cost the sixty-six-year-old Texan this time out of his estimated $3 billion fortune was another question of consequence. In 1992, playing by his own rules, he was estimated to have spent $60 to $70 million of his own money—no limit applied because he was using no federal campaign funding. That night, however, his people were already asking their supporters and the TV audience for public contributions; and so federal limits applied to him in 1996.

On the basis of their parties' showing in 1992, President Clinton and Dole each collected nearly $62 million in what were called federal matching funds, under which they were bound to limit themselves to raise and spend no more than an identical amount for their own respective campaigns. That sum was also automatically the limit Perot could raise, minus the $29.1 million in federal campaign funds that were due him for his own total vote in 1992.

Under federal rules for contributions, there were further limitations for the current Perot campaign. No contribution could be larger than $1,000, except for Political Action Committee grants that could not be more than $5,000. But because Perot was quite honestly committed to campaign financial reform and opposed the PACs, that kind of money was barred for him on personal grounds. He also couldn't accept the huge "soft money" contributions given to Democratic organizations by such allied forces as the AFL-CIO and to the Republicans by, say Big Tobacco or the National Rifle Association, a process he also opposed.

Therefore, assuming that he maintained his legal and personal funding obligations, all he could contribute out of his own fortune this year was $50,000. But that night at the Radio City Music Hall in New York, President Clinton was raising $10 million in gifts—which was quite a contrast.

And so now, even if Perot as an independent campaigner had dropped out in 1992, then returned shortly before election day and was still given a surprising independent total, few familiar with the field expected him to do that well this time. He would assuredly do better than the 3 percent of a sampling given him in a current *Newsweek* poll and the 7 percent in a *USA Today* poll; but that was quite a distance from the nearly 20 percent of his actual total vote in 1992.

Still, when as expert a correspondent as David Broder of the Washington *Post* gave Perot's candidacy respectful attention and said that he might very well play a critical role in a close campaign, the Texan couldn't be disregarded. How many Republicans might shift from Dole to Perot or desert President Clinton in the last days of the fall drive might well determine the outcome if the voting was as close as some expected.

That night at Valley Forge, Pennsylvania, Perot had become his Reform Party's candidate when the delegates gave him their vote on the basis of his victory over former Governor Richard D. Lamm of Colorado. Out of a claimed membership of 1.1 million people who had been declared eligible to vote for a party nominee, fewer than 50,000 had actually cast ballots by mail, telephone, or the Internet, that new medium created by the computers' invasion of cyberspace.

A party spokesman at the outset of the Valley Forge meeting had announced this count of Reform Party voters in Perot's favor: 32,145 votes, or about 65.2 percent as against the Lamm total of 17,121 votes, or about 34.8 percent. The Colorado governor, in his address to the convention directly afterward, had neither conceded nor challenged the result but merely thanked those among the delegates who had voted for him. He also did not endorse the victor. Later, in an interview with CNN, he readily acknowledged his continued loyalty to the principles of the Reform Party, saying that he was committed to an attempt to end the dominance of the two old parties.

But he was equally reluctant to explain his refusal either to congratulate or even to endorse Perot. At first, he pleaded that he'd rather not try to explain his position, that he just wanted time to think things over. But when he was badgered for a reason, even for criticism of his successful opponent, he replied curtly that he didn't want to appear to be a bad loser, insisted on withholding either a yes or a no in support of Perot, and at last walked off more in seeming confusion than any exhibition of hurt feelings.

All in all, it was quite a comedown from the 19,741,065 votes Perot had received as an independent in the 1992 election against the president-to-be, Clinton, and the retiring chief executive, Bush.

Even if those in charge of the mailings from Perot's office in Dallas had done their work with maximum efficiency, there were bound to be difficulties in so many mailings and returns within so short a time. It wasn't surprising, in consequence, that complaints of nonreceipt of ballots were general among the registered Reform membership within little more than a week of the supposed mailings between August 1 and 5.

The reactions were equally predictable. Some had hurt feelings, others philosophical resignation, still others had dark suspicions, and a few bubbled over with outright charges of fraud. In so strained a situation, the original Happy Warrior, former Governor Alfred Emanuel Smith of New York, so named as the 1928 Democratic presidential nominee by Franklin D. Roosevelt, might with reason have choked on his campaign theme song, "The Sidewalks of New York."

Meanwhile, having designed and very largely paid for the creation of the Reform Party, Perot set up the machinery for the split-site convention, the opening day being August 11 at Long Beach, California, and the closing at Valley Forge a week later. But once the delegates assembled at Long Beach for the first featured debate between Messrs. Perot and Lamm, the former Colorado governor blew his top over not having received a ballot along with his daughter and his father, although his wife had been sent such a mailing.

That embarrassment seemed to have been papered over for the time being because the Reform Party opponents staged their debate, as scheduled at that first meeting at Long Beach, while the Republicans were assembling at San Diego. There really wasn't very much difference between the rivals' views, which were unmistakably conservative to the point of old-fashioned isolationism of the pre-World War II variety.

If they didn't have Communism to combat as miasma ferociously as the old-time isolationists who fought the New Deal in general and Franklin Roosevelt's third term in particular, they took it out on foreigners and their children generally, demanding sharp restrictions on immigration in a way that the senior Hearst of the 1930s would have recognized with sage approval.

Lamm said to the Reform delegates, "We are no longer an empty continent that can absorb all the world's 'huddled masses.' We must place as a first priority for our own 'huddled masses.' We must understand that the Statue of Liberty stands for liberty, not for unlimited immigration."

This turned out to be a popular theme for the Reformers as well as the Republican platform that was unveiled the next day. "*Down with Immigration!*" seemed to be a conservative cause with oomph second only to demands for American dissociation with international trade treaties like the North American Free Trade Agreement (NAFTA) and some of the nation's best customers, Canada and Mexico. Somehow, out of the miasma of mistrust, no one bothered to recall that President Clinton, in his State of the Union message, had announced cutting the national debt in half, reducing unemployment by 53 percent, and keeping down inflation.

Lamm argued, however, without challenge by Perot that both major parties were heading the nation toward bankruptcy with "reckless spending" and therefore demanded cuts in Social Security, Medicare, Medicaid, a balanced budget amendment, and so on in the familiar litany of programs agreeable to prosperous conservative opinion. Lamm went on in another passage familiar to conservative ideologues:

> We've transformed an economically powerful nation into the world's largest debtor nation. And we do this to maintain a lifestyle which we have not earned for ourselves. My generation inherited a strong, united country; and we are on the verge of leaving a weakened and dangerously divided America.

Just how much the dedicated conservatives and industrial downsizing had contributed to this questionable phenomenon, of course, neither speaker ever bothered to estimate and thereby put themselves above the battle. But the assembled delegates at Long Beach didn't seem to mind. Nor did Perot, who added little to the debate if there was one because there seemed to be no difference between Lamm, the conservative Democrat, and his opposite number, the conservative Republican.

It was on this somewhat less than combative note among the rivals that the first day's phase of the Reform Party's convention ended as the Republicans took over in San Diego next day. If, under the circumstances, there was little press or TV coverage at Long Beach, except for CNN's enterprise in long-distance reporting from San Diego, that was the measure of outside interest in Perot's newest arrangement for attracting the public. In short, the billionaire was still more of a public curiosity than a threat to the two-party system.

Lamm accepted what he called errors of omission and commission in the ballot distribution from Perot's headquarters with admirable calm for a while, saying that he was in the business of building a third party for the long run, not merely for three months. But eventually, before the returned ballots had been counted and the result announced at the resumed party convention on August 18 at Valley Forge, he became upset and declared that he had been "lied to" about his presumed role as Perot's challenger.

Still, when Perot was publicly declared to be the victor at Valley Forge, Lamm did not challenge the outcome, although he and Perot knew perfectly well that the result had been based on only about 4 percent of the ballots legally returned by party members. Regardless of such shortcomings, the reality Lamm had to accept was that the 1996 election would now be decided once again in a three-way race.

Lamm, therefore, quietly bowed out with thanks to his supporters but not a word of support or derogation for Perot, although he pledged loyalty to the Reform Party, saying, "Our two major parties are not going to govern our country in the best long-term interests of our children."

When Perot took over, it was with a mild demonstration from the delegates as he accepted their nomination based on the result of the voting. He had already been given a grandiose introduction in a film that traced his rise from Annapolis cadet to IBM salesman and billionaire entrepreneur, but what he told the crowd and the TV audience after that was pretty much a rerun of his previous campaign.

There were a few added touches that were Perotean in context, such as the revelation that one of his wife's relatives had supplied General Washington's barefoot soldiers, about 10,000 in number at their Valley Forge encampment nearby in the winter of 1777–1778, with hand-sewn shoes to ease their misery in the snows of the Pennsylvania highlands.

To which he trumpeted the challenge: "Valley Forge will once again represent the turning point in American history." And the delegates once again applauded and cheered because the evening's developments seemed to call for it. Knowing that he was in a contest with dissatisfied conservatives for the rank-and-file loyalty of an undetermined number of Republicans, the one decided change in his mostly ad-lib oratory was to center more of his attention on the Democrats.

It was for this reason, in all probability, that he aimed some of his barbs at President Clinton directly, among them an observation that the president owed the American public straight talk instead of telling people that he feels the pain of the deprived.

Perot also wandered off into the stratosphere of the next century at one point by adding up the supposed immigration totals for the United States at a designated time and producing a population figure of around 1 billion people. "Do you want to make us the size of India?" he demanded. At the notion of turning America into the counterpart of the land of Jawaharlal Nehru, Indira Gandhi, and those who have followed them, the delegates roared, "No!"

The old America First crowd of the 1930s couldn't have made a greater fuss; but many seemed to enjoy themselves, and Perot certainly did. He timed his last remarks to the minute just before 9:00 P.M., exactly his time to move on to an hour-long exchange with an expert interviewer, the proprietor of CNN's *Larry King Live,* who was hard pressed to maintain control of his own show during the gabby flow of Perotean comment.

The 1996 edition of Henry Ross Perot added little to the scenario that was played out in 1992, at least during the introductory phase of the candidate's latest adventure in the presidential arena. Ed Rollins, a Republican operative whom Perot fired after a month in 1992, got back at the founder of the Reform Party by calling him ignorant and wanting to dominate a world he didn't understand. In a sense, Rollins, in talking about the Texan, began to sound like him—a danger that Larry King probably had sensed more than once in the one-on-one interviews he'd conducted with the financier on CNN.

Sometimes, Perot had felt so deeply about an issue that he'd caused a book to be written about it under his own name. Such a one was the volume about NAFTA, which he promoted in his cross-country travels until he came up against Vice-President Al Gore, an old debater in the Tennessee style. The result: Perot bogged down and wound up mumbling to himself.

He also strayed off course during the 1992 campaign when, out of sheer frustration at one point he seemed convinced that Republicans were trying to interfere with his daughter's wedding—an imaginary cause célèbre that became public during his temporary retirement from the hustings. Yet, he came back to make the best third-man showing in a presidential election since Theodore Roosevelt's 1912 Bull Moose independent race brought him 27 percent of the total vote and resulted in Woodrow Wilson's election over President William Howard Taft.

And so it would pay Perot's opponents this year to keep a wary eye out for the Reform Party's nominee, especially if there was a possibility of a close race between President Clinton and Bob Dole. Perot was likely at the end to be closer to 20 percent of the total vote than to the 3 to 7 percent he was allowed by pollsters directly after the end of his self-financed party convention.

At the outset of his campaign, which would be waged mainly through guest appearances on a variety of radio and TV talk shows, Perot made the Dole 15-percent-across-the-board tax cut program one of his major targets. That first night on CNN, he had said that the proposal hadn't worked in 1980 and couldn't work now. Therefore, Dole's tax-cutting proposal would have two opponents to contend with — President Clinton from the White House and the nervy little Texas billionaire from the electronic talk-show circuit.

24 Clinton at Fifty

When President Clinton climaxed his fiftieth birthday week by ordering regulation of cigarette sales and marketing for the nation's youth, he faced the opposition of many in tobacco-growing states as well as the enmity of Big Tobacco itself.

The decision at best became a calculated risk. What the president may have lost by attacking smoking, he hoped to gain through the gratitude of families that sought to protect their young from harm. The issue thereby was more than political. It also became emotionally compelling.

To the applause of leading citizens on the south lawn of the White House August 23, the president announced, "Joe Camel and the Marlboro Man have been put out of our children's reach forever." In authorizing the Food and Drug Administration to control tobacco as an addictive drug, he added pointedly that the 450,000 deaths annually from tobacco-related causes exceeded the nation's combined fatalities from AIDS, auto accidents, murders, suicides, and fires. "This," he said, "is the most significant public hazard facing our people."

Despite the enormous public support for the presidential decision that day, it wasn't certain that the Supreme Court would uphold the FDA's authority to regulate advertising and sales of cigarettes directed at young people, the crux of the Clinton decision. In one case that summer, the high court had nullified a ban on liquor ads and called for the review of another decision prohibiting billboard ads, both involving commercial free speech; but neither had anything to do with protecting the right to life of children being poisoned by cigarette smoke.

Regardless of these decisions, the president argued control of sales and marketing of the weed for children had become a public necessity when 3,000 of them daily took up smoking, the onset of a life-shortening experience. What he wanted the FDA to do, therefore, was to force tobacco firms to restrict cigarette ads appealing to youth under eighteen, halt sales to them by most vending machines, limit appeals directed at them through billboards near schools and other places, require proof of age beyond eighteen in questionable cases, and forbid sales of single cigarettes.

Even more important, as Senator Kennedy emphasized, the FDA's oversight to halt underage cigarette sales had become mandatory to slam shut one of the gateways to narcotic drug addiction that even now was hooking children as young as fifth and sixth graders.

To former Senator Dole and others in the Republican opposition, however, the presidential action seemed to be merely a cynical Democratic attempt to gain political advantage. Dole went so far as to call the attempted limitation of cigarette sales and marketing a fake issue. And yet, earlier, the Republican nominee had had no hesitation about expressing his doubts that all cigarette smoking was addictive, even though he agreed that people generally shouldn't smoke. But for him, even so, it still seemed not always to be true that human rights as far as tobacco was concerned should exceed company privileges to force-feed the poison to the young.

Dole's doubts about cigarette addictiveness had been ridiculed by Dr. C. Everett Koop, the surgeon general in the Reagan administration, who recalled that he had found nicotine to be an addictive drug during his own government service from 1981 to 1989. Dole, however, chose to remain on the side of Big Tobacco and the farmers in the tobacco-growing states of the South in seeking to overturn the Clinton initiative either in the courts or in the voting booths on election day.

What the pro-tobacco forces feared was not so much the loss of the youth trade in the United States, the next generation of American smokers. It was the ever-growing popular belief across the country that smoking in general should be curbed in the best interest of national health. Except in the tobacco-growing states, there appeared to be little popular support for the cause of the tobacco farmers, some even arguing that Big Tobacco was now counting more on expanding its overseas markets as smoking in America declined. This was an issue that would remain in the forefront of public interest well into the next century.

Another cause affecting the Southland in which President Clinton took a leading part was the popular outrage, especially among African Americans, over the torching of black churches below the Mason-Dixon line.

The president, in blue jeans and open-collared shirt, had spent a part of his fiftieth birthday on August 19 helping to rebuild one such black church in rural west Tennessee that had been destroyed in an arsenous attack.

It was 1 of 216 such churches that had been attacked by ghouls, half in the past 18 months. During his birthday's work there, the president greeted a sympathetic crowd from a stage in front of the partly rebuilt Salem Missionary Baptist Church near Fruitland, Tennessee, and was rewarded with a chorus of "Happy Birthday."

With him were the first lady, Hillary Rodham Clinton; their daughter, Chelsea; Vice-President and Mrs. Al Gore and 3 of their 4 children, Karenna, Sarah, and Albert III. It was also Tipper Gore's birthday, her forty-eighth; and so she was also saluted in song and later exchanged gifts with the president after observing their birthdays with what a construction foreman called "good, honest work."

The presidential party had come to Salem church that day after a visit to a neighboring white church, the New Shiloh United Methodist Church, also at Fruitland, that had been rebuilt after being destroyed in 1994 by a fire of accidental origin. The New Shiloh congregation and others from the countryside had been helping rebuild the Salem church as well.

The church-burning problem had been one issue in which former Senator Dole had been the first to seek coordinated federal and state action to find and punish what he called "the cowards responsible." It was immediately afterward that President Clinton had summoned the governors of the southern states to the White House for a strategy conference to deal with the spread of arsenous blazes that had torched so many black churches.

The most recent Justice Department report detailing the number of church fires and other attacks against black communities, however, had listed but few arrests; and President Clinton that afternoon could add only scant progress, although he still pledged himself to renewed efforts to find and seize more culprits. As for rebuilding, in which white congregations like the one in Fruitland participated, the presidential visit added zest to the work that was being done by so many willing hands.

Clinton praised the efforts of the black and white congregations to help each other in the emergency. They had been taking up joint collections during the summer and otherwise trying to bolster support for each other. As the president observed that day:

> When the two congregations got together, when people began to reach across the lines that divide us, when people began to reassert their beliefs in the freedom of religion—every time you do that, you are sticking up for what's made America great.
>
> I've spent a lot of time on this church-burning issue because I think it is a test of our character as a people. We've worked hard to try to rally the American people to deal with the problem of church burning, too, because we don't want to see it start in America.

Turning to the far worse religious and ethnic conflicts that divide the world's peoples from the Middle East and Africa to Bosnia-Herzegovina and Northern Ireland, the president's talk took a philosophical turn:

> Not a single soul here can say that you've not been guilty some time in your life of defining yourself because you could look down on somebody else and say,"Well, I may not be perfect, but at least I'm not like that other person."
>
> Every one of us is guilty of that. And we know there's something in human nature that makes people do that. But when it's uncontrolled, you have all this slaughter and heartache.

Until the completion of reconstruction at the Salem church, its Sunday services were joined with those of the nearby Morning Star Baptist Church, whose members had also been among those attending the reception of the presidential party. As one of the grateful people from Morning Star observed after the visit ended, "That they could find their way to this little old cotton patch is amazing."

A *Newsweek* poll taken at the end of the Republican National Convention on August 15 had shown President Clinton and former Senator Dole to be in a virtual dead heat, shattering what had been a 20- to 25-point lead for the president during much of the summer. It was a reminder, if one had been needed, that the Republican challenger was not to be taken lightly.

Yet, by the time of the president's birthday when a New York *Times*–CBS poll was taken of the standing of the major party contenders, he was back on top by an 11-point spread, 50 to 39 percent. The professional interpretation at the time was that the expected post-convention bounce for Dole hadn't lasted very long. And as for Perot's chances, he was given 8 percent in the New York *Times*–CBS poll, a gain over the 3 percent registered in the *Newsweek* poll but still far from his nearly 20-point high in the 1992 election.

Still, the president didn't let the pollsters' findings interfere with his own campaigning for the rest of that week before the Democratic convention, during which he signed into law the major pieces of legislation sent to him by Congress. The leadoff on August 20 was the celebration marking the president's signature on the minimum-wage bill, which Dole and his Republican colleagues had opposed for months.

As the 90-cent-an-hour wage rise was signed into law, with the first 50-cent increase due October 1, one month before election day, the president said of those who would benefit that day and a year later, "These 10 million Americans will become a part of America's success story." The success, as the first minimum-wage rise in six years was called, would ultimately move the total per hour from $4.75 to $5.15 in the following year. At the Republicans' insistence, the package also gave to employers a few modest gains, mainly in tax benefits.

The next day, August 21, was, in effect, a time for remembrance as well as achievement for President and Mrs. Clinton. Together, they had begun his term at the White House in 1993 by boldly holding out the promise of major health care for every American, something both had planned based on the generous model offered by the major nations of Europe, where so great a privilege has almost been taken for granted for many years.

The Clintons, however, had failed dismally to realize their ambitious goal, even with a Democratic Congress, which had permitted the Republicans to block health-care reform at every step on the ground that it was too inclusive and far too expensive for the federal government to undertake. What finally happened, in the later Republican-controlled Congress, was a bipartisan bill that permitted workers covered by health insurance to take it with them if they changed jobs and barred insurance companies from refusing coverage to people with preexisting conditions injurious to health.

Senator Kennedy, who cosponsored the bill with the Republican senator from Kansas, Nancy Kassebaum, told the president at the ceremonial signing of the act at the White House, "Every valuable part of this legislation — from insurance reform to help with long-term care, to assistance for the self-employed — was originally conceived and contained in the broad-based health-care reform proposal that you submitted to Congress in 1993."

Former Senator Dole, however, remained an intractable opponent of anything resembling major health care for Americans at government expense. In accepting the mild Kennedy-Kassebaum substitute, he commented, "The new law should end once and for all the prescription of big government health care. The American people should ask why it took President Clinton more than three years to support these commonsense reforms which he previously threatened to veto."

And so, with a modest increase in the minimum wage and a small forward movement in insured health care, the President next faced up to the welfare reform bill he proposed to sign, despite the opposition of some of the most prominent Democratic members of Congress, whose wishes had been overshadowed by the demands of the Republican majority before any kind of a welfare bill was passed.

The angry voices of massed protestors outside the White House rose garden and the absence of leading Democrats inside the fence marked President Clinton's signing of the Republican Congress's welfare reform bill on August 22. Although the measure was only a little better than two other congressional welfare efforts he had vetoed, the president signed it into law but, at the same time, promised to fight for improvements; but these could come about only with his reelection and the return of a Democratic Congress to power.

That wasn't good enough for three high officials in the Department of Health and Human Services, Peter Edelman, Mary Jo Bane, and Wendell E. Primus, who resigned in protest. Still, the president pledged, "This is not the end of welfare reform. This is the beginning. And we all have to assume responsibility."

In particular, he had a warning for the governors of the fifty states who now would inherit from the federal government the major burden of caring for the poor, the aged, the sick, and the infirm: "The governors asked for the responsibility. Now they've got to live with it." As if to reassure himself as well as others, he went on, "This is a historic chance to make welfare what it was meant to be."

That in itself would be a big job. Among the shortcomings of the Republican-approved bill that the president signed, to the dismay of at least half his White House staff, were a $24 billion cut in food stamps for poor people, totaling more than 25 million, and the congressional failure to set up job-creation programs for those who were to be thrown off welfare while still unable to find work.

These, along with measures against further care and support for at least 1 million poor children, were other shortcomings of an unmerciful Republican bill. Just how the president intended to avoid such calamitous occurrences, he didn't say at the time; but the shrill voices of hundreds of women protestors outside the White House fence were a continuous reminder that they weren't satisfied with this part of his performance as a "new" Democrat.

Nor was the absence of major Democratic figures for this welfare rally any easier for the president to disregard that day. Among the backers he didn't see beside him then were Senator Christopher J. Dodd, chairman of the Democratic National Committee; the old faithful from Boston, Senator Kennedy; and others, including most of the Democratic leadership in Congress.

Like the opposition of the women protestors outside the White House fence and at least half the presidential White House staff, the refusal of these people to go along demonstrated what the president had lost morally, if not politically, by making good on his campaign pledge "to end welfare as we know it." No wonder the Republicans present at the signing were jubilant.

Bob Dole, too, was having his troubles sticking to Republican positions of which he didn't approve. The day after Clinton's embarrassment at signing welfare reform into law, his Republican rival rejected still another of his party's platform planks in his first campaign appearance before black voters.

Adding to his objection to the party's position on abortion by selecting a prochoice keynoter (who didn't discuss her views), Dole told the National Association of Black Journalists in Nashville that he also didn't approve of automatically barring citizenship to children of aliens illegally in America. He also expressed his regret at having refused to address the National Association for the Advancement of Colored People.

It didn't seem to help him with a largely unsympathetic black audience. The most any recent Republican presidential candidate had received from black voters was the short end of a 5–1 ratio by President Gerald Ford in his 1976 defeat by Jimmy Carter. Usually, that ratio in most presidential races since had been about 10–1 against the Republican candidate.

In refusing, however, to settle for Republican control of much of what was once the Democratic "Solid South," Dole said, "I deeply believe that the Republican Party will never be whole until it earns the broad support of African Americans and others by speaking to their hopes." Still, his audience couldn't be blamed for its skepticism because of his repudiation of affirmative action, a position he defended but never convincingly by saying blacks had the right now to compete. This time, at least, he appeared before a black audience.

That was the position when President Clinton began his four-day campaign train trip to Chicago for his renomination and acceptance speech before the Democratic National Convention. Like the Republican meeting that had preceded it, the Democrats were putting on a scripted, controlled TV show but making no visible effort to silence liberal members' protests over welfare reform, tightened immigration policy, and other known differences with Clinton's "new" Democrats.

The President conceded as much at the outset, saying there was "tension" in the ranks but that "we're not going to push anybody in a corner—we're not ashamed of anybody." That, of course, was a thrust at the forced harmony of the TV show that the Republicans put on at San Diego.

Anyway, the Democrats were staging many of the same acts that the Republicans put on — the common folk and their dreams of the future and so on. But despite the fervent hope of the Democratic leadership to bury the past — the violence that disrupted the Democrats in Chicago in 1968 with the demonstrations against the Vietnam War — plus the promise of a major address from President Clinton raised the hopes of the delegates for a banner four days to start a winning presidential reelection campaign in style.

This was the presidential theme at fifty, with four years of an up-and-down experience in the White House behind him, as he began his train ride to Chicago and the Democratic convention that would renominate him: "I want America to know we're on the right track in this country, and we're going forward. We're not turning back."

It was to be the theme of his campaign to win reelection and to bring a Democratic-controlled Congress back to Washington with him for a more heartening and productive four years. What were his chances? For himself, as he headed for the convention, they were better than even. For pulling a Democratic Congress back to Washington, it looked like an uphill struggle all the way.

25 Return to Chicago

A boisterous Democratic National Convention renominated Bill Clinton with a roar of approval on August 29, expecting him to become its first presidential candidate in sixty years to be reelected. The last had been FDR's fabulous 46–2 state victory in 1936.

As an added show of confidence, the 4,320 delegates also stopped singing and swaying to big band macarena music long enough to bellow their renomination of Vice-President Gore, who had the night before delivered the best speech of the four-day meeting in Chicago. To do it, he had topped Hillary Rodham Clinton's celebration of family values that also drew cheers from the crowd.

The most fervent demonstration of all at the United Center, however, was touched off by Clinton's sixty-six minute acceptance speech amid a red, white, and blue blizzard of floating balloons. At the end, he was more tired and still more excited than any who heard him.

Although this meeting, like its Republican predecessor in San Diego, had been carefully scripted, nobody even thought of muzzling such old stalwarts as the Reverend Jesse Jackson, former Governor Mario Cuomo of New York, and Senator Edward M. Kennedy of Massachusetts—and nobody had guts enough to try.

In any event, it would have amounted to a scandal. Jackson and Cuomo therefore lamented President Clinton's signature on a Republican welfare reform bill; but both also joined with Kennedy in refusing to let such shortcomings split the party, as had happened during the Vietnam War period in 1968, the last time the Democrats had convened in Chicago. In fact, Kennedy didn't even mention his own differences with the president on reform.

What happened instead was a general agreement thereafter that it would take the return of a Democratic Congress on election day, together with the president, to undo the harm done to the poorest, youngest, and others least able to defend themselves against the shortcomings of welfare reform under Republican auspices.

It was just as well that the Democrats averted disunion; for by evening, although there had been no mention of it on the floor, the delegates were buzzing over the news of the forced resignation of a presidential adviser, Dick Morris, over charges in a scandal sheet, the *Star*, that he had been consorting with a prostitute and had even let her listen to his phone talks with the president.

Although Morris refused to confirm or deny the allegation as he exited with his wife for their Connecticut home, the accusations were broadcast quickly enough to the public by evening. As for the reaction outside the convention hall, Mayor Richard M. Daley of Chicago, a Democratic leader like his father before him, predicted in another broadcast that Morris's downfall would have no effect on the presidential campaign because nobody was voting for Morris in this election. A check of the news media in the next forty-eight hours indicated that most public comment on the affair began with a puzzled "Morris who?" or the equivalent. Daley had called it right.

As the delegates departed for their homes once the convention ended, the bottom line to the incident was provided by the ABC-TV network with an announcement that its daily tracking poll, which had given Clinton a 19-point lead before the convention, was now showing him 20 points better than his Republican challenger, Bob Dole, and counting.

Still, at a Democratic National Committee meeting next morning, Clinton cautioned that he'd known of candidates who'd blown a 20-point lead before election day, adding, "It's not over till it's over." The not-very-original conclusion served as his going-away line for his first bus tour with the first lady and Vice-President and Mrs. Gore into the American heartland.

The Democratic high command, in its post-convention operations, remained just as cautious as the president over the party's chances to recapture Congress, despite a CBS-TV poll in late August that showed a 45–36 percent Democratic lead for control of both houses. Even though that was the figure by which the Republicans had seized Congress in 1994, the Democratic leadership was well aware that sixty-five days still remained before election day, November 5, and nothing could be taken for granted.

Just as both Clinton and Gore had given convention exposure to the most threatened among their congressional colleagues, hoping to stimulate a favorable reaction at home, so the party's directorate scheduled bumper advertising campaigns for the national ticket in districts with tight local races for the Senate and House. By that time, the party's war chest was well stocked; but everybody also realized that ballyhoo by itself had never elected anybody.

The major efforts expended by each major party at its national convention were the best evidence that no candidate for high office, either at the executive or legislative level, could be sold to a skeptical public as easily as a bar of soap or a package of chewing gum. Political talent counted for much more.

President Clinton, in his acceptance address, demonstrated once again his skill as a campaigner when he seized upon an unfortunate Dole theme at San Diego and turned it to Democratic advantage. What Dole had said, out of the wisdom of his seventy-three years, was that his party's mission and his own were to build a bridge to the glorious past — conceivably the bullish 1920s before the bottom dropped from the economy. Against that flawed vision, Clinton countered in his own address:

> We don't need to build a bridge to the past. We need to build a bridge to the future. And this is what I count on you [the delegates] to do. Tonight, let us resolve to build that bridge to the twenty-first century to meet our challenges and protect our values.

That led him directly into the major themes that he had used in his five-state train trip on the way to the Chicago convention on his aptly named "Twenty-first Century Express." These included more government support for a strong economy that had already created 10 million new jobs and cut the national debt by 60 percent; billions more for education, including a new literacy campaign and a public school rebuilding program; a major attack on crime through a broadened gun-control program; and 100,000 new police on the streets of cities and towns; a mounting war on illicit drugs; regulation of tobacco through branding nicotine as a habit-forming drug; freedom of choice for women considering abortions; more support for affirmative action policies; and, above all, necessary changes for the much-criticized welfare reform plan.

There were new ideas, too, that the president put forward in addition to a summation of what he considered he had accomplished in his first term. Among them were proposed tax breaks for new home owners and for businesses that create the necessary jobs that should be waiting for people forced off welfare.

But he also added, as the Reverend Jackson had so insistently urged, that the White House would need the assistance of a Democratic return to leadership of the coming One hundred-fifth Congress if any of his programs, especially the new parts of welfare reform, were to be made the law of the land.

The climactic fourth evening of the Democratic National Convention began with an elaborate Hollywood-type production of Clinton's past as the man from Hope, Arkansas; his modest home life and schooling, and his steady progress in public life until the film ended, the lights went up, and the president appeared on stage to be greeted with a five-minute standing ovation.

With his facile, bridge-building opening theme, broken by almost continual applause, he listed the major accomplishments of his first term; increasing the minimum wage for the first time in six years, saving (with the help of Senators Kennedy and Kassebaum) his health insurance portable provision from job to job with its pledge that insurance could not be denied to an applicant for a precontracted illness, the family leave/medical leave law, and the major attention he continued to direct at increasing the opportunities for national public education.

Before launching into his newest proposals and summing up the ones that he had made on his train trip to the convention, he paid graceful tribute to his rivals, former Senator Dole and H. Ross Perot, the candidate now of his self-financed Reform Party, praising their patriotism, their careers, and their service to the nation. Clinton also pledged himself not to conduct a negative campaign against them or to allow others to do so. "This," he said, "must be a campaign of ideas, not a campaign of insults."

Right off, the president repeated his objections to the much-publicized Dole 15 percent tax-cut proposal while promising once again to balance the federal budget by the year 2002. By contrast, he emphasized his own budget cuts of a less sweeping nature, assuring his audience that he had made certain that the funding of all tax breaks had been assured "line by line, item by item," together with a reminder that he'd never submit to a pressure program such as the two government shutdowns engineered by the Republican congressional majority. "As long as I am president," he commented, "I'll never let it happen. We didn't let it happen before. We won't let it happen again."

Despite the disgrace of President Clinton's adviser Dick Morris, who in the past had also served such Republican senators as Trent Lott of Mississippi and Jesse Helms of North Carolina, the White House regrouped quickly enough. And as for the convention delegates, there were twice as many Democrats as there had been at the preceding Republican convention. Nor were they as compliant in muffling their differences as the Republicans had been to put up a false front of seeming unity, despite deep cleavages over women's rights to an abortion if they wanted one, among other issues.

Although nearly half of the Democrats were well-to-do with incomes listed at $75,000 annually or more plus a scattering of millionaires, almost matching the Republican display of great wealth, all but 5 percent of the Democrats described themselves as liberals in varying degrees—nearly the extent to which the Republicans styled themselves as conservatives.

As compiled by a New York *Times*–CBS survey among other sources, this phenomenon of close-to-exact opposites also appeared in their respective backgrounds, except for education, in which more than two-thirds of both delegations listed themselves as college graduates. But about 34 percent of the Democrats were also union members, compared to only a very few Republicans—4 percent to be exact.

In the categories of gender and race, 53 percent of the Democrats were women, 47 percent, men; 36 percent of the Republicans were women, 64 percent men. Seventy-one percent of the Democrats were white, 17 percent black; 71 percent of the Republicans were white, 3 percent black.

The delegates were just as divided on major issues. On abortion, so painful a problem in both parties, 61 percent of the Democrats were for choice, compared to 11 percent of the Republicans. On welfare reform, the main issue that divided Democrats, most Republicans sided with Messrs. Dole and Gingrich and the law signed by the president. The Democrats were split nearly in half.

Other issues showed divisions mainly along party lines. Democrats favored government action to help solve the nation's problems by 76 percent, Republicans by just 4 percent. By nearly as great a difference, Democrats also favored government help in regulating business and the environment. In Clinton's ban on nineteen types of assault weapons, he drew 91 percent support from Democrats, 34 percent from Republicans. On affirmative action, the Democratic margin was even wider, 81 to 9 percent.

On platforms, the Democratic document almost entirely reflected President Clinton's views as a self-styled "new" Democrat who sought a middle ground between laissez-faire capitalist economics and the welfare state of a bygone Democratic era. On welfare reform, the president met some of the objections of leading Democrats to the Congress's package by last-minute revisions in the platform against big cuts in food stamps. If reelected, he also promised among other changes to seek to restore public cash payments to poor children.

There were also disclaimers in the platform. In the majority belief in freedom of choice for abortions, there was recognition as well for "the individual conscience of each American on this difficult issue." And to counter Dole's 15 percent tax-cut initiative, there was Democratic support in general for reduced taxes for families with children, others for home buyers, and for families that were paying college tuition for sons or daughters.

Otherwise, the "new" Democrats made no change in such historic party positions as commitments to public education, tobacco regulation, affirmative action, civil rights for homosexuals, protection of the environment, and government-paid abortions for poor women if so desired. There were a few additions, the most important being the expansion of the death penalty as a deterrent to crime.

As for actual work of the Chicago convention, the first three days were shared with President Clinton as his "Twenty-first Century Express" loitered through West Virginia, Kentucky, Ohio, Michigan, and Indiana before arriving in Chicago the night before his renomination. This was where the president's love of campaigning and his exceptional ability as an off-the-cuff orator were much in evidence. It didn't matter that his routine by rail was different. He often managed to tie into the issues before the convention during his informal talks with crowds along his route and also in speeches that had been scheduled for him in his travels.

The night before the opening of the convention, Sunday, August 25, the president made a blistering attack on the 15 percent tax-cut proposal by former Senator Dole. During an interview with CNN staff people that was heard nationally, he argued that so large and unrestricted a tax cut simply wouldn't work in the current state of the American economy. He forecast that the result would be huge cuts in social services, including Social Security and Medicare, to pay for lost revenue; an increase in the national debt and consequent rise in inflationary pressures, along with further and as yet unlooked-for reductions in government services.

Each day thereafter, while Clinton was on the road, he hammered hard at a particular issue that also became a part of the day's proceedings in Chicago, where delegates could watch him in action on huge screens in the convention hall. What the Democratic planners were able to do thereby was to enlarge his daily audiences which, when combined with the national audience for televised excerpts from the convention, outstripped the totals of those who followed the Republican convention.

On August 26, for example, his major subject during the day was the attack on crime, during which he announced his proposal to include the forced removal of guns from homes marred by domestic violence as well as from criminal use. "If you commit an act of violence against your spouse," he warned, "you shouldn't have a gun."

That night in Chicago, Sarah and Jim Brady, both Republicans, were also featured at the convention's exposure to gun control. As a passionate advocate for keeping guns out of criminal hands from the time her husband was shot in the head during the 1981 attempt to assassinate his boss, President Ronald Reagan, Sarah Brady aroused the Democratic delegates with her pleas to stiffen gun laws.

Delegates were also aroused by another celebrity that night when the actor Christopher Reeve, who had played "Superman," appeared at the United Center in a wheel chair, paralyzed as the result of a horse-riding accident.

On the road at a rally in Arlington, Ohio, President Clinton again sounded his anticrime theme saying:

> We need to finish the job of putting 100,000 police on the streets. We need to build on the Brady bill. . . . Jim and Sarah Brady have spent their lives, not as Republicans, not switching parties to the Democratic Party, but just being Americans, trying to say this is crazy for us to keep letting felons get guns.

The next day at the Chicago convention, "Family First" for the delegates, also became a showpiece for the president at the public library in Wyandotte, Michigan, a suburb of Detroit. There, national TV showed him being read to by Elizabeth Schweye, nine, and Justin Whitney, seven, who took turns quoting passages from *The Little Engine That Couldn't*.

From that scene, after applauding the children and their classmates before a crowd of parents and teachers, the president announced a national literacy program costing $2.75 billion over four years. Through the hiring of tutors and federal grants to public schools, he called for a nationwide effort to make certain that all children in the third grade could read. And instead of criticizing teachers because they belonged to a union, as Dole had done, Clinton praised the teachers for their devotion to duty and pleaded for their help once his literacy campaign became law.

The previous night, in Toledo, Ohio, he had been cheered by a crowd of 15,000 people outside a Chrysler Jeep factory that had been revived to full production during his administration, turning out its 2 millionth Jeep in his presence. It was, he said, a demonstration that the United States had now regained from the Japanese the position as the world's number 1 auto producer.

It mattered not a bit to him that Democratic Representative Marcy Kaptur criticized his signing the North American Free Trade Agreement, which had stimulated American trade with two of its best customers, Canada and Mexico. For response, he invited the crowd to join his "new" Democratic Party and was cheered again.

This spirited acceptance of criticism of his policies brought President Clinton a heartening reward the night of August 27 in Chicago while he was still on the road. It was when the party's most distinguished liberals, Jesse Jackson and Mario Cuomo, addressed the Chicago convention to urge his reelection and the election of a Democratic Congress, although they differed with him over his signature of the welfare bill.

To tumultuous applause in the convention auditorium, the Reverend Jackson said:

> Now that we have ended welfare as we know it, we must provide jobs and job training and education and day care as we ought to know it. . . . On this issue, many of us differ with the president. Patricia Ireland and I even picketed the White House. But we can disagree and debate and still work together. Diversity is the measure of this party's strength; how we handle adversity, the measure of our character. We must find the bridge, keep our tent intact. And we must make the commitment to right the wrongs in this bill.

To that, former Governor Cuomo added a passionate amen. He agreed with Jackson that "in 1996, Clinton is our best option," then added, "Many of us, and I am among them, believe that the risk to children was too great to justify the action of signing the [welfare] bill, no matter what its political benefits." But out of party loyalty, he continued, "The president is confident that we can avert this risk by further legislation before children are actually harmed. We should hope and pray that the president is right."

For the rest of that evening, there were better moments for the president, particularly when the keynoter, Governor Evan Bayh of Indiana, invoked the family values that still distinguish America by saying, "They are the values that President Clinton has worked to restore to meet the challenges of our time. Opportunity for all Americans, responsibility from all Americans, and a sense of community among all Americans."

But doubtless, the speech that pleased the president most that night in Chicago while he was still on his "Twenty-first Century Express" was Hillary Rodham Clinton's own exposition of family values. She told how she and the president had engaged in

> no experience more challenging, more rewarding, and more humbling than raising our daughter. And we have learned from experience how to raise a happy, healthy, and hopeful child.
>
> It takes other family members, it takes teachers, it takes clergy, it takes business people, it takes community leaders. It takes all of us. Yes, it takes a village. And it takes a president.
>
> It takes a president who believes not only in the potential of his own child, but of all children; who believes not only in the strength of his own family, but of the American family; who believes not only in the promise of each of us as individuals but in our promise together as a nation.
>
> It takes a president who not only holds these beliefs but acts on them. It takes Bill Clinton.

As for sixteen-year-old Chelsea, whose privacy had been so fanatically guarded by her parents, she had her own coming-out party during the convention — a date at the most talked-about affair of Democratic convention week, the host being John F. Kennedy Jr., John-John to his father's surviving genereration, now the publisher of a magazine called *George*.

For August 29, just before the president's arrival at Chicago, he paused at Kalamazoo, Michigan, to announce his newest environmental package, a commitment, if reelected, to spend $1.9 billion over the next four years as follows:

> In the last three years, not counting this year, we have cleaned up 197 toxic-waste sites, more than in the previous twelve years. In the next four years, we'll clean up another 500 toxic-waste sites . . . and by the year 2000, we will clean up two-thirds — the two-thirds worst toxic-waste dumps in the country. We will get them out of the neighborhoods where children live.

The main speaker of the evening, Vice-President Gore, already featured in many a news account of the convention as a likely Democratic presidential candidate in the year 2000, reminded his TV audience of the major Republican error of this election year, when they twice shut down the federal government under the leadership of Messrs. Gingrich and Dole.

The vice-president went on, "They thought Bill Clinton would buckle under pressure, cave in to their demands. But they did not know the true measure of this man. He never flinched nor wavered. He never stooped to their level. And, of course, he never attacked his opponent's wife," a reference to the continual Republican attacks on Mrs. Clinton. The vice-president concluded his account: "Bill Clinton took Speaker Gingrich and Senator Dole into the Oval Office. I was there, I remember. And the president said, 'As long as I occupy this office, you will never enact this [shutdown] plan. Because as long as I am president, I won't let you.'"

There was still another moving commentary by the vice-president, a former tobacco farmer himself, in his discussion of the administration's attack against Big Tobacco's continued advertising appeals to young people to smoke more cigarettes. In his recollection of a sister's death from causes directly attributable to her smoking habit, he brought tears to many among his audience, including his own parents, and was himself deeply affected. He had long ago ceased to raise tobacco.

In placing the president's name in nomination before the convention in which there was no opposition candidate, Senator Christopher J. Dodd of Connecticut went out of his way to thank his former colleague, Dole, for his wartime sacrifices while under fire with his army unit in Italy. Dodd also said that he didn't question the Republican nominee's reputation but, instead, "It is his agenda for America. Sometimes a fine person has flawed ideas. This is such a time."

With Clinton's continued lead in the polls at the time, it cost little or nothing for the Democratic Party's chairman to have a few kind words for the opposition and it contrasted with Dole's own daily denunciations of the president. And then, at last, after the parade of seconding speeches, the convention unanimously adopted the president as its candidate for reelection, together with Gore as vice-president. It set the stage thereby for the president's acceptance speech the following night, marking the onset of the fall campaign.

After the rousing success of the acceptance speech, the president was so revved up that he got very little sleep. And so when he met Vice-President Gore at an early meeting of the Democratic National Committee in Chicago next morning, Firday, August 30, a bleary-eyed president asked forlornly, "Why are we here?"

To which Gore replied on cue, "We've got to beat Dole"—all of which set the committee members for a reconsideration of both party conventions as the president summed them up, saying that he felt much better about his party's showing because there was no effort to cover up differences of opinion, the flaw he saw in the Republican performance.

He sent his party's delegates and leaders on their way then for the Labor Day opening of the decisive fall campaign with a brisk listing of the most critical issues—crime and drug-use reduction, expansion of welfare reform, and other difficulties saying, "These are all difficult issues. There will always be differences of opinion about them because if somebody knew all the answers, we'd have no problems."

Then, with a promise of his full support and a fervent "God bless you," he sent his auditors on their way for the big push to reelection while he and Gore flew to a small town in Missouri, Cape Girardeau, for a reunion with their wives and the onset of a two-day barnstorming bus trip through Missouri, Illinois, Kentucky, and Tennessee — a dress rehearsal for the campaign that would start in earnest with Labor Day.

It was, as the president repeated to the crowds that greeted their red, white, and blue bus caravan, the beginning of the trip across the bridge he so fervently sought to the twenty-first century.

PART FOUR
The Fall Campaign

26 Labor Day Kickoff

Bill Clinton and Bob Dole weren't the only combatants that Labor Day, the traditional kickoff for the fall presidential campaign. Unexpectedly, Saddam Hussein of Iraq also dealt himself in.

Apparently tempted by the notion that America's leadership would be politically engaged that weekend, the Middle East troublemaker decided to invade a Kurdish city forbidden to him in a UN resolution that warned him against further persecution of its desperate minority. It was when 30,000 tank-led Iraqi troops entered the city that President Clinton acted with two missile attacks directed against Saddam's military installations closer to the Persian Gulf.

Unlike the wide support given President Bush in his 1991 Gulf War against Saddam, however, this American action drew little backing abroad. Those who refused support included most of the NATO allies, except Britain and the Middle East Arab lands dependent on American arms—Saudi Arabia, Kuwait, Jordan, and Egypt. In so doing, whether intended or not, they encouraged a brutal dictator, who still terrorized his neighbors just as he did in taking Kuwait, the cause of the Gulf War. Only Kuwait now offered the Americans air bases.

Those with long memories could only sigh over what happened in the 1930s, when so many nations also refused to take up arms against a savage Austrian named Hitler because he was only beating Jews, the start of his reign of terror that climaxed in World War II. And so there was a sense of history in President Clinton's explanation of the American position against Saddam:

> We must make it clear that reckless acts have consequences or those acts will increase. We must reduce Iraq's ability to strike out at its neighbors, and we must increase America's ability to contain Iraq over the long run.

The summation of the Middle East position was apt. Left to his own devices, Saddam's Iraq could quickly have become an even greater threat to its palpably weaker oil-rich neighbors in the next century than Nazi Germany had been to its fellow Europeans in the first half of this century. What Saddam had done to the Kurds was warning enough of his intentions elsewhere. And as for the United States, there was an additional urgency to act against him. As Defense Secretary William J. Perry said in a discussion of the missile strikes, "We must maintain the flow of oil," a necessity for American industry and automotive transport.

As far as foreign comment was concerned, however, there seemed to be little hope that the American strikes against Saddam in themselves would deter him from further adventures for as long as he remained in power. In 1993, the president had also tried such a missile attack on the Iraqi capital, Baghdad, with even greater resultant damage, as a punitive measure against what was called a plot to kill former President Bush; but Saddam had come out of that stronger than ever.

Although a large part of the American electorate was hazy about this latest American adventure in the Middle East, given the uncertain results, former Senator Dole moderated his criticism of the president's foreign policy as "weak-kneed" by saying at an American Legion convention:

> In matters like this, all of us think not as Republicans or Democrats, but as Americans. And as Americans, we wish our troops success and safety. They are freedom's heroes; and we support them without hesitation or reservation.

From the position of a Republican challenger who had already dropped still more in the polls after the Democratic National Convention renominated President Clinton, now figured at a disadvantaged 20 to 25 points, it might have seemed logical for this decorated, wounded veteran of World War II to pursue his advantage over a rival without a war record; but for the time being, he turned to other issues.

This much was certain about the relationship of the presidential contenders that Labor Day weekend: There had never been a Labor Day kickoff campaign in the latter part of this century quite like this one eleven weeks before election day. How it developed could well decide in large part whether the outcome would be a bridge to the future, as Clinton expected, or to the modern realization of a bridge to the past, as Dole had suggested. As for Saddam, he seemed intent on burning his bridges, no matter what happened.

Sadddam Hussein al-Tikriti, now in his sixtieth year, had been in power in Baghdad since 1979 as an iron-fisted Iraqi dictator, ruling over more than 20 million mostly Arab Sunni Muslim people in an area about the size of California. One month after assuming authority with the self-imposed title of president, he had staged a bloody purge to rid himself of some of his major opponents. That kind of villainous conduct had continued on and off even as late as the previous year, when he had succeeded in persuading two close relatives who had fled the country to return. Of course, he shot them.

Like his predecessors, Saddam had been a vengeful foe of Iraq's Kurdish minority, now figured at about 20 percent of the population and sequestered in northern Iraq around what was called its "capital city" of Irbil — a protected zone by edict of the UN Security Council, from which Iraqi air assaults were barred. As for ground troops, Council resolution number 688 warned Iraq against prejudicial conduct against the Kurds; but, otherwise, there was no actual rule to prevent the entry of ground troops.

The reason for the UN gesture to prevent further brutal conduct against the Kurds, even in a part of the country that was still Iraqi territory, was based on the tragic history of the people. To romantics, they were held to be the lineal descendants of the Saracens of the Crusades with Saladin, the conqueror of Richard the Lion-Hearted, as their ancient leader.

But in the Middle East today, the Kurds are ragged, homeless wanderers who have appealed for help at international gatherings for much of this century. At Versailles after World War I, in calling for "the self-determination of peoples," President Woodrow Wilson doubtless had had the Kurds in mind among others and had sought, with the help of his European allies, to lessen their suffering.

During and after World War II, the Kurds appeared to be centered mainly in the mountainous areas north of the Persian Gulf but still without a land of their own. Briefly, there had been a Soviet Kurdistan; it had vanished beyond recall. Finally, in 1973, after a losing war with Saddam's predecessors, the Kurds were split between Turkey, with 4 million, and Iran, with 2 million, while the rest in Iraq were centered around Irbil and were given, by the United Nations, a surrounding protected area, an enclave, that they presumed to call their own.

During the Iran-Iraq War in the early 1980s, Saddam and his army had driven into Iranian territory and burned Kurdish villages there, leading to American-supported pleas before the UN Security Council to ease the suffering of these nomadic peoples. And so, the Kurdish enclave gradually gained support.

Whether this had anything to do with Saddam's open hostility toward the United States, there is no way of knowing; but American displeasure came to a head when an Iraqi missile killed thirty-three American sailors on a frigate, the USS *Stark,* in the Persian Gulf in 1987. The Iraqi government called it an "accident"; nevertheless, from then on, US Navy vessels began escorting most oil tankers leaving the Persian Gulf for the United States.

Saddam's ambition, however, knew no bounds. And on August 2, 1990, without provocation, he sent his troops storming across the border to oil-rich Kuwait, which also shares a border with Saudi Arabia, and announced three weeks later that the nation of 1.8 million people in an area the size of Connecticut had become Iraq's nineteenth province.

Why Saddam thought that he could get away with such brazen violation of the independence of a small, defenseless nation has never been explained. But President Bush, at the head of a multinational force that included Britain, France, and Arab states such as Saudi Arabia, Egypt, and Jordan, battered Iraq from the air for almost two months, then launched a ground war on February 23, 1991, that ended four days later with Saddam's surrender and Kuwait's liberation.

The worst damage the United States suffered was the deaths of twenty-eight American soldiers at Dhahran, Saudi Arabia, when a Scud missile hit them. It cost the Kuwaitis $5 billion to repair the sabotage the Iraqis had caused in their oilfields and another substantial sum was apportioned with Saudi Arabia to care for 400,000 Kuwaiti refugees who had fled across Saudi borders.

But in the end, the American mistake was to permit Saddam to remain in power in Iraq, continue to sell billions of dollars in oil annually from his resources, build up a new army, conduct experiments in nuclear explosives and chemical weapons, and all too soon resume threatening his neighbors.

What complicated the latest American effort to seek punitive action by allied states against Saddam's forces in the fall of 1996, aside from the conduct of the presidential campaign at home, was the anomalous position of the Kurdish population. What had happened in the Kurd enclave around Irbil for several years was that Iraqi and Iranian agents had succeeded in splitting the Kurdish community so that one group appealed to Iran for help and the larger accepted Saddam's dubious offer of armed support.

This was what preceded the dictator's orders to his tank-led troops to invade the Kurd enclave and to search the city, disposing of those Kurds who were sympathetic to Iran—something that refugees reported after fleeing the enclave and the country. This developed at about the time of the Democratic National Convention; before and directly afterward, President Clinton was kept in touch with developments by the Defense Department and the CIA while authorizing warnings to Saddam to cease and desist.

Such warnings, three in all and given privately, were ignored. As Saddam's government later claimed, his forces had been invited to Irbil by one of the two warring factions of Kurds and had responded. It became obvious, therefore, that the United States would have been in an awkward position to intervene in a dispute between two Kurdish factions as well as the Iraqis; but the consensus at the White House was that something had to be done to make Saddam "pay a price," as the president put it, when he was held to have violated a UN resolution against Kurdish persecution.

Because it was evident that Saddam was testing American resolve to protect its own interests as well as the Kurds in this push into Irbil, the president finally decided the most effective punishment for Saddam would be to reduce his air force and his protective installations against air attack with a missile offensive against a number of Iraqi air installations between the thirty-second and the thirty-third parallels, just south of Baghdad.

After the Gulf War, the United States had established a "no fly" zone for Saddam's aircraft below the thirty-second parallel, where Iraq's ground forces were mostly stationed. The effect of the missile attack, if successful, would be to deprive Saddam of air cover for his army if he moved south toward the Persian Gulf while, at the same time, sending a stiff warning to Baghdad to pull out of Irbil at once.

This is what hapened when two American warships in the Persian Gulf, plus B-52s that flew all the way from Guam and back, fired twenty-seven missiles at the airfields and air defenses at 1:00 A.M., EDT, which was 9:00 A.M. in Baghdad. The United States followed up the next day with seventeen more missiles that wiped out installations that were missed in the first attack. The casualties, as announced by Saddam's people, were relatively few; but the assessment of the damage by the missiles served to delay any Iraqi strike for some time to come — or so the Pentagon hoped. It was more damaging to Iraq that UN permission to sell its oil supplies to buy food and medicine for its people had been suspended.

The pullback of Saddam's forces from Irbil was also completed, after which refugees spread tales of mass executions of some of the leaders of the Iran-supported Kurd faction. There was, however, no solid reaction among the American electorate, which seemed to be divided between those who were annoyed that the United States had to go it alone against Saddam's forces (Britain supplied no forces, ships, or missiles) and those who were so indifferent to the entire, complicated business that President Clinton could derive very little satisfaction from this phase of the start of his fall political campaign.

Regardless of what happened thereafter in the course of diplomatic or economic measures against Iraq, informed opinion in the United States concluded that whoever was elected president on November 5 would have to finish, sooner rather than later, the Gulf War that President Bush had ended with Saddam Hussein still in authority in Iraq. It would either be that or endless provocations against the Kurds, Kuwaitis, and other virtually defenseless peoples and the continual threat of interdiction of American oil supplies from the Gulf states.

The rising tide of Muslim fundamentalism that was spreading from Pakistan across Asia and North Africa to Libya was no myth, nor was there any sign that it would moderate in the near future. This was mainly what Saddam Hussein was counting on to remain in power in Baghdad for the rest of his days.

It was against this devious background that Messrs. Clinton and Dole opened their respective fall campaigns for the presidency on Labor Day. Neither had anything very original to say at their outdoor gatherings, which seemed to be more of a convivial celebration of a sunny early autumn in a prosperous land than ill-natured political combat for the highest office in the land.

Clinton was at a picnic for 25,000 people just outside Green Bay, Wisconsin, at the end of a sweeping nine-state tour he had completed that September 2 after the end of the Democratic National Convention. At pleasant Voyaguer Park in DePere, near Green Bay, the president felt encouraged enough to talk about balancing the budget, his opponent's favorite theme. But he did it with a twist as always, saying:

> This is Labor Day. We can be grateful that we have over 10 million new jobs, but we know we'll have to keep this recovery going. That means we have to continue to balance the budget, but do it in a way that grows the economy and keeps us together.

The easy Clinton Labor Day formula was to insist that the budget could be balanced without going into horrendous financial details, as follows:

> We can balance the budget without wrecking Medicare; turning our backs on the medical commitments of Medicaid, which includes families with disabilities; little babies that are poor; pregnant women; and

the elderly in nursing homes. We can balance the budget and increase our commitment to education and to research and to the environment, not walk away from it. Will you help us balance the budget that way? [A roar of support.]

Later, as the guest of John J. Sweeney, the president of the AFL-CIO in Milwaukee, the president took his usual swipe at his opponent's 15-percent tax cut proposed to tumultuous applause, saying:

> If you thought the budget I vetoed was bad, you ain't seen nothing yet. If they pass this tax plan, they'll come back with deeper cuts. Is that what you want for the future? Of course not!

And, proclaiming that he and his party were for both business and labor, with easy confidence, he said that he would build his much-desired bridge to the twenty-first century.

It was old-fashioned oratory, familiar to highly partisan Democratic crowds that Labor Day, and it went over well. After such enthusiasm over political pleasantries, it must have been a cold-water shock to an amiable president to return to the White House that night and face up to the grim realities of growing tension in the Middle East. But then, few among his entourage had ever expected him to be confident of his grasp of the nation's foreign problems.

Dole, too, had a relaxing Labor Day on the banks of the Mississippi before the Gateway Arch in St. Louis and a cheering crowd as large if not larger than the president's audience in Wisconsin. It was also loud and seemingly happy with a candidate who was frank enough to admit his concern that he was behind in the polls by two-digit figures but hopeful of coming through as a winner in the fashion made famous by Harry Truman, Missouri's favorite son. Truman had come from behind in 1948 at the age of sixty-four to win the presidency that many had though irretrievably lost, as the seventy-three-year-old Republican candidate told the story, saying,

> Like Harry Truman, I represented a Midwestern state in the Senate. I was honored to serve my country in uniform. And, like Truman, I'm going to win a come-from-behind victory for president of the United States.

Dole's themes were also familiar—his 15-percent tax cut, a conservative vision of smaller government that he favored against a liberal vision of big government, and "an administration you can trust."

"Our opponents offer an old-style liberal vision that puts government first," he shouted above the encouraging cheers of the crowd, "and Jack Kemp and I offer an optimistic vision that puts the American people first. That's the difference. That's the key dividing line in this campaign. They believe in government and we believe in you."

Then, too, the Republican nominee had to take his own swipe at the president for extolling bridge-building to the future. Dole proclaimed:

> My opponent wants to build a bridge to the future. But as Jack Kemp has said, he's a toll bridge. You pay every inch of the way, every step of the way. You pay and you pay and you pay.
>
> That's what we're afraid of because he would be a bridge to the future of higher taxes, more teenagers using drugs, a govenment-run health-care system, more liberal judges, America defenseless against incoming ballistic missiles, an economy producing too few jobs, and on and on and on with more government and more government in our lives every day and every day and every day.

Except for the president's private telephone call to former Senator Dole to inform him of the missile offensive against Iraq and the old soldier's warm pledge of support, it had been just another sunny Labor Day election kickoff—and the partisan crowds had thoroughly enjoyed it. For that matter, Dole's problem had been tougher than Truman's, for as a septuagenarian, he was up against a younger, more vigorous president instead of President Truman's overconfident rival, the New York racket-buster Thomas E. Dewey.

And so the Labor Day kickoff passed for both Republicans and Democrats with exaggerated if harmless rhetoric that few thoughtful people were able to take seriously. It was far more important, later in the first week of the fall campaign, that the Pentagon realized that Saddam Hussein, despite the blows that his military defenses had suffered from two missile attacks, was still "out of his box." That was how the position was put by General Colin Powell, the American Gulf War commander, now retired.

Despite reports that Saddam's tank-led forces remained active in Kurdish territory outside the city of Irban and that phony reports were being spread of American missile attacks on Baghdad, President Clinton declined for the time being to order a third missile strike, even though General Powell, now a Republican consultant, recommended it. The Pentagon seemed satisfied that Saddam's ground forces, without their protective air cover, could be heavily damaged if they became too dangerous to American interests in the Persian Gulf.

It was in this manner that the presidential campaign entered its crucial final phase heading toward election day.

27 Advantage: Clinton

Bob Dole had to face up to still another emergency at the onset of his post-Labor Day campaign.

The Republican challenger was trailing President Clinton so badly, sometimes by as much as 15 to 20 points in the polls, that he had to shake up his campaign staff for the second time in six months. It became a matter of deep concern to the Republican high command, therefore, when the top of their ticket took aboard three new advisers and dropped the two who had been with him since his first drastic reorganization in February.

The switch emphasized the candidate's own worries, clearly evident at his Labor Day rallies, over his failure to maintain the boost that he had received across the land after almost catching up with the president in the aftermath of the Republican National Convention. But with official and unofficial Republican advertising estimated at $100 million about to begin for the fall campaign, the candidate had seemingly lost confidence in two of his closest advisers, Don Sipple and Mike Murphy, who resigned and were at once replaced by three veteran strategists, Greg Stevens, Chris Mottola, and Alex Castellanos.

It now became the responsibility of the campaign manager, Scott Reed, to meld the new strategists into a confused, even resentful campaign organization on which Dole would now have to depend for the major thrust of his campaign. The outlook, at best, was cloudy that September, for one major poll was already reporting that 64 percent of respondents across the land remained unconvinced that, if elected president, the former senator from Kansas could cut taxes by 15 percent across the board, the issue he had made the heart of his campaign.

Sipple, the top strategist who quit under pressure, had been the closest campaign adviser since taking over the previous February from Bill Lacy, the original deputy campaign chairman. Perhaps, at seventy-three, the elderly candidate hadn't been easy to manage; and his clashing position on abortion and other key issues had alienated too many women voters. But the criticism of the Sipple/Murphy strategy within the Republican organization seemed to have glossed over such basics as these to descend to personalities, a situation not unusual among people working for trailing nominees.

Murphy, for example, had seemed amused while representing the Dole campaign staff at a CNN-TV discussion of the resignation of President Clinton's top strategist, Dick Morris, over an affair with a prostitute that he refused to confirm or deny. Without such complications, apparently, Murphy had had his own detractors, along with Sipple's, in the Republican organization. Whether winning or losing, the careers of political advisers are seldom as secure as they would wish.

But now, with different people new to the Dole presidential organization, the nominee's position seemed to be the most difficult of all in the eight weeks that remained before election day. Between the presidential TV debates, the multimillion-dollar advertising war, and the day-to-day grind of trying to get through to a doubting electorate, Bob Dole was in a make-or-break situation in which he needed a strong, devoted campaign organization on which he could depend. Did he have it? At the moment, he couldn't be sure.

Clinton's political stock, by contrast, continued to rise after the Democratic National Convention. A high of 73 percent of respondents in a current New York *Times*-CBS poll after Labor Day reported feeling economically secure in the Clinton administration, as compared with only 27 percent who still worried about economic insecurity. Even Clinton's foreign policy rating, directly after the United States had to go it almost alone against Saddam Hussein's Iraq, reached almost 53 percent. And with regard to the Dick Morris resignation, only 9 percent said that it made them think worse of the president.

The importance to the poll respondents of the president's role in bolstering the economy could not be overemphasized. By a margin of 6–1, those participating in the poll said they would vote for him in November. And in terms of approving his management of the nation's economy, the ratio was 55 percent—the highest he had ever received in that particular set of poll-taken values.

The respondents who called the nation's economy good also backed the president over Dole 2–1. As for the significance of these findings, the New York *Times* stressed the modern polling record that every presidential nominee who was ahead by double digits at or around the Labor Day kickoff had gone on to win the election.

It was not only the economy but the president's support of Social

Security, Medicare, and Medicaid that gave him a lift in his first venture into Florida after Labor Day—a state designated as Republican territory for twenty years, although he only narrowly lost it in 1992. In addressing elderly audiences throughout the state in his two-day barnstorming tour, the president plugged hard at the health-care program that he lost so disastrously during his earliest years in the White House and yet managed to salvage a few key provisions like portable health insurance and insurance for people with preexisting conditions injurious to health.

To a delighted audience of older people at one stop in Florida, Sunrise, he made everybody feel good with this kind of approach to Medicare:

> Everybody wants us to save Medicare. Everybody knows that we're all living longer and staying healthier, and that's good, isn't it?
>
> So when somebody tells me we've got this terrible problem with Medicare, I don't understand all this handwringing. That's a high-class problem if we've got people living longer and being healthier and hanging around and doing things. I think that's a very high-class problem. . . . Now, we have the highest life expectancy of any country in the world among people who live to be sixty-five going forward.

The president, his advisers, and campaign staff were serious about taking Florida on election day and adding its twenty-five Electoral College votes to his total. Other southern states that he and his people were also refusing to concede to the Republicans were Georgia, Louisiana, North Carolina, Tennessee, and Kentucky. He won all except North Carolina in 1992.

As Clinton developed his campaign in Florida, notably with a display of Bible-quoting oratory before the National Baptist Convention at Orlando, he received one of his biggest boosts from the Labor Department's September report, which put unemployment at a seven-year low of 5.2 percent for August. What this meant was that 467,000 people had been added to the nation's payrolls that summer, dropping unemployment below 7 million for the first time since the summer of 1990.

Admittedly, a part of the record was based on more summer jobs for young people, and there were also less encouraging statistics for minorities. As compared with the white jobless rate of 4.4 percent, down 3/10 of a point, black unemployment remained at 10.5 percent, and Hispanics dropped from 9 to 8.7 percent.

Average hourly earnings also increased to $11.87, a gain of 6 cents, all of which led to a 52.9-point gain in the Dow Jones Industrial Averages to 5,659 after Labor Day on September 6 and predictions of a rise in Federal Reserve interest rates to forestall an inflationary situation.

It was such good news for the president at his appearance before the Baptist convention, the largest black church organization in the nation, with more than 30,000 churches and 8 million members, that he cried out for help from each church to hire someone off welfare, saying as a fellow Baptist:

> The Scripture commands us in Nehemiah to rise up and build and strengthen our hands for the good work. Today, I ask your help in building that bridge to the twenty-first century I have been talking about all across America.

He then outlined the core of his own appeal:

> If every church in America hired one person off welfare, if every church in America could get some work to do that, it would set an example that would require the business community to follow, that would require charitable and other nonprofit organizations to follow. We cannot create a government jobs program big enough to solve this whole thing; but if everybody did it, one by one, we could do this job.

The enthusiastic response of his audience was a rising chant of "Four more years!"

For former Senator Dole, the report scarcely added to his chances, as he recognized, saying," People are working, but many are working because they have to work to pay the federal taxes. We have very slow growth."

And as for his hardworking teammate, the vice-presidential nominee, Jack Kemp, he became the first Republican candidate for high office in almost one hundred years to seek votes in New York's Harlem, the largest and most influential black community in the nation, saying, "We weren't there with Dr. King. But we are here today and have an obligation to this community to make this country what it was supposed to be, a city on a hill."

It was safe to predict that he didn't change many votes, welcome though a visit to Harlem may have been from at least a part of the Republican presidential ticket.

What Dole was actually counting on now to revive his political fortunes was the three presidential debates that would begin toward the end of September. Just as Clinton had hazarded a guess in a TV interview that he "felt in my bones that this is a closer presidential race than the polls show," so Dole added that he believed "in my bones" that he was only 7 or 8 points behind the president, instead of the double-digit margin separating the contenders in every major poll.

In a radio interview, the Republican nominee added that he was "going to get into the ring" with the president in what appeared to be his best hope at the time for a change in his political fortunes. He continued, however, to insist that the Reform Party's candidate, Ross Perot, should not be invited because he didn't have a chance of being elected but was being supported for the debates by the Democratic campaign committee.

What Perot was actually doing after Labor Day was to put forward a hard-hitting campaign directed mainly against President Clinton, apparently hoping thereby to blunt the Republican argument that his candidacy — as happened in 1992 — only gave the Democrats a greater advantage.

From the $29 million he received from the federal government in matching funds for his surprise showing in 1992 of almost 19 million votes as an independent candidate, he was now planning a series of thirty-minute lectures on TV, "infomercials," as he called them, although the information he used was merely material to support his own views, rather than the flip thirty-second spots that the Republicans and Democrats specialized in for their TV attacks.

One of these lectures, a substantial part of an address that Perot delivered before an American Legion convention in Salt Lake City on September 4, was re-broadcast over ABC-TV the next night. Another, on taxes, was heard over NBC four days later. And over the course of the campaign, his plans were to hew to the thirty-minute paid lecture series for as long as he believed them to be effective.

This was his own electronic recipe, assuming at the time that he would be on the ballot in all fifty states on election day. To be sure, he would be limited now in what he personally could spend as the presidential candidate of the Reform Party; but the "soft money" available to the two major parties without limit could also be used by the Reform Party, although Perot wasn't any more specific about such funding than his rivals were.

The one certainty was that this would still be the costliest of all presidential elections, particularly in the buying of TV time.

Perot was also following neither major party candidate in his proposals for foreign affairs, especially in situations likely to lead to the further engagement of American forces abroad. In his American Legion lecture, he attacked President Clinton repeatedly, although not by name, saying at one point, "War is not a place for politicians to create a positive image and gain a bump in the polls."

He elaborated in this manner:

> What did we accomplish in Somalia? Nothing.
> The people in Bosnia have been chewing on one another and fighting for hundreds of years. How many of you think that in nine months our troops can solve the problems in Bosnia?
> We've been on the thirty-eighth paralled in Korea for forty years,

keeping that crowd apart. And now, in less that a year, we are bringing our troops home from Bosnia — just before the election.

It was hard to tell what objection Perot had to the policies of Presidents Truman and Eisenhower in the conduct and settlement of the Korean War, but there was no doubt about his interest in the protection of the ill and the captive war veterans he had tried to help in the Vietnam and Gulf Wars.

The only time that he came down to specifics about the presidential interest in war itself was when he took off again on President Clinton, saying, "If you won't go, how could you send someone else?" Then he added, "Today, war is presented to the American people on television as a Super Bowl sporting event."

It was here that Perot, a graduate of the Naval Academy at Annapolis, differed with the position of the old soldier Bob Dole, who supported the president's actions against Iraq "without hesitation or reservation." The Reform Party's candidate also proposed a war tax to be paid by the American people whenever there was a foreign mission for the nation's armed forces.

"Every American," he said, "would pay a war tax so that they'd get a tap on the shoulder every time they get a pay check that we have people fighting and dying. That would get the nation's attention."

But in arguing for more manufacturing of war materiel at home rather than abroad, he apparently assumed that Puerto Rico, a part of the United States since 1898, was a foreign country we might call on for supplies for troops wounded in combat. In any event, the Legionnaires were polite about his talk toward the end of their convention, although more than one might have wondered about his preoccupation with Democratic politics when it was the Republicans who were trying to bar him from the forthcoming presidential debates.

From a 1996 campaign beginning at only 4 percent in most opinion polls, he had progressed by Labor Day to 7 or 8 percent; but by any conceivable standard, he still was far afield from the 19.7 million votes he had received in 1992. Few believed, regardless of how much TV time he bought and how many TV lectures he delivered, that he could approach that showing in 1996. It was still Clinton's race to lose as a sitting president.

28 Rehearsal for A.D. 2000?

The contest for vice-president, usually an afterthought in most presidential elections, assumed more importance in 1996, mainly because of the strength of the contenders—forty-eight-year-old Vice-President Al Gore and his Republican rival, sixty-one-year-old Jack Kemp.

Despite President Clinton's impressive lead in the polls and his talent as a fifty-year-old campaigner, it was apparent that he placed great confidence in his vice-president's judgment and, if reelected to a constitutionally limited second term, could very well support what was now a developing presidential boomlet for Gore for A.D. 2000.

The show of strength that Kemp was also bringing to the trailing Dole campaign was not lost on the Republican leadership. And while the greatest effort for the ticket lay directly ahead in the fewer than eight weeks that remained of the current campaign, Kemp had already demonstrated his usefulness to the former senator's cause and very likely would have to assume an even more forceful role at the climax. It seemed a certainty, therefore, win or lose, that Kemp's services would be rewarded, whether or not he made it to the White House this time.

Aside from the prominence of the vice-presidential contenders, the greater emphasis that was being placed on the office itself with the reduction in the size of the federal government made it mandatory that the importance of the number 2 role should be emphasized both inside and outside the White House.

After all, the time had long passed since the vice-presidency itself was regarded as a bad joke by down-at-the-heels vaudeville comedians. In this century alone, seven of eighteen vice-presidents had become presidents. In the ninety-six years ending with President Clinton's current term, former vice-presidents had served as presidents for thirty-eight years—almost 40 percent of the period.

The prominence of some of the vice-presidents who became presidents was also worth greater public attention with the coming of the next century and its broadened challenges to a nation that values its democratic heritage. Presidents Theodore Roosevelt and Lyndon Johnson respectively succeeded the assassinated McKinley and Kennedy. When Presidents Warren G. Harding and Franklin Roosevelt died, they were replaced by Vice-Presidents Coolidge and Truman.

Vice-Presidents Nixon and Bush, who served under Presidents Eisenhower and Reagan, were later elected presidents themselves. And Nixon, unhappily, became the first president in history to resign under fire, being replaced by Vice-President Gerald Ford, himself the successor as Speaker of the House to the resigned Vice-President Spiro Agnew.

On balance, therefore, the record would seem to indicate that the greater effort to increase the usefulness of the vice-presidency has not been misplaced. Along with the three presidential debates as an important factor in this campaign, the single vice-presidential debate scheduled by the Bipartisan Commission would bear watching, not only for this election but, perhaps for one or the other candidate and maybe both, for the next one in A.D. 2000.

More than any vice-president within my own memory, which covers most of this century, Albert Gore Jr. has broadened both the office and its inherent responsibilities by accepting and delivering on more presidential assignments than any of his predecessors.

This was no accident. From his earliest days in the political arena in Tennessee, he never made any great secret of his ambition to be president; but he was also tactful and patient. As a United States senator and the son of a senator, Albert Gore Sr., who served in the upper house for thirty years, the younger Gore devoted himself meticulously to the vice-presidency once he entered the White House.

"I don't see this primarily as a preparatory job," he once explained. He added that his purpose was to do first whatever President Clinton asked him to do.

Born in Washington, D.C., on March 31, 1948, Al Gore enjoyed the many advantages that come to a conscientious youth whose parents could afford private schooling for him and life with them in a hotel in the nation's capital while his father served in Congress. During vacations and summers, he was at the family estate at Carthage, Tennessee, which was also a large farm, on which he sometimes worked with the help. He was also close enough to Nashville to become familiar with the operations of the State of Tennessee as well as the federal government.

At Harvard, he became a University Scholar and took his bachelor of arts degree cum laude in 1969, when he was only twenty-one. And in the following year, in a whirl of activity, he was married to Mary Elizabeth (Tipper) Aitcheson, who became the mother of their four children; but more immediately, he enlisted in the army and spent a year in Vietnam. Then, he returned to Tennessee, where he joined the staff of the Nashville *Tennessean* as an investigative reporter and editorial writer. Later, he also studied law at Vanderbilt University Law School between 1974 and 1976.

It was then that he turned to politics by winning election as a member of the House of Representatives from Tennessee in the Ninety-fifth to the Ninety-eighth Congresses, before moving up to succeed his father in the Senate between 1985 and 1993. In the latter year, having been elected vice-president during Bill Clinton's successful presidential campaign, his next move was to the White House.

There, his office was only a few steps from the Oval Office, where the president often welcomed him, valuing his advice and giving him more work to do between 1993 and 1997 than anybody else in the number 2 spot had ever tried to handle. Yet, this vice-president was never known to have protested the overload and performed useful service throughout. In the 1996 campaign, he was also much more active than most vice-presidents in this century, which was just as well, given the energetic activity of his Republican rival, Kemp.

At home meanwhile, the Gores enjoyed a fortunate marriage with their four children—Karenna, now twenty-three; Kristin, nineteen; Sarah, seventeen; and Albert III, thirteen. As for the father's greatest ambition, the presidency itself, that still remained a distant goal during the 1996 campaign, when he was commissioned more often than not to perform major services for President Clinton both at the White House and on the campaign trail. As a thirty-nine-year-old senator in 1988, he had entered the presidential primaries but won only the experience.

One of the most important projects the vice-president undertook for the president after their election in 1992 was to reduce the size of the federal government without markedly affecting its usefulness for the bulk of the American public. This was the program called "Re-inventing Government," in which Gore, after careful study, proposed and received authority to eliminate 240,000 jobs by January 1, 1996, as existed by White House standards.

As a result, President Clinton went into the reelection campaign at the head of a federal work force with fewer positions in it than at any time since President Kennedy took over more than thirty years ago. It says something for Gore's tact that there was no passionate outcry from the union of federal and state employees against the cuts, which were made in a time of mounting prosperity for the nation and pleas by the Republican high command against "big government"—a major part of the Dole campaign.

Another successful Gore initiative, again on assignment from the president, was his part in the expansion of the administration's campaign against the outrageous efforts that cigarette companies waged to lure children of tender years to begin smoking. The vice-president had a personal reason for his concern in this assignment, having seen his older sister, Nancy, a large-scale smoker, die of smoke-induced lung cancer in 1984 — something that touched the heart of many across the nation when he recalled it in his speech accepting his vice-presidential renomination.

This was the genesis of the presidential effort to prevent cigarette companies from advertising their product within reach of any public school as well as other restraints suggested first by Gore primarily to save the lives of small boys and girls from possible fatal consequences through addiction to nicotine at a time when they should have been encouraged instead to more healthful playtime in fresh air and sunlight.

Other presidential programs in which Vice-President Gore exerted a compelling influence at the White House included environmental protection, in which he also had a deep personal interest, and the enlargement of the government's efforts to examine outer space — certainly a major project for the next century. Through his own studies in telecommunications, grounded in his experience as a journalist after returning from Vietnam, he also contributed markedly to the president's efforts to regulate this ever-expanding industry in its latest ventures into cyberspace.

Perhaps the vice-president's most important addition to the national interest, however, came with his more than two dozen trips abroad in his first four years in the White House, during which he contributed markedly to the formulation of the Clinton administration's foreign policies. A major factor in this regard came with the realization that President Boris Yeltsin, always a heavy drinker, had suffered heart problems that affected his reelection campaign against renewed Communist opposition.

Even though a pale and seldom active Yeltsin was able to stave off a Communist comeback in the voting, his disapearance from Moscow for weeks both during and after his campaign created problems for the United States as well as for his own constituency. It was during this period, before Yeltsin's crucial heart operation in the early fall of 1996, that Gore and Secretary of State Warren Christopher were able to work out with Russia's Prime Minister Viktor S. Chernomyrdin the creation of a commission of cabinet experts from both Russia and the United States to formulate agreements on major policies such as arms control; international trade rivalries; and, probably the most significant of all, measures to maintain watchfulness over dangerous experiments in the Middle East involving chemical, biological, and nuclear warfare.

It was at the time of the 1996 national conventions in August, however, that the president turned to his vice-president for solid support with the downfall of the principal presidential adviser, Dick Morris, following his forced resignation over a prostitute's bought-and-paid-for story of a year-long affair with him. Whatever the complaints over Gore's rigidly straight mannerisms and his impeccable family presence, this was exactly what helped get the Democratic National Convention out of a rough start.

At a time when the Republicans were hoping to make political capital once again from the "character" issue — a thinly disguised repeat performance of the 1992 allegations of Gennifer Flowers, together with broad hints of other presidential improprieties — Vice-President Gore, together with his Tipper and their four children, presented the party and the nation with an imposing family portrait of togetherness, love, and devotion. And it was against so sympathetic a background, beyond the criticism of the most wild-eyed of tabloid reporters, that the president's formal renomination proceeded in Chicago for the benefit of a national TV audience.

In leading a procession of distinguished speakers proposing the president for renomination, Gore said:

> Make no mistake, there is a profound difference in outlook between the president and the man who seeks his office. In his speech from San Diego, Senator Dole offered himself as a bridge to the past. Tonight, Bill Clinton and I offer ourselves as a bridge to the future.

The Democrats' target, of course, was Speaker Gingrich, the most unpopular figure in Congress, as the author of two failed government shutdowns at the start of the presidential year, not so much Dole or even Jack Kemp. And it was Gingrich whom Gore held out to an all-labor rally in Chicago sponsored by the AFL-CIO, saying:

> With equal portions of ignorance and audacity, this two-headed monster of Dole and Gingrich has been launching an all-out assault on decades of progress on behalf of working men and women.

Like the convention crowd, the labor rally outside took up the victory chant for Clinton and Gore: "Four more years!" It was such scenes as this rather than the unsavory retreat of Dick Morris that lingered in the public memory, as shown by the subsequent polls in which the president's high standing quickly recovered from its temporary descent at the end of the Republican National Convention. Nor did Dole's chant of an unbelievable 15-percent tax cut for everybody while still balancing the budget seem to make any better impression on the electorate if the rising Clinton poll figures were any indication of the public mood.

Jack French Kemp, Gore's Republican opponent, was by no means your average politician. Nor did he act his sixty-one years after his career as a professional football quarterback. He wasn't stumped by the poll figures that showed how far down the scale Dole had fallen with the rise of the Clinton/Gore ticket after the end of the Democratic National Convention. Although some of the threatened Republicans in Congress were already quietly distancing themselves from the admitted difficulties of the national ticket, Kemp kept tackling the Democrats, even in places like New York City's Harlem, where most people in the largest black community in the United States generally considered themselves to be 90 percent for Clinton/Gore.

Until Kemp ventured into Harlem on a hot Friday, September 6, the closest any major Republican figure had come to the lively scene on the Harlem plain was in the early 1950s on Morningside Heights. There, General Dwight David Eisenhower and his Mamie were occupying the Columbia University President's House while he awaited the Republican presidential nomination in 1952.

Having been a Columbia professor at the time, I remember no record that Ike ever actually descended into Harlem from the heights; but he certainly saw it frequently enough while looking out his Columbia presidential windows and won two elections in 1952 and 1956 without Harlem's support.

And so Kemp, at the very least, was due credit for bringing America's other major party to the direct attention of the Harlem electorate, even if he had no illusions about making progress there against the overwhelming Democratic support that quickly made itself evident. As the cheerful Republican candidate put it, "All too often, the Democratic Party has taken the black vote for granted; and all too often, the Republican Party has written it off."

But having played football for Buffalo at the other end of New York State, he couldn't be expected to know the ins and outs of New York City politics; and so he made a capital error in lauding the career of the black leader of the Nation of Islam, Louis Farrakhan, in a weekend in Boston, in advance of a meeting with national Jewish leaders a few days later.

Although the Republican vice-presidential nominee was well aware of Farrakhan's reputed anti-Semitic attitudes and was careful to specify disagreement with some of the ideas of the leader of the "Million Man March on Washington," he still alluded with admiration to some of Farrakhan's attitudes. In any event, it didn't make for great enthusiasm among his Jewish audience soon afterward, especially when Vice-President Gore followed him on the platform.

What Kemp was discovering through actual experience as a vigorous campaigner for the national ticket was that not every audience in the land could be addressed as if it were predominantly white, male, and well-to-do, the traditional group at the core of the Republican Party's support. But he couldn't have hurt the ticket any more than Dole's continued emphasis on his 15-percent-tax-cut proposal in the face of growing public skepticism. The difference, however, was that Dole was near the end of his career, while his running mate still had a way to go, win or lose.

Kemp, the former congressman from Los Angeles and the former secretary of Housing and Urban Development in the Reagan administration, was born July 13, 1935. He and his wife, the former Joanne Main, have four children—Jeffrey, Jennifer, Judith, and James.

After taking his bachelor of arts degree from Occidental College in California with postgraduate study at two other colleges in the Golden State, he made a name for himself as a professional football quarterback for thirteen seasons in Buffalo, San Diego, and elsewhere.

Then, turning to politics, he became a Republican representative from New York's thirty-first district, Buffalo, serving in the Ninety-second to the One hundredth Congress. Under President Reagan, his most important experience in government then followed as the secretary of Housing and Urban Development from 1989 to 1992.

Once he left the government in the latter year, however, he made his fortune mainly as a public speaker until 1996, when he reported total earnings of $6.9 million, mainly in fees for his speeches plus added compensation as a member of the boards of at least one dozen corporations. Up to that time, he had not precisely been underpaid, either, having earned $189,000 a year in his Reagan cabinet job.

Despite the favorable impression he made elsewhere across the land as a Republican vice-presidential nominee, sometimes eclipsing the somewhat strait-laced Vice-President Gore, he still had something to learn about the usefulness of principle in public life. Having abandoned a lifelong belief in affirmative action and other parts of a liberal personal creed to conform to the positions taken by Dole as his party's presidential candidate, Kemp was caught short now and then when asked to explain his sudden change of front.

That was particularly noticeable when he and the former senator addressed a convention of the National Association of Black Journalists in Nashville late in August that year and he was floored by a question such as this: "What credibility do you now have with African American voters after turning your back on affirmative action in the mere space of two days?"

The response was not particularly enlightening, beginning with the candidate's fulsome belief "with all my heart that affirmative action is very much needed, but the right kind of affirmative action, small *a*." Only the *a* seemed to be very small and confused, concluding with, "All government action is affirmative." That, unfortunately, was what hurt the Republican ticket's campaign, along with similar waffling on other issues, including that affront to a majority of women in the nation who favored freedom of choice.

As the presidential candidate and chief financial supporter of the new Reform Party, Ross Perot had expected to have difficulty in obtaining the third spot in the presidential debates that he gratuitously received in 1992. What he didn't really expect for 1996, however, was still more trouble in persuading anybody of substance to become his vice-presidential nominee; but he was repeatedly turned down until September 10, when he was finally able to announce the acceptance of a writer with radical economic ideas, Pat Choate, with whom he had had an up-and-down relationship for years.

Choate had earned a doctorate in economics at the University of Oklahoma with a dissertation on the role of government in economic policy. He had also held state jobs in economic development offices in Oklahoma and Tennessee, then became director of research for the federal government's Office of Economic Research in 1975 but lasted only until the Carter administration took office after being elected in 1976.

From then on, Choate had a relationship with Perot, first as an economic adviser, then occasionally as a guide and coauthor, along with others in and out of government. As an unabashed isolationist in economics, Choate has opposed the North American Free Trade Agreement, also a favorite belief of Perot's; but they both fell afoul of Vice-President Gore in a 1993 debate and didn't do very well when Gore stoutly supported NAFTA.

But with Choate as his vice-presidential nominee, Perot's Reform Party at last had a complete ticket. All the two needed now was an invitation to the forthcoming debates to try to improve their standing in the polls. From nearly 20 percent of the total vote in 1992, Perot, by early fall four years later, had slipped to only 4 or 5 percent in most major polls, despite his investment of so much effort and money in what was, for him, a billionaire's adventure of a lifetime.

29 The Republican Dilemma

President Clinton was campaigning that fall in states that the Democrats hadn't carried in a generation or more, raising the party's hope for resuming control of Congress as well as the White House.

Although the Democratic high command still wasn't inclined to make extravagant claims with the presidential debates directly ahead, there was an unmistakable air of optimism about its headquarters in the nation's capital. Some Republicans, by contrast, were clearly worried about the consequences on election day.

The position was such that the Republican leadership, with fifty-four days still to go before election day, asked Bob Dole to address Republican members of Congress in what was apparently supposed to be a pep rally, only there wasn't too much pep on Capitol Hill that otherwise pleasant September 11; and fewer than half of the 288 party members serving in the Senate and House showed up for the great event.

The presidential candidate was in good humor for the occasion, fortunately, reminding his congressional following that he had called himself "the most optimistic man in America" during his acceptance speech at the San Diego convention. Then, trying to put spirit into the Capitol Hill troops, he added pointedly, "I want to say to the fainthearted people in this audience—there are probably not very many—don't worry about this election. We're going to win."

He talked of Republican leadership in the White House, in Congress, and of moving forward with the party into the next century and "making it happen." He went on in a philosophical vein, "Each of us have been in close, tough races. The polls go up and down and people get discouraged. But the candidate can never get discouraged. The candidate has to be optimistic."

It didn't seem to be too convincing a performance. The mood among many in the audience was thoughtful, even dour; for some painful statistics were being tossed about by congressional candidates seeking reelection who reported downbeat showings for the leader of the ticket that were bound to hurt their own campaigns. One who blurted out some bad news from a Massachusetts district on national TV had Dole trailing there by 39 percent, which inevitably affected his own race. A few others, also heard on TV at the time, were almost as bad; but there was no way of knowing whether the fault lay with the congressional candidates or the head of the ticket or both.

What seemed to matter most to the assemblage in the relatively brief time of Dole's appearance was that this was not a year when very many expected to ride to victory on the presidential candidate's slender coattails. There were some who grumbled audibly that their problem was quite the opposite.

In retrospect, having conducted their experiment in morale building with the presidential candidate's help, the Republican leadership problem was how and where to use the party's enormous financial resources — both the declared presidential funds and the vast pool of much larger contributions to the party organization and the party itself for which there was no legal limit.

These funds either could be devoted to a nationwide advertising attack on Clinton's credibility, his policies, and his personal life in order to benefit the flagging Dole cause or they could be spread judiciously across the several states where crucial Senate and House races might very well determine the composition of the One hundred-fifth Congress and its political dominance. But it was doubtful whether both causes could be served simultaneously.

And this, in brief, was the Republican dilemma: whether to favor the presidential candidate with a blizzard of commercials in the concluding weeks of the campaign or to emphasize the continued control of Congress, which in effect would be giving up on Dole's still-faltering presidential drive. Nobody, of course, expected that the Republican high command would be making so prejudicial a choice publicly or even shifting from its declared objective of electing both a president and a supportive Congress until it became absolutely necessary.

Scott Reed, the Dole campaign manager, hinted at a deadline for a decision at the Labor Day kickoff by acknowledging President Clinton's double-digit lead in the polls and observing, "We have recovered and put our base back in place. We have a viable candidacy right now. Our goal is to get this to single digits by the middle of October."

Given the extent of Clinton's lead on Labor Day, that in itself amounted to a major undertaking, particularly when Dole and his campaign staff still kept emphasizing the 15-percent tax cut as their supposedly winning issue through much of September, without cutting the president's lead by very much.

True, in the flurry of charges and countercharges growing out of the attacks on Saddam Hussein's Iraq, Dole had also begun to question the effectiveness of the president's Middle East policies in a mild way in the apparent belief that the head of the opposition ticket shouldn't markedly differ from the White House's military decisions, except in the degree of force used against the enemy. In the case of Iraq, of course, Dole was the first to suggest that the opening limited missile attack would be ineffective, as indeed it was.

The burden of the criticism of the Clinton policies against Iraq, therefore, was shouldered by the vice-presidential nominee, Jack Kemp. And although he was both direct and forthright in demanding something more from the White House than random air attacks on a powerful Middle East foe, perhaps the best-armed and most united in the region, that in itself also didn't immediately indicate any forthcoming change in public sentiment supporting the Clinton/Gore ticket, rated in one poll at 57 percent.

By mid-September, however, there was evidence that a number of congressional candidates in tight races with their Democratic rivals were quietly separating themselves from the Dole cause. Instead, they were trying to save themselves in the event of a possible Democratic landslide that was now being suggested by independent commentators, although not by the Democratic high command itself.

A Republican polltaker, Bill McInturff, indicated in a casual comment that if enough Republican candidates in the House and Senate decided to go it alone, without necessarily notifying headquarters or any other major source, that in itself would tend to detract from the presidential race and, in the end, would substantially alter the Republican turnout for the entire ticket. That, too, eventually became a problem for the party's campaign committee, especially in the block of thirteen southern states that had become the backbone of Dole's effort.

The position in Tennessee, which Bush had carried for the Republican ticket in 1992 by a substantial margin, was such an instance four years later, when a September poll showed Clinton leading Dole there by 48–37 percent, with Perot getting only 2 percent. Looking behind the polls for an answer to the turnaround, this was a state in which Vice-President Gore was both a resident and a tough campaigner. What he emphasized throughout was a charge that Dole, if elected, meant to close down the important and valuable national nuclear laboratory in Oak Ridge by eliminating the Energy Department and eventually consolidating it with the Defense Department.

Whatever Dole did to reassure Tennesseans in general and Oak Ridge in particular while campaigning in the state, he evidently didn't satisfy a dubious electorate; and his 15-percent-tax-cut proposal also drew him no new votes. Nor did Perot, for all his anti-major-party campaigning, come within reach of his 10.1 percent of the total vote for president cast in the state in 1992.

Such "down home" issues as this, together with the failure of many southern voters to be impressed by Dole's tax-cutting promises or his attacks on the president's character, also led to Clinton's lead in mid-September in other states below the Mason-Dixon line, including Arkansas, Florida, Georgia, Kentucky, Louisiana, and West Virginia.

Robert Joffe, a pollster familiar with southern conditions, commented, "If Dole has to fight for states like Florida, North Carolina, and Virginia, he's fighting behind his own 40-yard line. These states were won by Bush in 1992."

There was something more to the disclosure of Dole's surprising weakness in the South than the possible loss of more states there in November than Bush had carried easily in 1992. For if Dole had to spend more time shoring up his base in the South, a region that the Republicans were supposed to dominate, then he would perforce have to abandon time he could have devoted with possibly greater advantage to critical midwestern states, including, among others, Michigan, Illinois, Wisconsin, and Ohio.

With Dole's candidacy slipping and the outcome of key races for control of Congress in doubt in the final weeks of the 1996 campaign, the Republican dilemma deepened on how best to use its still awesome financial resources. This was the overall position:

In the House, the Republicans' 235 out of the 435 seats were all up for election or reelection. Of the Senate's 100 seats, the Republicans held a 53–47 majority. But in both chambers, the retirement of Democratic veterans complicated the problem and made it more difficult for the Democrats to seize control of the Senate than the House, despite the fewer seats involved in the upper chamber.

With a normal turnout of voters in a presidential year, any analyst familiar with congressional elections might well have anticipated Republican retention of control in at least one chamber and, with a break or two, also its congressional leadership in both houses, though at a reduced margin. But if, by any stretch of the imagination, discouraged Republican voters stayed home in droves—the chilling possibility based on a stalled Dole rally before election day—then the Democrats had a chance to score. The question that could scarcely be answered until November 6, the day after the election, was by how much.

To be sure, the Republican Party's platform, the work very largely of the Christian Coalition that dominated the National Covention, was responsible for some of Dole's major difficulties, headed by the demand for a constitutional amendment banning all forms of abortion. This, basically, was accounted to be the reason Dole lost a majority of the women's vote, which was usually given as the principal reason for the troubles that bedeviled his candidacy from the outside.

It didn't help him to contend that he was much more moderate on the abortion question than the platform, that he had never read the platform, and didn't feel bound by it. If anything, that avowal only enraged the professional women even more and sent them by the hundreds of thousands into the Clinton column. Nor was Dole able to make headway with women's organizations by showing how much he appreciated the efforts of Republican women in government, regardless of their position on abortion.

That only solidified the continued exodus of influential women's organizations and much of their memberships from supporting either the top of the ticket or many of the illiberal members of Congress who were seeking reelection.

If ever there was a lesson in the preservation of the traditional separation of church and state in America, this was it. Instead of the glorious victory expected through heaven-sent guidance exclusively to Republican true believers and nobody else, what the Republican high command had to contemplate in the concluding weeks of the presidential campaign was a surging majority of the electorate that favored President Clinton's reelection. Also, if September polls were any guidance, there was a doubtful outcome in the close struggle being waged by both major parties at the time for control of Congress.

The desertion of women's organizations and their membership from the Dole standard, however, while a major political disaster for the Dole presidential candidacy, was not in itself decisive.

The elderly Republican nominee had also not been particularly fortunate in campaigning for both a 15-percent tax cut and a balanced budget in the same election while failing to emphasize that these measures, if he was elected, would be put into effect over a period of years. What happened thereafter was perhaps inevitable; for although the over-sixty-five generation of Americans was not the largest block of voters, its members were the most faithful to cast their ballots and to make their influence felt.

Despite Dole's protests that he also meant to "save" such core measures for the elderly as Social Security, Medicare, and Medicaid, it did not take any great degree of budgetary knowledge to conclude that the billions stuffed in the pockets of those who benefited most from a 15-percent tax cut were likely to come in large part from drastic cuts in entitlements. Despite the loudest of Republican disclaimers, that lost to Dole a large majority of the vote of elderly Americans.

Similarly, the discrimination against immigrants who did not become American citizens and their several million children also became a losing issue for him and most of the Republicans seeking election or reelection to Congress. What happened was a virtually unprecedented surge in American-domiciled immigrants who became citizens by the end of the fiscal year on September 30 and thereby would become eligible to vote in the presidential election if they registered for the privilege at the designated period before election day.

The total, as announced by the Immigration and Naturalization Service, was a record of more than 1 million new citizens for fiscal 1996, added to 445,853 naturalizations for 1995. The previous record for new citizens had been set in 1944, with 441,979. The immigration service estimated there are about 10 million other immigrants in the United States who are eligible for citizenship by having lived here for five years, with no criminal record, provided they pass a language and civics test and pay $95 before taking the oath of loyalty to the United States.

Actually, as Republicans were well aware, it was the Democrats, under the leadership of Vice-President Gore, who began the "Citizenship USA" campaign in 1995 after the Republican-controlled Congress approved a budget item for the drive. And although President Clinton signed the welfare reform bill that increased the threat to many noncitizen immigrants of losing many current privileges, he was also likely to be the beneficiary of most of those who registered to vote in the November presidential election.

Because most of the new immigrant-citizens live in large cities, mainly New York and Chicago, both heavily Democratic politically, Republican critics quickly enough were charging that the citizenship drive was instituted to favor the Democratic cause. They cited a Gore memorandum to President Clinton, prepared for internal White House use, that fell into Republican hands, reading, "I.N.S. warns that if we are too aggressive at removing roadblocks to success . . . we might be publicly criticized for running a pro-Democratic voter mill and even risk having Congress stop us."

At the time of the mass swearing in of new citizens for 1996, however, it was nearly time for members of the One hundred-fourth Congress to adjourn in September to devote the remaining weeks of the fall to campaigning for themselves or their presidential nominees or perhaps both. And so the fears of Republicans of vast masses of new citizens at the polls to vote Democratic were vastly exaggerated.

Both Dole and the Republicans seeking election to Congress would have trouble enough in this election year, contending with far more numerous defections from their cause than the addition of perhaps a relatively few new immigrant-citizen voters. Many a descendant of the immigrants who helped found this country would see to that.

While the Republican campaign directors mulled their problem in the closing weeks of the campaign, they had to face up to a discouraging barrage of independent forecasts and unsolicited advice from professionals in the field who saw Dole struggling to maintain his base of support.

One of the most caustic was Andrew Kohut, director of the Pew Research Center for the People and the Press, who commented:

> It is not clear that Dole has really pulled together his base, He has to get some of those Republican defectors back and make sure he keeps them. And he needs more than 90 percent of the Republicans — he needs a good number of independents who now think he's out of touch with them, women in particular.
>
> The bottom line is, at this point, it's Clinton's to lose. But unless the Dole campaign really revives itself, it's going to be a struggle because the economy's good and Clinton is a much better campaigner. The danger for Clinton is that there are still a lot of reservations about his character.

A more practical-minded Republican from Connecticut seeking re-election, Representative Christopher Shays, viewed these possibilities for the House alone without regard to what happened elsewhere on election day:

> If Dole wins, we pick up seats in significant numbers. If he loses 55–45, we hold our own, winning some and losing some. Anything close to 60 percent, then we're out of power.

For the Senate just then, the outcome seemed too close to call, except for the Democratic enthusiasts who predicted a landslide. But the complications, particularly in a Middle East bristling with American air power and armor, called for cool judgment in the White House so close to election day. And this, finally, was the most important test of all that the Clinton administration had to face together with the nation itself.

30 The War on Terror, II

Iraqi dictator Saddam Hussein ordered his missile defense guns to fire on American aircraft patrolling over his territory early in September. That they missed their targets didn't matter. President Clinton, pausing on the campaign trail in Arizona, at once ordered mobilization against Saddam's threat.

At the time, it looked as if the United States would have to renew the Persian Gulf War, during which the Americans, at the head of a powerful allied force in 1991, had forced Saddam to sue for peace. Only this time, President Clinton had the immediate support mainly of the British out of the coalition that President Bush had put together five years before.

Regardless of the risks that Clinton was taking in an election year, this was also scarcely a favorable positon for the United States in an area where Western powers were always suspect—and this was particularly true now in the midst of what seemed to be turning into a fanatical revival of Muslim fundamentalism. As the United States had learned to its cost in Vietnam and the Russians in Chechnya, native peoples fighting for their lives were a power in themselves. And Saddam knew how to use fanatical Muslims, especially after France, Egypt, Jordan, and other Arab states appeared to have withdrawn from the victorious Gulf War coalition earlier in the decade.

Still, carrying out the president's orders, Defense Secretary Perry warned Iraq and its missile batteries, "We aren't playing games." He had already dispatched eight F-117 Stealth fighter aircraft carrying 2,000-pound bombs from their American bases and four B-52 bombers with Cruise missiles from Guam to a closer British base in the Indian Ocean. Army tank troops had also been alerted in Texas for immediate service in the Middle East.

Except for shouted support from an Arizona campaign crowd for President Clinton when he vowed to protect American pilots, the public took the mobilization in stride. Although Dole quietly pledged support to the armed forces, a proper position for a wounded veteran of World War II, that didn't keep other Republican speakers from yammering against Clinton for moving without coalition backing. And in Iraq, Saddam's people were told to repel American "aggression against our sovereignty."

Actually, what had happened after the Gulf War was that the United States, Britain, France, and their Arab allies had put Saddam "in a box" — that is, the three Western powers had agreed to install "no fly zones" in northern and southern Iraq, where Saddam was forbidden to exert air power to protect his own territory. He had also been warned not to try to take over parts of northern Iraq, where, by the grace of the United Nations, the persecuted Kurds occupied a protected zone.

But by backing one Kurd faction against another in the north earlier that year, Saddam had secured an "invitation" from his own Kurds to move his troops and tanks into the north and beat the opposition Kurds who had the support of neighboring Iran. Thus, if the United States used ground troops in the north, it would, in effect, be intervening in what was, technically, a civil war.

This is what caused most of the Arab allies in the Gulf War to hesitate about backing the United States again, and even the French turned against American interests for the time being. What had renewed the threat of another conflict was at least six missile attacks by Saddam's defense batteries in the northern "no fly zone" against American patrolling aircraft that had missed their mark.

In reply, what the United States did at once was to fire missiles to knock out Saddam's two air bases and missile batteries in the *southern* "no fly zone." Also, the southern zone was extended to a point just below the Iraqi capital of Baghdad, uncomfortably close to Saddam himself — only the French refused to fly their patrol routes in the area.

Finally, on Friday, September 13, about forty-eight hours after the presidential mobilization order for the Persian Gulf began taking effect, Saddam signaled that he had had enough. The Iraqi government at once halted repairs on its damaged southern defense sites and called off further missile shots at patrolling aircraft, which now included the British and the French, the latter meanwhile having rejoined scheduled flights over Iraq. But the former Arab allies in the Persian Gulf War, particularly Egypt and Jordan, still stayed out of the fracas on the apparent supposition that the Americans and Europeans would withdraw soon enough but Saddam and his rebuilt army would still remain to be dealt with.

There was a caveat, of course. With Saddam, that was usually the case. And this time, it came through the government-operated Iraqi

News Agency, which confirmed suspension of its "military reaction" but still maintained that the American and allied imposition of "no fly zones" north and south was illegal because they infringed on Iraqi sovereignty.

Meanwhile, the Pentagon continued the movement of American forces ordered to the Persian Gulf, except that it reduced the number of army troops affected from 5,000 to 3,000 pending settlement with Kuwait of when, where, and how they would be based. Now, as the president himself conceded, the fuss over what Kuwait would and would not do in connection with the American buildup began because somebody in the American chain of command forgot to ask the Kuwaitis for permission to base more American aircraft and troops on their territory. That, apparently, hurt their feelings, even though the 1990–1991 Gulf War had spared them from becoming Saddam's nineteenth Iraqi province.

In any event, although the Defense Department accepted the Iraqi agreement to stop shooting and rebuilding defenses as "encouraging," Secretary Perry again warned that Saddam's actions rather than his words would be carefully watched and that a renewed American assault on Iraq was still a possibility.

What remained to be done in this foreign extension of terrorism against American interests was to see to it that the several thousand surviving Kurds who had worked for the United States in northern Iraq should be helped, so far as possible, to leave the country for evacuation to Turkey.

These people were among the losers in the minority segment of the Kurdish population. They had been set upon by the treacherous Kurdish majority, armed by Saddam Hussein, who had welcomed his forces as their "protector" while inflicting large casualties on the helpless minority Kurds. An undetermined number of survivors then fled east into Iran, while some sought safety by heading west for the Turkish border. Others also gathered near the latter border in the Iraqi city of Zakho in the hope that the American authorities would persuade Turkey to accept them.

As for Saddam's offer of amnesty to the Kurds who had opposed him, that did not apply — as the victims speedily learned — to those who had worked for "foreign interests," mainly American. Those refugees who despaired of any agency whatever helping them took their own chances on flight in all directions, but most were either caught by the pro-Saddam Kurds or executed by the remaining Iraqi tank forces and foot soldiers who remained in the area for mop-up operations.

For those refugees who had papers showing that they had been employed by various American agencies—primarily the Military Cooperative Center or the various branches of the State Department in Iraq—there was a bit more hope, provided they could find an American team that would help them to the Turkish border. But such American operatives, wary of Saddam's remaining tank columns, were bound to have trouble themselves getting to safety.

In the event of a renewed American strike force against Saddam, little hope was left for any of the Kurdish refugees in the north and the American relief people who had tried to protect them. An all-out war would have been a tragedy on a far greater scale than the survivors of the bungled CIA 1961 attack on Castro's Cuba at the Bay of Pigs—a shameful sacrifice of the lives of a brave people.

For the fight against terrorism within the United States itself at about the same time, President Clinton received a detailed proposal of a billion-dollar-a-year investment in enlarged FBI and police forces. Also included were expensive airline security equipment, increased staffing for federal courts prosecutors, the Federal Aviation Administration and its adjuncts.

These were the recommendations that had been prepared within the forty-five-day emergency limit set by the White House for Vice-President Al Gore and other high government officials with added suggestions from the air travel industry itself.

"We have to take the fight to the terrorists," the president said in making public the Gore proposals. "If we have the will, we can find the way."

With Congress approaching an early fall recess to prepare for the last stage of the presidential and congressional elections, however, Vice-President Gore's own estimate of his contribution was both cautious and reserved.

"There's no silver bullet or single magic answer," he said. "So we're presenting a combination of approaches—some high tech, some low tech, some even no tech."

Right off, the Republican Congress served notice through Senator Orrin G. Hatch of Utah, the chairman of the Senate Judiciary Committee, that no further funding for a new Middle East war could be expected before adjournment because a billion-dollar antiterrorism bill had already been approved by Congress.

It was also discouraging that a former Bush administration official, Kenneth Quinn, observed:

> The whole rapid response concept of fighting terrorism has gotten out of hand.

The main response from some in the industry was doubt about the cost of the expensive new machines that the Gore report proposed for checking baggage for bombs and even more complicated systems for checking the backgrounds of airline passengers.

The most solid reaction came from the Federal Aviation Administration that signed what may develop into a billion-dollar campaign to modernize most of the nation's civilian and military control centers for aircraft within 50 miles of airports.

Secretary of Transportation Federico F. Peña predicted with the completion of the first contract, modernization of the Boston area by the end of 1998. He added that the whole system would be safer and more reliable if all turns out well for the contractor, the Raytheon Co. of Marlborough, Massachusetts. Florida's Eglin Air Force Base, a US Air Force installation, was included in this operation for a total of $80 million.

Provided these results are satisfactory, Peña said, the government plans to extend the contract to modernize 192 military centers and 172 civilian operations by 2007.

If all went well, what the FAA hoped to do within the next ten years was to build on a program that began modernizing long-distance control centers in 1993. The FAA planned to use a system called Terminal Radar Approach Controls in a computerized network of stations within 50 miles of airports. Raytheon was asked to supply the necessary software for the new computer system, to be tested in stages as it is completed.

Additionally, all three major airports in the New York region, begining with Kennedy International, undertook to upgrade both their security and other critical parts of their operation. Among the immediate steps to make these airports safer was the installation of better lighting, more inclusive fencing, the use of bomb-sniffing dogs throughout critical areas and tighter police protection.

Kennedy, in particular, had been severely criticized for years for lax security, a failing that was emphasized after the crash of TWA flight 800 off Long Island soon after takeoff on July 17, 1996.

A member of Vice-President Gore's investigative commission, Kathleen Flynn, who had lost a son in the blast that wrecked Pan Am 103 over Scotland in 1988, emphasized the need for broader action to insure public safety aloft, saying,

"The climate in America is such that the public is frustrated and ready, willing, and able to do something about it. We have a long, long road and it's going to take a lot of work. The key is oversight and implementation."

What President Clinton demanded immediately in emergency funding was about $600 million to tighten security at major American military and diplomtic outposts around the world that are prime targets for native terrorists. What he proposed to do with the money if Congress provided it was to safeguard the government's people and military detachments abroad from explosive attacks and exposure to infectious diseases.

After Saddam Hussein's threatened germ warfare with the spread of strange illnesses among American troops following the first Persian Gulf War, nobody wanted to take any more chances with American lives, even though proof of Iraqi germ warfare remained elusive.

When Saddam backed down in his most recent threat to American forces and President Clinton held up a pending new American offensive, Dole questioned his judgment by giving his approval to a thoughtfully drafted Republican statement commenting on Clinton's turnaround strategy as follows:

> In Iran, as in Bosnia, the Clinton administration should be careful about making claims of success that events on the ground may not substantiate and about giving assurances that it is unable or unwilling to fulfill because the credibility of the United States in at stake.

The warning could have been applied as well to what many now believed was the Pentagon's failure at the time of the Bush administration to investigate the exposure of thousands of American troops to an Iraqi nerve gas called Sarin during the Persian Gulf War of 1990–1991. After refusing for five years to acknowledge the seriousness of the nerve gas risks that caused so many complaints of illness among Gulf War veterans, a Pentagon spokesman in June 1996 finally suggested in a tentative manner that perhaps a few American troops in the Gulf War may have been exposed to debilitating gases.

Then at last, in the midst of the latter part of the presidential campaign in October, another authorized Pentagon source agreed to be quoted for publication that as many as 15,000 American soldiers could have suffered from exposure to nerve gas — and some even speculated that thousands of others might also have been exposed to such risks.

From published reports, fragmentary in nature and still lacking formal authorization at the Pentagon, it appeared that a series of American intelligence reports had linked the possibility of nerve-gas dispersion in combat areas to the destruction, through air strikes by the American military in 1991, of a vast Iraqi ammunition dump at Kamisiyah.

These reports, later withdrawn from public attention, were said by congressional sources to have raised the possibility that nerve-gas shells at Kamisiyah might have been destroyed in the bombings, releasing gas clouds that drifted over areas where large bodies of American troop landings were being conducted in the latter stages of the Gulf War.

There was still no direct, confirming evidence, however, of when and where the nerve gas may have been released. Nor was it possible for nongovernmental investigators to fix responsibility for the alleged failure of the various military commands affected to take sufficient protective action, effective use of gas masks, and the like before the gas attacks created harm.

But from the standpoint of the Gulf War veterans who complained of various illnesses during the ensuing years after Saddam Hussein was permitted to resume his arms buildup, there was never any question that they believed they had been victimized by Iraqi nerve gases. The symptoms mainly consisted of painful movements of arm and leg joints; trouble with digestion; and, most of all, a debilitating weakness and physical fatigue.

During the brief show of American force against Saddam and his rebuilt Iraqi war machine in 1996, the extent of damage inflicted by forty-four long-range American missiles was limited to Iraq's southernmost air defenses. After that, belatedly, the Kuwaitis got over their sulkiness and accepted 3,000 American tank combat troops from Fort Hood in Texas to operate tanks and armor left behind from previous engagements in the Gulf. Even the French thereafter got over their nervousness and resumed scheduled patrols in the "no fly zones" that they had agreed to inspect daily.

And so with the reluctant Turkish acceptance of about 2,000 minority Kurd refugees from Iraq, most of whom were flown from there to Guam, the latest American confrontation with Saddam was put on hold. It was the most that President Clinton wanted to attempt toward the end of his reelection campaign.

31 The Race Tightens

With the elimination of Ross Perot from the presidential debates that fall because he was given no chance to be elected, the race tightened: but it was mainly to President Clinton's advantage.

Bob Dole, however, gamely fought on, trying by every conceivable device to reduce the double-digit odds against him in the polls.

In the big states like Florida and California, among others, he worked at such a pace that many a younger man would have been fazed. Once, he was so eager to make an impression that he took a bad tumble off a three-foot California stage but fortunately averted serious injury.

And so Perot seemed nearly out of it now, although he had won almost one-fifth of the 1992 presidential vote. He had even been refused prime network time, for which he was willing to pay, and had to settle for what he could get and whatever TV guest shots he could scrounge. He was, as luck would have it, nowhere near his almost 19 percent of the 1992 total vote; and his Reform Party was far from a match for the two old-line major parties. His polls had now dropped to 4 or 5 percent.

With neither Dole nor Perot any match for the president, he was dividing his time between the White House, the One hundred-fourth Congress, an appearance before the United Nations, and periodic sallies by bus on the campaign trail with Hillary and Al and Tipper Gore. Except for an occasional spell of hoarseness, he showed no sign of damage from the strain of almost constant electioneering. Once, he even took the time to invite a ferocious radio critic of his presidency to the White House and, to show no ill will, gave him a personally conducted tour of the premises.

The basis of the widespread TV and press reports favorable to his candidacy was his continued two-digit lead over Dole in the polls that had been viturally unchanged for months. No matter what the distinguished Republican did in shifting issues from the economy to crime, drugs, his proposed 15-percent tax cut, and praise of family values, the president's lead seldom narrowed, and then only briefly, with but a few weeks now left before election day.

The president usually remained relaxed, with every appearance of confidence, despite grievous attacks on his character, often by Dole but echoed by a host of Republican speakers spread across the land. Of course, the Democrats responded in kind, mostly against Speaker Gingrich, who was also forced to answer to ethics charges before a House committee composed equally of his fellow Republicans and opposition Democrats. But there seemed to be only an outside chance that the special prosecutors' inquiries into the backgrounds of either the president or the Speaker would end before election day.

As far as the general public was concerned, such exhibitions, for the time being, amounted to little more than campaign rhetoric of a most indecisive nature.

The president let none of this bother him unduly. In the week before the first debate, he signed a $256.6 billion congressional spending bill that included a 3-percent military pay rise.

"This bill," he said at the ceremonial signing, "makes good our pledge to keep our armed forces the best trained, the best equipped fighting force on earth. It gives us the technological edge to prevail on the battlefields of tomorrow."

As a bonus, the Republican-controlled Congress had passed along with its military-support act an entirely separate measure that made the stalking and persecution of women across state lines a federal offense, whether or not the criminal was a spouse or others intent on harming women. The proud sponsor of the legislation, Senator Kay Bailey Hutchison, a Texas Republican who had been the victim of such abuse, was in the Oval Office for the signing and won the president's heartfelt recognition for her efforts.

What both measures demonstrated so late in this presidential campaign was that it was not foreordained that a Congress of one party and a president of another would collapse inevitably into gridlock when nothing of consequence was accomplished. It was belated, but necessary, assurance that a reelected Congress with Republican leadership, still a distinct possibility, could not be considered an unmitigated disaster if the president also won reelection.

Braced by such evidence of a cooperative Republican mood in the national legislature, the president pressed for additional measures he sought before congressional adjournment for preelection day campaigning.

Meanwhile, in his annual appearance before the UN General Assembly in New York City, he appealed for a halt in the spread of nuclear weaponry before signing a newer and broader test-ban treaty forbidding all such explosions of nuclear weapons, something a likely new nuclear power, India, had already refused to do.

Here, too, congressional help would be useful, for its consent to the proposed treaty as well as the president's signature were necessary before the nation was bound to restrict nuclear testing.

What was also important in the president's appearance before the United Nations was his continued insistence on behalf of the United States that UN Secretary General Boutros Boutros-Ghali of Egypt would have to be replaced at the end of his current five-year term. What both Congress and the president were agreed upon was that the onset of American repayment of the nation's UN debt of more than $1 billion would be contingent on the naming of a new secretary general who would have to reduce the commitment of the world organization to such necessities as peace keeping and the upholding of human rights as ordained by the Security Council.

In campaigning on the home front in the closing weeks, President Clinton also had a pleasant surprise for environmentalists. West of the Mississippi that September, he had announced the creation of a new scenic wonderland—the canyons of the Escalante National Monument in Utah. Although millions of tourists were bound to be thrilled by the new federal parkland of massive red cliffs linked to the nearby Grand Canyon of the Colorado River, the president's decision displeased the entire Utah congressional delegation.

It so happened that beneath the new scenic layout lay a great coal deposit—the largest in North America—for which a Dutch concern was bidding and offering a proposed commitment of jobs for nine hundred workers. The estimated value of the unmined coal, put at $1 trillion in published accounts, was reason enough for the outrage of the Utah lawmakers; but the president stood by his decision.

It should not be supposed, however, that as shrewd a politician as President Clinton was wool gathering when he created so spectacular a new tourist attraction in Utah that added 2 million of the state's acres to the 80 million acres already under the control of the National Park Service. From the outset, Clinton had known of the prospective coalmine deal. He must also have been aware that he had scant hope of winning Utah's five electoral votes in the upcoming presidential election, for he had finished third there in 1992 behind President Bush and Ross Perot.

Those who knew the president well theorized that what he may have sought in this environmental venture was a chance at neighboring

Arizona's eight votes, for he had taken the unusual precaution of announcing his creation of the new federal park in Utah from Arizona's side of the Grand Canyon. True, Arizona hadn't gone Democratic in any presidential campaign since Truman's in 1948; and so this particular theory may have been wishful thinking.

In any event, the new Utah park was bound to interest any nearby state with environmental tourist attractions, including Yellowstone, on the borders of Wyoming, Montana, and Idaho; Sequoia and other scenic attractions in California; Rocky Mountain National Park and other ski areas in Colorado; and Mount Rushmore in South Dakota with its four massive heads of presidents hewn into its stone sides.

Former Senator Dole seemed to have paid little attention to the Utah controversy during the latter part of the presidential campaign; nor were there other hostile reactions of a piece with those of the Utah congressional delegation.

But on foreign policy aside from the United Nations, not often a contentious subject for presidential campaigns in prosperous times of peace, Clinton had to take his licks from one of Dole's advisers, Senator John McCain of Arizona. McCain had called the president "weak and indecisive" in confronting Iraq's Saddam Hussein late that summer.

Referring to Saddam's firing of Iraqi missiles at American aircraft on patrol over one of the allied "no fly zones" in southern Iraq, McCain had said:

> The administration unfortunately did not match deeds with rhetoric. Saddam Hussein is far better off than he was two weeks ago. You judge success by results.

To that, the president replied in kind. Saddam, he said, had been forced to pay a price for his hostility. He went on:

> The response we gave was one designed to improve the strategic position of the United States and our allies to keep Saddam Hussein in a box and to limit his ability to threaten his neighbors.

That barrage of American missiles was followed by troop and armament reinforcements in the area to overwhelm any further show of force that the Iraqi leader might undertake against the American buildup. On the home front, however, there was very little public concern either about the disciplining of Saddam Hussein or his part in the latter stages of the presidential campaign.

On his part, Dole had tried many a device to break the president's hold on a commanding lead in the polls before the first of the debates.

The Kansan began with his proposed 15-percent tax cut for everybody but without any marked effect, except against his own credibility.

Even die-hard Republicans were disappointed when the public refused to believe on the whole that Clinton wasn't as vulnerable on the crime issue that Dole had plugged so diligently when the tax cut failed him. The basic reason, it turned out, was Dole's own abysmal neglect while in the Senate of the necessities of gun control when he refused to vote for a ban of nineteen different kinds of assault weapons as well as the Brady gun-control bill.

When he reversed himself after quitting the Senate, it was too late to have any real effect on public opinion.

That failure, in all probability, helped lead to Clinton's endorsement by the 270,000-member Fraternal Order of Police — the first ever for a Democratic presidential nominee — together with others by the National Association of Police Organizations and the International Union of Police Associations. It also helped the president's cause when the Justice Department announced a decrease of more than 9 percent in violent crime in 1995. After calling for the addition of 100,000 police in cities across the nation, Clinton vowed to maintain the continual drop in criminal activity by further strengthening the machinery of law enforcement.

It was the war on drugs, drug pushers, and drug smugglers that the president didn't do as well. Despite a general decline in offenses attributable to the illicit drug trade, the latest statistics showed that teenage drug use had increased from 5.3 percent of those who used drugs at least once a month in 1992 to 10.9 percent in 1995. It was fortunate, however, that Clinton had substantially increased the federal forces assigned to cracking down on the drug trade after reducing them directly upon assuming office.

At any other time, perhaps, there might not have been much public feeling about the president's laughing confession early in his stay in the White House that he'd once tried marijuana but hadn't inhaled. And later, again on TV, he'd had a little more fun with the general subject by admitting that he'd have inhaled if he'd been able to do so. To the righteous Republicans, desperate now for an issue, both presidential images were included in a TV ad rebuking him for not having set a better example for children who might be tempted to try drugs.

As might have been expected, the Democrats retaliated. Another TV ad, featuring the president standing tall gainst a waving American flag, accused Dole of having voted against the White House's creation of General Barry R. McCaffrey, a four-star retired officer, as the nation's drug czar. It was true enough until Dole decided to reverse himself. Clinton meanwhile had increased the drug-fighting appropriation in the federal budget from $13.3 billion in fiscal 1995 to $15.1 billion in fiscal 1997.

During the current campaign, the president had also taken notice of findings that 60 percent of heroin and cocaine use was attributed to suspects out on probation, parole, or bail. In a Colorado campaign speech, he said that he'd make federal aid to states for building more prisons conditional on state drug testing and treatment programs both for people on parole and for prisoners.

At least one former cabinet veteran welcomed the candidates' argument over which one had done the most to fight drugs. That was when Joseph A. Califano Jr., a former Democratic secretary of health, education, and welfare, remarked, "However the debate turns out, it will have the effect of reducing drug use among teens."

Toward the end of the campaign, Dole also experimented with the use of the term *liberal*, honored from the time of Franklin Roosevelt in this country, as a substitute for the word *Communist*, as used so frequently to discredit real or imagined supporters of what used to be the Soviet Union. Apparently, the theory was that only certified conservatives by grace of the Republican Party could be trusted in the service of government in the United States.

In criticizing President Clinton's massive health plan that was rejected by Congress early in his years in the White House, Dole predicted that Clinton would try it again if reelected with consequent passive costs to the nation should he also have a Democratic Congress.

Then, assuming that all the conditions had been fulfilled and a reelected Clinton had his health plan, Dole concluded:

> President Clinton came to town a liberal, he's still a liberal. The only thing that stopped him in his tracks was a Republican Congress in 1994. That's all that happened.

The president's response at the White House was brief, pointing out merely that he hadn't thought of reviving a health plan in particular that had failed in 1993. And as to his liberalism, he observed with a smile that Dole seemed to think he was a "closet liberal," adding, "There aren't closets large enough in the White House to hide in."

He might have added, but didn't, that he was in deep trouble with Democratic liberals over his signature on the Republican-approved welfare bill, including three members of his own White House staff who had resigned in protest. Dole was still looking for a payoff issue when he returned to the condition of the nation's economy, which he warned would cause the president "to increase the size of government as he decreases the size of your wallet."

In a speech before the Detroit Economic Club, Dole used still more exaggeration to try to broaden his campaign appeal but with dubious results. This time, he attacked Interior Secretary Bruce Babbitt for proposing a tax on birdseed. Probably, it was good for a laugh among the less-critical Detroiters; but it didn't go over very well with the International Association of Fish and Wildlife Agencies, a collection of 1,200 organizations that had sought to protect wildlife and conservation projects with what they called a user fee on outdoor products, one of them birdseed.

One of the wildlife directors, Naomi Edelson, said neither Secretary Babbitt nor the Clinton administration had anything to do with their projects, which had originated because most states were too strapped to provide such necessities, particularly in the winter. Still, Dole ignored the opposition and rallied his Detroit audience, asking, "Have you paid your taxes, have you fed the birds?"

As for the American economy itself, he argued that it was in "bad shape" and, in his view, was getting worse, something that would have astonished Wall Street. Running for president seemed to have changed the former senator's perceptions.

But the most difficult of all Dole's campaign tactics to understand was his seeming belief that it was to his advantage to keep reminding people of his fall from the platform in Chico, California, on September 19 while making a routine speech. At a rally in Las Vegas next day, he joked with an audience that people shouldn't be afraid to sit in the first row because he wasn't likely to fall again.

That attitude continued for days on end, encouraged by his press people, who argued that it was proof of his courage and grit under pressure. The candidate evidently agreed. In his Detroit appearance, for example, he couldn't resist his version of a wisecrack when a previous speaker told of taking a dive in a submarine. Said Dole when it came his turn, "The last dive I took was in Chico, California."

The trouble with such humorous asides is that they didn't always work very well, as witness Dole's embarrassment at another California town, West Hills, where he compared himself to Hideo Nomo, the Los Angeles Dodger who had just pitched a no-hit, no-run baseball game against the Colorado Rockies in Denver. Said the Republican candidate for president, "The Brooklyn Dodgers had a no-hitter last night, and I'm going to follow what Nomo did. And we're going to wipe them out from now until November 5."

The audience could not be blamed for wondering. The Dodgers had left Ebbets Field in Brooklyn in 1958, as a silent spectator reminded Dole upon his arival in Los Angeles by hoisting a sign: "Welcome to Brooklyn."

For the candidate of the Reform Party, Perot, there was nothing but bad news that September. It was tough enough to be excluded from the presidential debates by a decision of the bipartisan Commission on Presidential Debates. But as he was contesting that ruling with scant hope of success on the basis of earlier judicial precedent, he was continually being refused TV network prime time, even though he had the funds to pay for the privilege.

Russell J. Verney, Perot's campaign coordinator, had rejected less favorable time periods for his candidate's "infomercials" — thirty-minute lectures giving the billionaire's views on issues he believed to be of importance in the campaign. As far as Perot himself was concerned, it was prime time or nothing after he had been barred from the presidential debates.

What happened was that the Republicans didn't want Perot as a third participant because a major part of his 1992 vote had been taken from President Bush, the failed Republican candidate for reelection that year. Although President Clinton had made no objection to Perot's presence in the debates in 1996, what the Democrats wanted was only two debates with a third for the vice-presidential candidates and no debates at all after October 16, the date for the last presidential debate.

That, briefly, is how matters turned out, with Perot barred and the Democrats getting everything else they wanted in a two-sided agreement. On NBC's *Meet the Press,* Perot commented plaintively,

> Only in America, when 76 percent of the voters want a candidate included could the debate commission exclude a candidate.

Still, the arrangements remained unchanged for the first Clinton-Dole debate on October 6, a vice-presidential Gore-Kemp debate October 9, and a final Clinton-Dole session, town-meeting style, for October 16.

The rest of the campaign would supposedly feature a TV advertising blitz, scarcely a spectacle in which the electorate could readily separate truth from fantasy.

32 Congress Goes Home

The One hundred-fourth Congress passed into history with its election day recess after failing to force significant cuts in government services. The Republican leaders contended, however, that they remained on schedule by moving toward a balanced budget in 2002.

Still, despite President Clinton's concession after two congressional shutdowns that "the era of big government is over," there was scant evidence of such a state of affairs in the huge mass of spending bills for fiscal 1997.

The total 1997 budget cost to the nation after months of haggling between the White House and Capitol Hill was put at about $600 billion. But the most meaningful reduction that the Republicans could claim was $53 billion, of which $23 billion consisted of savings taken from the 1996 budget. Even so, the total would have meant an overall cut of only 9 percent.

In signing the catch-all part of the appropriations, therefore, President Clinton could claim at least partial victory in maintaining sufficient funding for such major administration interests as support for education and environmental advances, attacks on the illegal drug trade, and funding for 100,000 additional police nationwide. The main people who suffered were welfare recipients, many of whom were deprived even of food stamps—a chintzy business for a great power.

Equally important overall, Speaker Gingrich and other Republican leaders agreed there would be no further government shutdowns, even though they narrowly completed the 1997 budget by a scant few hours before the deadline of 12:01 A.M., Tuesday, October 1. In any event, the performance was added proof that the Republican leadership was finally convinced that it didn't pay to add to the two earlier shutdowns with payless twenty-six-day holidays for 800,000 government workers at the end of 1995 and early 1996.

Gingrich also had a growing personal problem as Congress went into recess with the entire House membership and one-third of the Senate plus retiree vacancies up for reelection in the face of President Clinton's commanding lead in the polls for his own reelection.

All members of the House's bipartisan Ethics Committee had agreed on an expanded Gingrich inquiry before adjournment into whether he had given them "accurate, reliable, and complete" information regarding allegations of wrongdoing in campaign financing by his political action committee, GOPAC, and his own part in his 1990 campaign.

The House's Speaker and GOPAC had both insisted that the charges originally made by the Democratic Natonal Committee before the Federal Election Commission were groundless. Said a GOPAC press release:

> The most outrageous of the charges was that GOPAC had unlawfully supported Mr. Gingrich's 1990 congressional race in Georgia by paying for his travel and research expenses—the so-called $250,000 of "Newt Support."

The 1996 congressional session had come upon still another Republican problem—the Senate's failure to override Clinton's veto of an abortion bill opposed by prochoice women's majorities. The veto killed the bill that would have banned what is known as a "partial birth" abortion—a rarely used procedure that is involved mainly to save a woman's life.

Despite the rarity of this process of abortion, the issue was important to the presidential campaign as well as to some of the close congressional contests. It was still true, as it had been almost from the beginning of the year, that prochoice advocates like President Clinton and his congressional leaders continued to receive assurance from current polls that they commanded a majority of the always crucial women's vote.

The issue remained dominant toward the end in the struggle for the White House and control of Capitol Hill.

When the Republicans took possession of Congress for 1995–1996 for the first time in forty years, they came to the bargaining table with their Democratic counterparts and the president's people displaying a symbolic collection of knives, even machetes. What the new masters of Congress wanted to convey to their opponents was their fervent desire to reduce the size of government by cutting all forms of spending, a laudable if somewhat rash legislative program for century's end in the greatest military and industrial power on earth.

Right off, there wasn't anything that could be done about the national rite of military defense. What happened there was that the Republicans prodded Congress as a whole to give the Defense Department $255 billion, which was $9.4 billion more than the President had requested. But then, he didn't object to the financial overkill, either, considering how swiftly the American public was likely to respond negatively to cuts in national defense in an increasingly dangerous world.

Next, the entitlements — Social Security, Medicare, and Medicaid — had already been widely advertised by the Democratic National Committee's TV ads as the target of Dole's own machete if he were elected president. Despite his fervent denials, the large vote of the elderly in a once-safe Republican state like Florida had now shown that state edging into the Democratic column. It was reason enough for sedulous care by the Republicans in Congress who were seeking reelection to exercise caution, which is what they appeared to do.

The main part of a $30 billion reduction in the 1997 fiscal-year budget came from cuts in more than three hundred federal programs that had doubtful support in Congress, including, among others, such grants as those for an African development bank; a United States–Japan Friendship Commission; many separate health-research projects; and some parts of immigration services. But there were also some direct Republican targets, like the Corporation for Public Broadcasting, which was denounced as a "too liberal" organization. Even some no-nos like veterans' services were trimmed.

Among the major departments of government, such as State, Justice, Interior, Labor, and Commerce, Republican committees also produced reductions wherever possible. But it was mainly in anything having to do with education and training that the White House stood fast as well as in such necessary environmental matters as fighting forest fires, helping clean up the devastation of successive coastal hurricanes, and producing a better program to maintain the freedom of drinking water from polluting elements.

Immigration seemed to be a favorite Republican target throughout; but the sons and daughters of immigrants in Congress, including both Republicans and Democrats, fought hard to ward off what were regarded as punitive excesses against immigrants who were not citizens. Moreover, as repeatedly shown on TV before the whole nation, tens of thousands of illegal immigrants hastened to become citizens in large mass oath-taking ceremonials from coast to coast.

That, perhaps as much as anything else, may have led the parties to the negotiations to drop such provisions in the bill for the Immigration and Naturalization Service as excluding children of noncitizen immigrants from services like attending school and denial of other benefits, even help for AIDS victims who become citizens. But overall, INS funds for 1997 were put at $3.1 billion, a $500-million increase, to help pay for 1,000 additional border-patrol officers and 2,700 additional detention cells.

Probably the most frustrating part of the negotiations for both sides was the discussion over health care. The Republicans, knowing of the lengths to which Dole was going in charging that the president, if re-elected, would revive his failed massive health-protection program, were necessarily cautious about such appropriations. The Democrats, encouraged by the White House, wanted much more done in the fiscal 1997 budget.

But the best that Congress was able to accomplish for 1996 was the bipartisan Kassebaum-Kennedy bill that provided for portable health insurance for workers changing jobs.

Still, with the funding for Health and Human Services for 1997 at $187 billion, it became possible for the negotiators to agree on a 7 percent increase to $12.7 billion for the National Institute of Health and a separate boost for the Head Start program for kindergartens of $412 million, for a new total of $4 billion.

There was little doubt, therefore, that Congress would remain under increasing pressure to do more rather than less for the nation's health and education in the years yet to come, which meant much more than finding some acceptable way, if there is such a thing, of cutting entitlements, a favorite topic among conservatives, regardless of party.

The usual warning that increases in the next century of old people by age and number would bankrupt the system were in themselves a precautionary move, not a cut. Nor were the complaints of the under-sixty-fives against "supporting" the over-sixty-fives to be taken at face value.

This matter was far from a simplistic problem that could be resolved in a twinkling; nor was there any solution that would satisfy everybody. But sooner or later, it would have to be faced, if not in this administration or the next, then certainly later in the coming century of a vastly more populated America, which would be even more eager for health protection than its elders had been.

Next to the agenda for Health and Human Services, perhaps the most confusing problem that the congressional negotiators faced in putting together the fiscal 1997 budget was the somewhat revised Republican bill on welfare reform. As it was signed by President Clinton, together with well-meaning Democratic hopes for revision if they returned to power in Congress, the measure was basically short-sighted in its approach and unfair in expecting all states to pick up the federal welfare burden with equal diligence and financing.

The president himself was the first to express concern over what would happen to the children of parents who were forced off welfare for being unable to find jobs before reaching the limit of their stay on the state rolls.

Even if there were some magical way of assuring all welfare recipients of jobs, provided they were capable of holding them, that might reduce the welfare rolls. But it couldn't cancel out the needs of either their children or even the sometimes desperate condition of the most disadvantaged people in our society for some form of government help.

As for the immigrants, the most numerous people affected by the new statute, the founder of a fund to help them, George Soros, wrote of the new welfare law when it took effect:

> It will bar most legal immigrants, including permanent residents and refugees granted asylum, from receiving food stamps and Supplemental Security Income, which benefits the elderly and the disabled. Legal immigrants will also be denied welfare and Medicaid benefits in their first five years in this country.
>
> According to the Congressional Budget Office, more than 500,000 immigrants are likely to lose Supplemental Security benefits; about 900,000 are likely to lose food stamps. Legal immigrants represent only about five per cent of those on public aid, yet they are absorbing more than 40 per cent of the cuts in welfare. . . .
>
> There is no question that the welfare system needs to be reformed so that it moves people from dependency to work. But to do so, we must spend more money, not less, in the short term because creating work requires increased public investment and spending on job training—for citizens and legal immigrants. Depriving legal immigrants creates false savings at the cost of perpetuating an injustice.*

In concluding this analysis of what was done, undone, and remains to be done after the egregious budget negotiations examined herein, it would seem that what now must be undertaken in good faith is a *real* Contract with American for the century yet to come. There should be no necessity, as happened in this budget deal, for midnight meetings, hasty compromises, and strivings to gain a point or force a concession.

This welfare bill is bound to be revised—and soon. Our Statue of Liberty with her raised torch in New York Harbor should still welcome the immigrants of tomorrow with the same assurance of freedom that it bestowed on their forebears. For that, as always, remains the promise of America.

*"Immigrants' Burden," by George Soros, op ed page, New York *Times,* Oct. 2, 1996.

During the only time in the 1996 campaign that the American people heard from their congressional leaders in a national TV debate over things done and left undone, little was said by either the Republican leadership or their Democratic opponents to revive public confidence in the legislative process.

As far as the average citizen was concerned, the four congressional leaders they saw and heard on the Public Broadcasting Service's *Debate Night* that September 30 merely illustrated how difficult it had become for the legislative branch to conduct the nation's business. In the hundred or more separate local and regional meetings of the opposing parties' representatives before smaller public audiences across the land, also a part of *Debate Night,* perhaps more agreeable conclusions could have been drawn.

But on the whole, it remained a fair assumption that the One hundred-fourth Congress, like the "Do Nothing" Eightieth that helped elect President Truman, might better have served the public interest if it had quarreled less.

What a national audience heard that night from the four congressional leaders viewed over TV from Williamsburg, Virginia, mainly was a rehash of their disagreements in the two-year session they were just concluding. In addition, the Democratic minority leaders, Representative Dick Gephardt and Senator Tom Daschle, saw to it that the public did not forget that their chief opponent, Speaker Gingrich, had been the key Republican figure in the two congressional shutdowns so critical to the outcome of the year's elections to the presidency and Congress. Gingrich, of course, replied in kind.

Gephardt, for example, sounded the Democratic theme that the American people "did not get the change they voted for" when they put the Republicans in control of Congress in 1994. And Senator Trent Lott, who had become majority leader of the upper house when Bob Dole resigned, claimed major accomplishments while admitting, "There is more to do." As for Gingrich, the least popular figure in this Congress, he remained as pugnacious as ever.

So whatever a national public learned that night of "The Future of Congress," the topic of that part of the countrywide debate, it was tinged throughout by the refusal of the leaders, with few exceptions, to recognize even the bare amenities of civilized discourse.

To be sure, the nation had also suffered disappointments in its choice of presidents as well as Congresses. In this century alone, there had been casualties on the Republican side from Harding and his friends in the Teapot Dome oil gang to the forced resignation of Nixon; on the Democratic side, Lyndon Johnson refused to seek reelection over his failed policies in the Vietnam War. But most Americans would agree that the nation had also been well served and sometime brilliantly by Wilson and the two Roosevelts, Truman, Eisenhower, and Reagan up to the 1996 elections.

Perhaps because the leaders of Congress didn't have the White House as a showcase or because the congressional requirement of reason and compromise is not as appealing to the public as the vitality of a leader like the assassinated John Kennedy, the legislative branch has seldom won the public acclaim that goes to the presidency. And yet, such Speakers as Cannon and Martin and such Senate majority leaders as Barkley and Taft became important figures in this century.

It follows that the increasing public reliance placed on the presidency is bound to make it even more dominant in the next century unless succeeding Congresses find a way to lessen the differences that unfairly and unjustly penalize the legislative branch. As a modest beginning, it should not be too much to ask the honorable members of the Senate and House to reconcile their different views in the same spirit as the equally important deliberations of the Supreme Court. Common civility is still not a crime in one of the largest and still the most successful of the world's democracies.

Congress has inherited a tradition of solemn deliberation among a concerned citizenry that led to the Declaration of Independence on July 4, 1776, and the adoption of the Constitution on March 4, 1789. To follow such inspired examples, it is time for a Congress facing the next century to close ranks.

33 Clinton Bids for Peace

The flames of still another Middle East war were threatening to consume President Clinton's hard-won agreement of 1993 between Israel and its Palestinian rebels that fall. But after almost eighty Palestinians and Israeli soldiers had been killed in three days of rioting, the president intervened.

It was then only thirty-five days before the November 5 election, a considerable risk to the president's future if he failed to achieve even as little as a lull in the fighting from Jerusalem to the West Bank of the Jordan River and the Gaza Strip.

With the larger and more basic Oslo Accords between the combatants also seriously weakened by the brutality of the renewed strife, the president by rare good fortune brought the two rival leaders back to the White House with King Hussein of Jordan to try to resume negotiations and thereby achieve at least a short truce — anything to stave off what seemed like a renewal of war.

For a little more than three hours on the first day of this incredible new summit at the White House on October 1, Prime Minister Netanyahu and his bitter foe, Chairman Arafat of the Palestine Authority, talked alone together with just a translator between them. But on the second day, the summit's end, reality intervened. In the East Room, with the principals listening silently, the president faced an unruly TV–print news conference. Alas, all he could say was that Messrs. Arafat and Netanyahu had agreed to meet for "continuous negotiations" beginning Sunday, October 6, at Erez, on the Gaza Strip border with Israel. But as for immediate concessions, especially by the Israelis, there were none.

The assembled representatives of the news media exploded in a fusillade of questions for which there were no answers, except a mild presidential suggestion as heard by the nation on TV: "Please, please, give us a chance to let this thing work in the days ahead." It seemed to at least one detached observer that this was a proper response to those who treated so sensitive a negotiation as if it were a ball game.

It was, all in all, quite a scene. One reporter went so far as to challenge the president to permit his three guests to speak, to which he promptly agreed. But they arose silently, posed with the president for some final pictures, and quickly departed. Later, at the Israeli embassy, Prime Minister Netanyahu issued a brief statement confirming his readiness for continual negotiations, which had been his original proposal. And although Chairman Arafat made no immediate comment before leaving, some of his people later called the White House session a failure. He did not.

From the standpoint of the embattled Israelis and Palestinians in Jerusalem and the West Bank, however, that day was one of relief for all but the family of a young protestor who was killed by an Israeli soldier in a West Bank village near Hebron and two others who were wounded. At least, for the time being, the mass protests and mass killings had stopped, although there was no guarantee, by any means, of even a degree of peace for the future.

The president had summed up the shaky position in his opening statement as well as possible at that tense phase of the renewed conflict:

> For three years now, the Israelis and the Palestinians have been moving forward along the path to a lasting peace. Every step is hard. It requires both sides to make difficult decisions and to keep their eyes fixed on the prize of lasting peace.
>
> But the progress they have made has proved to the world that progress is possible.
>
> Both sides know there is no turning back. Just as there can be no peace without security, there can be no true security without peace.

Each side blamed the other for inciting the renewed violence. Prime Ministe Netanyahu, who was in Paris on a round of talks with European leaders on September 25, blamed Arafat and other Palestinian leaders for spreading "wild and unfounded" accusations that the Israelis were endangering a sacred Muslim holy place, the al-Aksa Mosque in Jerusalem.

"This is a very dangerous game," he said, "and I do not advise anyone to play it."

But Arafat, aroused by what he believed was an Israeli threat to al-Aksa's safety as an ancient Muslim shrine, had called on Palestinians to protest, ordered a general strike, and encouraged protests by warning his Palestinian police guards not to break up such demonstrations.

It turned out that the Palestinians had lost patience with Prime Minister Netanyahu's regime that had only narrowly defeated the Labor

Party's administration in the June elections by calling for renewed Israeli security as the price of extending peace arrangements with the Palestinians under the Oslo Accords. Thus, Labor's policy of trading land for peace—that is, carrying out phased Israeli withdrawals from areas to be handed over to the new Palestinian Authority—had now been deliberately held up by the Netanyahu regime, pending his approval of better security arrangements.

What had bothered Arafat and his people in particular was that the scheduled Israeli withdrawal from the key city of Hebron on the West Bank had been indefinitely delayed by the Netanyahu regime. There were only an embattled group of five hundred Jewish settlers in Hebron among a surrounding Palestinian populace of about 100,000, and the previous Labor regime itself had stalled on pulling out at the long-passed Oslo deadline of March 22. Meanwhile, most other Palestinian areas on the West Bank had been turned over to the Palestinial Authority, headed by Arafat with his Palestinian police, who had been armed by the Israelis with some of their own rifles.

The Israelis, however, had still not been satisfied with the security arrangements offered by the Palestinian Authority to safeguard the thin ranks of Israeli settlers in Hebron, something that Netanyahu emphasized when he also extended his own delayed withdrawal from the ancient town without setting a time for the takeover by Arafat's people. But while continuing to pledge adherence to the Oslo Accords, the new prime minister also let it be known that there might yet be a sprinkling of more Israeli settlements on the West Bank not specifically marked for Palestinian takeover.

There had also been renewed agitation by the large and always influential Orthodox Jewish community in Jerusalem, which had helped put Netanyahu's conservatives in power, against yielding any more Israeli land to the Palestinian Authority. That, too, had made the minority Palestinians in Jerusalem uncomfortable, particularly when the prime minister continued to assure Arafat that the Oslo Accords would be honored once security arrangements were mutually approved. Only, once again, no definite dates were set.

The blowoff came on September 25, by coincidence the one-hundredth day of the new Likud regime's assumption of power, in what seemed to the Western view a most improbable immediate issue. It so hapened that the Netanyahu government, in what apparently began as a bid to extend tourist interest in Old Jerusalem, had opened a new entrance to an ancient archaeological tunnel in the old city that penetrated an area near, but not directly under, the al-Aksa Mosque on the Temple Mount. It was also of great interest to Jews as the site nearby of what had been Herod's Temple.

Although both Mayor Ehud Olmert of Jerusalem and Prime Minister Netanyahu gave assurances that the new tunnel entrance in no way threatened the safety of the Muslim holy place, the youngest and most implacable Palestinians in Jerusalem at once assumed that there had been a deliberate religious affront to their people. Arafat called next for demonstrations. In the light of what happened later, there is little doubt that neither Netanyahu nor Arafat realized the enormity of the tensions that the new tunnel opening had unleashed in Jerusalem.

Before calm could be restored, the rioting had spread from Jerusalem to the West Bank town of Ramallah, then Nablus and Bethlehem. The Israeli soldiers began their defense by firing rubber bullets, but that only infuriated the fiery young Palestinians.

All of a sudden, real bullets began flying, too; and before nightfall that Wednesday, at least five Palestinians were killed and scores were wounded, most being treated at a Ramallah hospital. It was the onset of what seemed at first to be the worst outbreak since the 1987 riots that had touched off civil unrest for six years, ending with the accords that President Clinton was able to negotiate with the parties in the White House Rose Garden.

Once the confrontation was resumed, more rioting flared next day centered in Nablus, the largest city on the West Bank, and extended as far as Gaza, bordering Egypt on the Mediterranean. The fighting, mainly stones from the Palestinian youths and bullets from the Palestinian police, answered by bullets from the Israeli troops, lasted until well into the night of the twenty-sixth.

It was the killing of six Israeli soldiers, along with eight Israeli civilians and forty-five Palestinians that jarred the Israeli public, who cried out time and again that the troops were slaughtered with guns their own government had given to the enemy. Several hundred wounded were also treated at various hospitals across the land that Thursday, as well.

And now, an angry Prime Minister Netanyahu, returning posthaste from his swing around Europe, found blame being attached mainly to Israel amid demands in Europe and the United States for the closing of the tunnel that had touched off the violence. Abruptly, Netanyahu again refused and tried to arrange a meeting with Arafat to stop the violence. The Palestinian leader, however, wouldn't meet the Israeli prime minister without some assurance of a resumption of the trading of land for peace that the Labor Party had begun.

On President Clinton's instructions, the United States also sent some of its Middle East diplomats to intervene with both sides, hoping to persuade either President Hosni Mubarak of Egypt or King Hussein of Jordan to act as a mediator. But it didn't work out, for Netanyahu was as defiant as Arafat. He charged Arafat with "deliberate incitement" to violence and a "cynical manipulation" of the youthful Palestinians who seemed to have become the chief victims.

As for suggestions that the Israeli prime minister should shut the new Jerusalem tunnel opening at once as a signal that he was ready to discuss peace again, he replied with still another refusal and an irate statement:

> I do not regret that we opened the Western Wall tunnel, which has no effect on the Temple Mount [where the mosque is located] and expresses our soverignty over Jerusalem.

That Friday, the third of the new riots, at least one dozen more deaths and scores more of wounded were attributed to the fighting. That day, it happened directly on the Temple Mount before the mosque, where more Palestinian youths were throwing rocks until the Israeli police dispersed them with a hurtling charge, tear gas, and more bullets.

Arafat responded with his own challenge:

> It is necessary to calm the situation down, but the attempt to attack worshipers inside the mosque is something we cannot tolerate.

This time, the Palestinian leader was said also to have ordered the Palestinian police to try to halt the attacks on the Israeli police. All he received for his pains, once a few of his police tried to quiet the young stone throwers, was more stones—some thrown at the Palestinian police as well.

In all truth, the situation was out of control, although there were relatively few incidents the fourth day, the twenty-eighth; and on the fifth, Sunday, the twenty-ninth, President Clinton was able to announce at the White House that Chairman Arafat, Prime Minister Netanyahu, and King Hussein had agreed to meet with him in Washington and that Arafat and Netanyahu were "concerned about the way events had spun out of control . . . the eruption of old tensions and bitternesses." The president concluded hopefully, "I believe they want to try to get beyond that."

There were only thirty-seven days, then, until the American election day; a week until the opening of Clinton's first televised debate with the Republican presidential challenger, Bob Dole; and barely a weekend until Clinton's opening meeting October 1 with the principals in this latest of Middle East tragedies.

It was not a position that any American president would have invited, much less welcomed; but, as the author of the Rose Garden Accords of 1993, Clinton had no choice. His prospects of success were minimal, of failure huge; and Israeli tanks and armed personnel carriers were already on the move in the Middle East to keep the major Palestinian cities and forces blocked off from each other as far as possible.

President Mubarak of Egypt hadn't accepted President Clinton's invitation to attend the search for peace between Israel and the Palestinians, probably as much for concern over his own domestic problems as for what seemed like very little hope for success among his feuding neighbors. The combative Muslim fundamentalists in such other hostile Egyptian neighbors as Libya and Sudan would have been as much of a menace to Mubarak as to Netanyahu in the event of the failure of the new White House summit, and the Israelis were better able to defend themselves than the less- well-armed Egyptians.

But with King Hussein as a friendly third party and President Clinton as host, there was a surprising development that first October day of this altogether White House summit. It came about when the chief antagonists, Chairman Arafat and Prime Minister Netanyahu, politely declined the offer of a mediator or referee and chose to go off in a room by themselves.

They took with them only a translator and talked together quietly for more than three hours but made no report on what they had accomplished, if anything. To a negative-minded Whate House Press Corps, of course, that seemed immediately to spell failure — a position easy to justify in any tough negotiation such as this one.

Still, the press verdict on this improbable summit had to be delayed for the second day and an expected summation by the parties of what had been decided. It was then that the first hasty judgments were made when President Clinton, speaking on behalf of all concerned, could announce only that continuous negotiations on the Gaza Strip between the principals would begin on Sunday, October 6, a few hours before the first presidential debate that evening.

Because Netanyahu had offered nothing and yielded nothing publicly in the two days at the White House, despite his long session with Arafat, it seemed to be taken for granted that President Clinton's intervention had failed to produce instant peace. It was not only Arafat's grim visage that appeared to tell the story; some of his people announced outright that the negotiation had failed.

The president's plea for time, therefore, was treated mainly by his domestic opponents as a pathetic side issue to soften the harsh judgment of instant history. Still, neither side had moved to resume the riots in Jerusalem, the West Bank, or Gaza, although there had been individual incidents testifying to the inherent dangers in the situation between the bitterly disappointed Palestinians and the still defensive and aloof Israeli prime minister.

Israel, however, did at last permit 10,000 Palestinian workers to cross from Gaza for long-deferred Israeli jobs; and two other crossing points at the same time were opened on the West Bank. It was a small but welcome gesture in support of an uncertain truce.

Moreover, when Chairman Arafat became discouraged over continued Israeli insistence on better protection for the few Jews in the 100,000-strong Palestinian city of Hebron on the West Bank, Prime Minister Netanyahu pleaded for continued negotiations, and President Clinton insisted that an agreement between the two sides was still possible.

It was under such straitened circumstances that a decidedly risky truce was extended in the Middle East in the closing weeks of the American presidential campaign.

And this, too, is how Prime Minister Netanyahu, with his shaky Likud coalition, tried to hold off an increasingly aggressive Arafat-led PLO from carrying out the pledges Israel made in the Oslo Accords at the price of more riots and more lives lost on both sides. The truce, luckily for Clinton, held through election day; but the bitter truth was, for all who would recognize it, that the spirit of Oslo was dying—and now there was no one to save it.

34 The Debates

President Clinton's double-digit lead in the polls over Bob Dole remained intact after their two widely heralded debates in October. A third meeting involving Vice-President Gore and his Republican challenger, Jack Kemp, also caused no material change in the election day outlook.

In essence, therefore, the debates made little impression on the electorate. Moreover, the TV audience was about 40 percent below that of 1992, with an average rating of only 26.1 percent on the basis of Neilsen Media Research standards—just about as low as any presidential debate could get. Partly, that could have been due to the telecast of the Atlanta Braves–St. Louis Cardinals championship baseball game at the same time period; but that wasn't the whole story.

The show, by TV criteria, wasn't very exciting, nor did the presidential contenders intend it to be. Dole, for the most part, was respectful; and the president was gracious, even after the last flareups in the final debate.

The pressure throughout was heaviest on Dole. From the outset, his candidacy had been clouded because of doubts among the elderly about his support of their entitlements. Then, too, at least 60 percent of women voters polled showed resentment of his attack on abortion rights. His continual rejection of affirmative action had also aroused opposition, particularly among blacks. And at seventy-three, young people scorned him as too old.

At the same time, with real wages for workers showing an increase for the first time in almost a generation and purchases of new homes at a new high, there was ample support for the president's contention that the nation's economy was thriving, despite Dole's contrary view. The six-year bull market's shattering of the 6,000 mark in the Dow Jones Industrial Averages also bolstered the president's position, even though polls showed that the financial community still favored Dole's candidacy. The public majority at large, however, remained faithful to Clinton through mid-October.

Dole still relied on his proposed 15-percent tax cut as the centerpiece of his presidential candidacy during the first debate with Clinton on October 6 at Hartford, Connecticut. The president, in response, quoted Dole's Republican colleague Senator Alphonse D'Amato, who long since had warned so steep a reduction could only be accomplished by chopping benefits for Social Security, Medicare, and Medicaid.

Another Dole staple, eliminating the Department of Education in favor of a voucher system to put more children in private or religious schools, also aroused vigorous presidential dissent. What Clinton wanted to do was to boost national support for public education. Among those who heard the debate on TV, there seemed to be support for Clinton's view that the private-school project was visionary at best.

The question of executive pardons, which Dole raised, could have been potentially dangerous to the president; for some of his partners in the Whitewater real-estate project had already been convicted and jailed. But when he refused to prejudge the matter, Dole snapped, "You should have said, 'No comment.'" And so when the challenger continued to argue, Clinton did say, "No comment," drawing a laugh from his in-house audience. End of danger.

As the debate continued, the president charged Dole with dodging the Big Tobacco issue by declining to penalize the efforts of major tobacco companies to popularize smoking among teenagers. Dole ducked. He brought up the federal government's admission that teenage drug use had increased. The president's defense was that Dole and the Republican majority in Congress should have been more cooperative in the administration's battle against increased drug smuggling. Dole thereby escaped being pinned down on the tobacco issue for the time being.

As for the challenger's criticism of the Clinton anticrime program generally, the president linked Dole with the National Rifle Association's opposition to government regulation of arms sales. Clinton also recalled the Republican nominee's own votes against the Brady gun-control bill and the ban on nineteen kinds of assault weapons. Congress, however, adopted both measures eventually.

The president had opened the session by asking the national TV audience, "Are you better off than you were four years ago?" To that, Dole answered, facing Clinton directly, "*He's* better off," which produced another laugh from the audience.

To the president's usual recital of his economic accomplishments, including the creation of 10 million new jobs and a 60-percent cut in the national debt, the Kansan observed that there was a greater gap among many families where one member worked to support the others and another labored to pay taxes.

Then, Dole charged that the president was a "tax-and-spend liberal" and drew a response from Clinton that he had reduced the size of the federal government to its lowest level in thirty years, regardless of whether the feat was called liberal, conservative, or whatever.

The least part of the performance on both sides was devoted to foreign affairs, considering the nation's position as a dominant world power and its dependence on foreign trade, including huge imports of oil from the Persian Gulf area. As for the renewed threat of Saddam Hussein's rebuilt Iraqi armed force in the Middle East, which had caused forty-four American missiles to be fired at the dictator's military targets, Dole grumbled that Saddam, too, was "better off than he had been four years ago." But the president justified the assault by saying that it had been done to halt the Iraqi attack on its Kurdish refugee population.

The even more critical presidential involvement in rising tension between Israel's Prime Minister Netanyahu and the challenge of Chairman Arafat's Palestinians received less attention in that debate. The reality was that a threat to peace was developing through Israel's delayed response in maintaining its pledged withdrawal from the West Bank city of Hebron, with a population of 100,000 Palestinians and only a token force of Israelis. What happened during the debate was rising American pressure on Israel to conform to the Oslo Peace Accords legitimized in the 1993 White House pact.

The ninety-minute first debate ended with Clinton offering his outstretched hand, which Dole grasped. Hillary Clinton, Elizabeth Dole, and others then joined the presidential debaters while the audience politely applauded both sides. In the instant polling that took place afterward, it was evident that the tit-for-tat exchanges had changed nothing.

The vice-presidential debate three days later also failed to make any decided change in the race. For while Messrs. Kemp and Gore vigorously contested the major issues, including abortion that had been neglected in the first presidential debate, they refused to enter into personal attacks. Kemp even seemed to have limited Dole's room for maneuver by saying "it would be beneath Bob Dole" to indulge in personal attacks on the president. That was the high point of the vice-presidential candidates' argument at St. Petersburg, Florida.

As a result, those in the Dole camp who were looking for a slam-bang, knockdown Republican offensive against Clinton in their final meeting were angry over Kemp's mild attitude. But it didn't make much difference to Dole's articulate running mate.

Kemp did his best to support Dole's proposed 15-percent tax cut, arguing that it could be done without slashing the entitlements and the public at large would still save $550 billion in taxes. Gore's response was to term the proposal risky, very much like "putting the American economy in a barrel and sending it over Niagara Falls." Again quoting Dole's colleague Senator D'Amato, the vice-president used the New Yorker's warning that so large a tax reduction inevitably would sharply reduce the nation's benefits to the elderly.

There were similar differences between the latest debaters over maintaining affirmative action, so critical to the black community. Vice-President Gore stressed that his rival had turned against the issue only after becoming the Republican vice-presidential nominee.

Such real changes, which also included the right of choice among women for abortions, were repeated during the second debate. Toward the end, Kemp veered toward the extremes, accusing the Clinton administration of a "reign of terror" to impose its policies on the nation. To that, Gore responded that federal regulation had been vastly reduced by setting aside or dropping 6,000 rules.

Kemp then contended that his party, through its 15-percent tax cut, would so greatly stimulate the American economy that it would be possible to continue the entitlements without any reduction. It was also Kemp's view that an economy with a 2-percent growth rate could be doubled in size with so big a tax cut.

No such supposed miracle was available, however, to persuade a majority of women voters that they should yield their right of choice for an abortion to a new Republican presidential administration. But where Gore was content merely to affirm his party's right of choice, Kemp lodged a strong attack on President Clinton's veto of a congressional measure that would have prohibited all so-called late abortions, even though they may have been necessary to save the life of the mother.

The veto, Kemp argued, was "gruesome." For justification, Gore contended that "the right of a woman to choose must never be taken away," whereas Kemp insisted that the protection of human life was at issue.

The most interesting part of the vice-presidential debate, billed by some as a preview of a likely presidential contest four years hence, was the civility with which the candidates treated each other. Kemp, at the outset, said that they were debating two divergent views of how the federal government should operate; Gore, in thanking his opponent, was equally careful to make no personal reference affecting either former Senator Dole or Kemp. The debaters thereafter took several bows with their families before an applauding audience.

During the week before the second and final presidential debate in southern California, Dole was deluged with advice from well-wishers about what he should do to demolish President Clinton's continuing double-digit lead in the polls. As a result, the hard-pressed Republican nominee let it be known that he was thinking of stepping up his attacks on President Clinton's "ethics in government." At the onset of the debate at the University of San Diego on October 16, however, the challenger's opening statement was so mild an assurance of his understanding of people's problems that he drew a few relieved handclaps from his audience.

Always the expert campaigner, Clinton moved right in with a big grin to reassure those who had begun to applaud, and said, "I wanted to applaud, too." Then, he went on with his usual effort "to build bridges to the twenty-first century" in the opening phase of the final presidential debate. The audience of about one hundred selected undecided voters by that time realized applause was unnecessary until the town-meeting session was over.

Jim Lehrer of the Public Broadcasting Service, the moderator, was to pick the public's questioners one by one from a small forest of waving hands, the usual process agreed on to avoid direct disputes between the candidates. It was a formula that now obliged Dole to scatter his critique of the Clinton administration as best he could between whatever questions that gave him an opportunity.

The alert Clinton, maintaining outward calm and a usually cheerful front, either ignored such oblique criticism or made a brief response covered by the general observation, "No attack ever created a job or educated a child or helped a family make ends meet. No insult ever cleaned up a toxic waste dump or helped an elderly person."

It stood to reason, therefore, that Dole was actually limited by both time and circumstance in mounting any attempted knockdown battle against so disciplined and well-prepared a presidential opponent.

This tit-for-tat style was illustrated by the way both candidates handled the opening question, a young teacher's request to describe what they would do in the next presidential term to unite our people and thereby strengthen the nation.

Dole said:

> There's no doubt about it that many people have lost faith in government. They see ethical problems in the White House today. They see

nine hundred FBI files . . . being gathered up by somebody in the White House. . . so there's a great deal of cynicism out there. But I've always tried in whatever I've done to bring people together . . . .

In response, Clinton followed with:

We've gotten some real progress in the last four years. I've done everything I could at every moment of the vision in this country, after Oklahoma City, when these churches were burned, to bring people together and remind them that we are stronger because of our diversity. We have to respect one another . . . .

It is important that we go beyond old partisan arguments and focus on people and their future. When we do that, instead of shutting down the government over a partisan fight on the budget, we're a better country; and that's why we're making progress now.

In a question over improving the nation's health care, the president got in another dig at his opponents by recalling that he had protected Medicare from a $270-billion cut in a Republican budget the he'd vetoed. After that, Dole recalled that the Republicans had killed the elaborate Clinton health plan in 1973 and predicted that an opposing Republican plan, far from cutting Medicare, would "increase it 39 percent."

Dole, however, had to scramble to answer a direct question about whether he still believed smoking tobacco was "nonaddictive." He began by saying that his brother's death might have been partly owing to cigarettes, then added, "Are they addictive? Maybe they're—they probably are addictive. I don't know. I'm not a doctor. You shouldn't smoke."

Soon enough, as he had in the first debate, the challenger veered to an attack on the Clinton administration for the admitted increase in teenage drug users. The president, however, stuck to the challenger's weak point, tobacco, saying that it was one of his biggest differences with the on-again, off-again Republican. He recalled that Dole had even opposed the regulation of cigarette advertising by the Food and Drug Administration, and went on:

No president has ever taken on the tobacco lobby before I did. Senator Dole opposed me. He went down and made a speech to those on his side saying I did the wrong thing. I think I did the right thing.

In response to a question on the future of Social Security, however, the president was quick to credit Dole as a member of a government panel in 1983 that made Social Security safe until well into the next century and suggested that the same kind of advisory panel should extend the life of Medicare beyond its current outlook for the next ten years.

But then, the president again criticized his opponent for having attempted to damage Medicare in the 1995 Republican budget that was vetoed at the White House. In it, Clinton specified, were anti-Medicare provisions that would have caused the closing of seven hundred hospitals. "We need to reform Medicare, not wreck it, " he concluded.

There was also an argument about reforming welfare, during which Dole commented, "What we need to do is to try to return people to work." He then elaborated by demanding that illegal immigrants should be denied welfare payments which, as Clinton promptly informed him, had been illegal for years. The president went on:

> I've got a plan with this new welfare reform law to work with the private sector to give employers specific tax incentives to hire people off welfare and do some other things which will create more jobs in the private sector, at least a million, to move more people off welfare to work.

Of course, there was no argument between the combatants about balancing the budget, but one questioner wanted to know from Dole how it could be done while still reducing taxes. And that, as had happened in the first debate, brought into question once more the $550 billion that Dole's 15-percent tax cut would cost.

Clinton argued that he had a less costly tax cut that would be fully paid for in his own budget while Dole assured the questioner that he'd sponsor a constitutional amendment to make a balanced budget a necessity. Just how that would pick up the $550 billion tab, however, was left hanging.

On affirmative action, the president insisted that such guarantees are still necessary as protection against discrimination; but he said that he was against creating quota systems. Dole argued that affirmative action benefited nobody, "except a very small group at the top." He said that he was still against "quotas and preferences."

Both had their pet projects and their pet peeves. The president's pet project, the Family Leave Act, was cited proudly as having already benefited 12 million families who were able to "take a little time off for the birth of a child or a family illness without losing their job." Dole's pet peeve was what he called the president's "public ethics," in which he charged, "You have thirty some in your administration who have either left or are being investigated or in jail or whatever, and you have an ethical problem."

In fairness to the president, however, it should be stressed that Dole did not offer any details. In any event, the president didn't take notice nor did he follow up later with either complaints or denials.

Throughout, there were only two questions about foreign affairs. On one, foreign trade, Clinton told of increased trade with Japan that had created more jobs in the United States, notably in automobile plants. And on the other, a question about whether he would send American troops to halt further outbursts between Israelis and Palestinians, the president counseled patience and predicted an eventual agreement between the parties that would make American troops on the West Bank of the Jordan unnecessary.

Once both debate summations had been completed, all evidence of ill will between the president and his opponent vanished. Again, they shook hands, Mrs. Clinton and Mrs. Dole joined them on the platform, the audience applauded, and the debates were over for another four years without any indication that they had changed the campaign in any respect. As incidental intelligence, the concurrent baseball game ended shortly afterward with Atlanta beating St. Louis 3–1.

But strangely, no one during any of the three debates had raised the question of the control of the next Congress that would also be decided together with the presidency on election day. Neither the president nor Dole could contend that the White House's relations with Congress were of no importance. Perhaps, in their infinite wisdom, both decided that anything they said about Congress could be used against them.

If so, that at least would have been one result of the debates. There weren't any others.

PART FIVE
The Election

35 Ending the Campaign

President Clinton's lead in the polls toward the last hours of the 1996 presidential campaign was so firmly settled in double digits that his Republican opponent, Bob Dole, frantically pleaded with Ross Perot to quit the race.

Perot, who then had only a 5-percent rating as his Reform Party's candidate, replied that he was in the current campaign "for the long haul" and dismissed Dole's suggestion as "weird and inconsequential." His reward was a slight rise in his poll rating, but even that was nowhere near the 19 percent of the presidential vote he drew in 1992.

The immediate effect of the Dole-Perot exchange, if any, was likely to be on congressional campaigns, where the gain or loss of a few votes might make a difference in some of the close House and Senate races. But despite the president's advanced standing, there was growing doubt across the land that he could bring a Democratic Congress back to power with him.

To do so, he would need a net gain of at least 19 seats in the 435-member House that Republicans dominated and a net gain of 3 in the Senate, where there were 34 vacancies, including a number in which Democrats were retiring.

The Republicans winced meanwhile when the supposedly secret appeal to Perot was disclosed. As for the candidate himself during a Florida campaign trip, he had to wave aside queries about the rejected bid with a wry smile and a discouraged flip of one hand. He varied the monotony of attacking the president by blaming his troubles on "the liberal media," then largely owned by some of America's largest corporations plus at least one foreign press magnate, Rupert Murdoch of Australia.

Like another Kansan, Governor Alf M. Landon, who faced the Democratic juggernaut of sixty years ago that reelected the last previous Democratic president for a second term, Franklin Roosevelt, Dole didn't seem to know what to do after Perot scorned his plea.

One day, the Republican challenger would try to revive hope that he could carry California, long since thought of as a lost cause by more practical-minded Republicans. Then, he'd reverse his field and pop up successively in New Jersey, New Hampshire, the Midwest, or the deep South and far West with whatever change in tactics came to mind.

But no matter how hard the Republican standard-bearer tried, he simply wasn't the accomplished campaigner of his younger rival, the president, who seemed so self-confident at fifty that he put comparatively little effort into his reelection drive until almost the end. By that time, the seventy-three-year-old Dole seemed more frustrated than he had been as the more moderate senator who had made a good name for himself in his long congressional career.

Dole had worked hard at this third and final attempt to become president. He had patiently experimented with varying tactics to find something that would work for him. Switching from blistering attacks on the president's character, he had tried denunciations of Clinton's conduct, particularly with references to the conviction of past presidential associates in the Whitewater affair; demands that none should receive a presidential pardon if he were reelected; and, finally, assaults on Democratic fund-raising tactics, including contributions from perfectly legal foreign interests through their American representatives, while overlooking even larger questions raised against Republican fund-raising.

But nothing Dole tried seemed to change the polls for the challenger from April to October, although he never slackened his efforts; traveled wherever he was wanted; and, in the last days, took responsibility for his renewed gamble in California. But for all that, President Clinton still managed to maintain his lead in most polls and his attitude of being above the battle as the nation's chief executive.

Hundreds of millions of dollars in bad-mouth TV advertising and even worse loud-mouth politicking, on which the Republican high command had depended to make Dole the next president, turned out to be the wrong way to go. Also, instead of being a come-on for the average American as Dole had hoped, his proposed 15-percent income-tax cut — the center of his campaign — never attracted much public attention and even less support.

Instead, the tax cut was profoundly mistrusted among working people and even more so at the professional level by all except theoretical "supply siders," the fancy name some conservative economists had invented for the old concept of the "trickle down" gain for the masses from the bountiful table of corporate America.

Dole had little else to offer that was of a positive nature and often heard complaints in his travels that people were actually interested in whatever future plans he had that might affect their lives, instead of the steady, almost monotonous repetitive drumbeat of critical comment about the Clinton administration — his major thrust.

What handicapped the challenger more than anything else was that there had been relatively little inducement for change among the electorate. The nation was at peace. The economy seemed steady, giving all but a reduced impoverished class very little to worry about. Home building was up; unemployment, down. And there was very little prospect, even on the horizon, that drastic change was likely.

Although there was no immediate evidence of a major challenge abroad, while the non-Communist Russians were having their own troubles in putting down the rebellious Chechnyans among other problems, the strength of American armed forces remained near a peacetime high, with more funding than the Pentagon bothered to request.

In a campaign speech in the Middle West during a late swing around the country, President Clinton even suggested opening the ranks of the North Atlantic Treaty Organization to such former Communist allies as Poland, Hungary, and the former Czechoslovakia, now split in two. They were admitted, however, after charges were made that it was done mainly to please Eastern Europeans.

It turned out in the last days of the presidential campaign that Clinton's main concern, aside from the in-and-out speculation over the control of Congress, was to win reelection by more than a majority of the vote. To keep him below 50 percent seemed to be the undeclared objective of the Republican high command after routing the unfortunate Dole on a cross-country whistle-stop schedule that at one point took him into an area at 4:30 A.M., where a few hundred of the faithful were waiting patiently for his usual sodden forecast of victory. It wasn't a pleasant sight, considering that this distinguished American was ending a major career of public service.

Meanwhile, President Clinton was trying to answer his critics with some of the more positive results of his four years in the White House. On October 28 at University City, Missouri, he was able to announce that the nation's debt had been reduced by 63 percent during his administration. From a record high of $290 billion in 1992, the figure he gave for the fall of 1996 was $107 billion, the lowest national deficit in twenty-two years and the smallest of any other major industrialized country in the world.

Among the theories floated by some of the president's economists about the reason for so remarkable a change in the nation's financial outlook was that millions of middle-class investors in the great bull market of the 1990s were cashing in their securities to reap their profits. At the same time, so the theory went, they were sending an enormous flow of capital-gain levies into the US Treasury.

There was some evidence to support this particular explanation, for the closing Dow Jones Industrial Averages had declined sharply from their high at more than 6,000, then rallied. At any rate, there appeared to be no concern among Wall Street's analysts that a major slump was in sight during the last week of the presidential campaign. Although there was a consensus that more moderate gains might be expected early on, it was clear enough that the financial community was entering a period of caution among experienced investors.

Said the president of his debt-reduction announcement:

> My friends, America has heard a lot of calls in the past several days. I would say that these results prove that America is awake and moving in the right direction to the twenty-first century. We are moving toward a balanced budget. We are going to continue building prosperity and create jobs.

As for the Republican majority in Congress whose budget he had vetoed in 1995, after which the Republican-controlled Congress produced its two shutdowns that lasted into early 1996, he recalled that the opposition had gambled on forcing him to accept their budget by keeping 800,000 government employees idle and unpaid during the period of closure. To which he added the comment, "And I said, 'I'd rather see you hurt people for three months than thirty years. No, thank you very much.'"

Another major aspect of his campaign that strengthened his position with the public toward election day was the manner in which he had co-opted the crime issue that had usually been a major Republican advantage in previous presidential contests in the latter part of the century.

A part of the reason for Clinton's success in winning more public support for his initiatives against crime was his decision to propose substantial funding to recompense victims of violent crimes, a popular proposal at any time. He explained that a new federal fund based on fines and other criminal penalties, usually money that ended up being distributed to the states, could help crime victims as well if as little as 10 percent of the total could be set aside to benefit them.

To illustrate the president's plan, it so happened that, within a short time in 1996, two large companies had been fined almost half a billion dollars — $340 million in a fraud case against the Daiwa Bank Ltd. and another $100 million fine against Archer Daniels Midland Co. for price-fixing — 10 percent of which sum could help the crime victims if set aside for them. The objective, of course, was to stimulate action for a Victims' Defense Fund in the next Congress, which was easier said than done.

Clinton also floated additional proposals for the advancement of public education to keep the issue in the forefront of his campaign. Along with substantial funding to rebuild the thousands of dilapidated school buildings across the land, engage more teachers, endow more scholarships, and grant more tax credits for families with children still in school, he proposed expanded educational standards to improve the quality of instruction.

He suggested connecting every classroom and school library in the United States to the Internet by the year 2000, a state report card on every school also to be placed on the Internet, a series of student competency tests at successive steps in their education, and a check on college entrance requirements for greater assurance of excellence at that level. As always, in every suggestion he made to improve public education, he emphasized his primary aim to see to it that every child would be able to read in the third grade.

No one, not even the most ardent Democrat, contended that such relatively modest proposals to advance education, reduce crime, recompense crime victims, and cut the national debt were likely to send the populace to dancing in the streets. But taken as a whole, what they did do was to support the notion, always in the forefront of the president's calculations, that anything he could do or even suggest in the way of public benefits would advance his campaign. Contrasted with the sour public reception of Dole's 15-percent-tax-reduction scheme, there was something to be said for Clinton's more measured approach.

But that didn't help him very much when the fury of critics of Democratic fund-raising, including his own principal role in that necessary effort, burst about him and his White House staff in the concluding days of his reelection campaign.

It developed that Perot and his Reform Party had been harping on the issue of campaign financial reform for weeks on end without attracting much public attention. But when it came to public notice that John Huang, a representative of a wealthy Indonesian family of Asian industrialists, had also been an official in the Commerce Department while acting as a Democratic fund-raiser, even the comatose Republican presidential campaign came to life.

The Democratic National Committee at once opted to return a questionable contribution to the presidential campaign from a South Korean source as illegal. Next, Huang, having solicited the Korean contribution, was suspended, pending an inquiry into his activities elsewhere in the Far East, including his wealthy Indonesian clients.

The pro-Republican press kept hammering at the campaign contribution issue from foreign sources until President Clinton on November 1 broke his silence at Santa Barbara, California, saying,

> Everybody knows the problems of campaigning money today. There's too much of it, it takes too much time to raise, and it raises too many questions.

Although he didn't mention Huang or the former fund-raiser's wealthy Indonesian connections, the president added in slight apology, "We have played by the rules. But you know and I know that we need to change the rules."

And so that was that. Despite the uproar of Republican protests, including a disclosure from the *Wall Street Journal* that there had been a record of at least fourteen White House visits by the Indonesian mogul, James T. Riady, the president went his own way, the White House clammed up, and a spokesman reflected that there was nothing illegal about White House visits from a foreign dignitary.

For the last weekend and right through to the early hours of election day itself, both presidential candidates became hoarse and travel weary in cross-country hippety-hops by aircraft and bus to wrap up the longest, least surprising, and most expensive presidential campaign within the memory of the oldest reporter extant. Few minds among prospective voters appeared to have changed, so the last polls suggested; but there still appeared to be 7 or 8 percent of undecided voters, even with Clinton's lead remaining high in the double digits.

No poll, however, was venturesome enough to predict which party would control the One hundred-fifth Congress. Despite all rival party claims, the position was still clearly too close to call.

In his ninety-six hours of travel from the eastern United States to California and back, an alert and combative former Senator Dole hoarsely emphasized his own personal set of values to try to persuade any undecided voters: "Integrity, character, honor, duty, country, decency," he said in Phoenix, Arizona. "And I keep my word."

But from California eastward on the last leg of this political ordeal, the plucky Kansan couldn't always address the modest-sized groups of voters who still wanted to see and hear him, even when his voice failed him. Instead, the equally courageous Elizabeth Dole argued his case for him with well-nigh fanatical zeal, no matter where they were and regardless of the lateness of the hour.

"Call everybody you know, tell them to get out and vote," she'd shout. "Get to your friends, your neighbors."

There were still regrets among the Dole contingent because Ross Perot had declined the Republican nominee's plea to abandon his Reform Party candidacy and to boost the Dole cause. In a weekend radio appeal, the Republican nominee said, "I'd just say to Perot's supporters, don't vote for Perot, you're just voting for Bill Clinton."

The only problem there was that Perot, in his own windup of TV "infomercials," for which he himself was paying, made an appeal to Clinton supporters to join the Reform movement and to deny the president reelection. It didn't seem to be working, however.

And so at last, when Bob and Elizabeth Dole finally reached Harry Truman's hometown of Independence, Missouri, before dawn on election day, the candidate could only reflect on how the tough Democrat had surprised the pollsters in 1948 by defeating the favored Governor Thomas E. Dewey of New York. Without much conviction, Dole predicted at Independence that he would emulate Truman's feat.

Otherwise, the visit to the Missouri shrine for beating impossible odds was purely ceremonial. But at the last stop, Dole's own hometown of Russell, Kansas, he finally appeared to be relieved that the presidential campaign had ended, except for the voting. Despite the hour, he seemed almost cheerful as he arrived home with Mrs. Dole for a few hours' sleep.

For Clinton, the finale was livelier. He had begun his own last tour in New Hampshire, where, in 1982, he had begged for a second chance after almost wrecking his first presidential bid. Before Manchester voters, he recalled how that second chance had come to him with a second-place, primary-election finish, which gave him the impetus he needed to win that early Democratic presidential nomination.

Now, facing his cheering supporters at the end of his 1996 campaign, he reflected that this would be the last day of his last political campaign, then added with a flourish, "There's still a lot of life left in the old dog." The crowd joined him in chanting the familiar phrase, laughing and applauding as he finished.

This was the kind of political adventure that Clinton had always enjoyed the most, and he handled it well. All through that last day and well into the first dark hours of election day, he was on the road with Hillary and Al and Tipper Gore, echoing his theme westward and back with superb confidence in his own destiny, "to seize the day, to keep our country moving in the right direction." And before dawn on election day, when his road show got home to Little Rock, Arkansas, he looked and acted the favorite for reelection as president.

36 The Presidential Election

President Clinton's reelection in 1996 topped the most expensive national political campaign in American history as well as one of the most divisive.

The president's 31–19 state lead plus the District of Columbia translated into a 379–159 electoral triumph, even though he lost Congress once again to the Republicans. When he was asked at a postelection news conference to comment on winning only 49 percent of the total vote instead of the 50 percent he had sought, he replied good-naturedly that the huge electoral count was "an enormous consolation prize."

As for the ill-tempered campaign of his Republican rival, former Senator Dole, which the president had often referred to as one of "insult rather than ideas," that evidently turned off more voters than it attracted. Rather than negative advertising, what seemed to count for more with the electorate was a surging economy, peace abroad, and 10.5 million new jobs in near-record unemployment.

There also appeared to be large-scale resentment of the "hate" campaigns that the major parties waged against each other, together with a lesser effort to the same effect by H. Ross Perot and his newly-formed Reform Party. But after a disappointed Perot drew only 8 percent of the presidential vote, as compared with almost 19 percent four years before, he now became a minor character in the field.

The real damage to Clinton came with the continuation of a sharply divided federal government that began with the Republican sweep of the 1994 Congressional elections, in which Speaker Gingrich rose to power. Although both the president and the Speaker offered conciliatory postelection gestures, there was scant hope that so precarious a postelection truce would last very long.

Still, the prospective renewal of partisan strife between the White House and Congress remained a matter of deep public concern. Within

Congress and the office of a special prosecutor, all the elements remained in place for a continuation of the various Republican inquiries into the Whitewater scandal, illicit fund-raising accusations, travel-office dismissals, and examinations of the FBI files of a number of Republicans.

The president, however, hadn't lowered his guard during the campaign; and he didn't do so now, despite a victory that he could have claimed as vindication after year-long assaults on his character, his trustfulness, his wife, and almost anything else his enemies aimed at, except — at least for the moment — his teenage daughter.

Instead, what he proposed to do was to go forward with his second-term cabinet, including his replacements, and with his plans for the advancement of education, financial protection of the entitlements so necessary to the elderly, renewed efforts at national health insurance, and repair of the damage caused by systematic welfare overhaul.

It was clear in Clinton's second term, therefore, that the stakes for the nation and the public were high, particularly if the election's adversaries failed to find the "common ground" that both said they wanted. It would seem that nobody else knew where to find it either. But in time, if divided government continued to produce little more than the black mud of controversy, blind partisanship could lead to something much worse than "big government" — perhaps no government at all.

The public had had as much of the camapign uproar as it could tolerate during almost one year before the election; but, strangely enough, the end came quickly shortly after 9:00 P.M., EST, on November 5. California and the Far West had yet to be heard from; but there were enough returns at that hour to cause the Voter News Service (VNS) to announce the reelection of President Clinton, news that at once was relayed by TV, radio, and the Associated Press to the nation and the world.

Dole conceded defeat shortly afterward in a telephone call to the president. Although Clinton's victory eventually turned out not to be as great as the more optimistic polls had estimated, it was big enough by VNS estimates to hold good until the last vote was counted some time later.

The VNS system, financed by the TV networks, the Fox, and Cable News systems, and the Associated Press, which itself is based on news membership support, had once again saved the nation countless hours of anxiety with its mass interviews of thousands of voters who were asked to tell, as they left the polls, how they voted on people and issues.

In this election, as in others in the recent past, the necessary 270 electoral-vote majority for the presidency had been exceeded from states where the polls had already closed. And so in Clinton's second election, California's 54 electoral votes, largest of all, hadn't even been needed.

The almost routine manner in which the results of that November 5 balloting were made known is worth more than a mere glance, a shrug, and a click of the TV channel selector, given the $1.6 billion estimated cost of this election and the conflicting emotions it seemed to arouse.

It should be recognized first of all that despite all the money, advertising campaigns, TV commercials, candidates' appearances, travel, and the like, there was relatively little change in President Clinton's advantage over Dole until the very last days when the gap narrowed, but only slighty.

Accordingly, the only real evidence of the result that the advertising and publicity of both major party campaigns were supposed to produce came in a statistic that is scarcely complimentary to either side. From 62.8 percent of the voting age population who cast ballots in the 1960 election of President John F. Kennedy, the figure in most parts of the nation declined in 1996 to less than half.

There were, of course, other causes of voter trauma than in the messiness and divisiveness of the various advertising campaigns. Included, one would suppose, were voter disillusionment with the candidates, overly long delays in the voter operation itself, dissatisfaction with the way campaign issues were presented (or de-emphasized in some cases), and the always dismal personal feeling of futility among the overly sensitive that one's vote would make a difference in the outcome of the election.

Even so, regardless of any party or other considerations affecting political organizations, it didn't take any scientific display of pollster expertise to determine that the negative nature of much of the advertising on both sides late in the year was troublesome to the average voter.

There were contributing causes, to a greater or lesser extent, that no campaign manager with any degree of responsibility can either countenance or even anticipate. For example, there were organized banks of anonymous phone calls in this campaign — in one of which I was apparently targeted for reasons unknown — but I disconnected at the suggestion that I was to be told some peculiar allegations of misconduct on the part of one of the candidates.

I was also asked by a prospective voter of strong religious beliefs whether I had heard anything of a threat by extremists to withhold Bibles from the public. Upon inquiry, it developed that such a question had actually been heard in a TV call-in program dealing with extremist attitudes in the presidential election.

I would agree that such experiences may be atypical, but I can't help wondering, in an election that involved tens of millions of voters across the land, how far such fanciful notions were passed along by word of mouth without record and without responsibility as to source.

What did appear prominently in postelection discussions was the admitted attempts to influence voters by targeting specific groups as various types of "gaps" beginning with gender and usually including race, national origin of first-generation citizens, religious preferences, the elderly, and less-prominent sets of prospective voters.

At its worst toward the end of the presidential campaign, this kind of thing amounted to a vastly distorted portrait of a political advertisers' America that could be and often was resented, whether eligible voters went to the polls or felt so outraged that they remained home. To some who found themselves listed willy-nilly among such target groups by energetic—and no doubt well-intentioned—questioners just before election day, it was understandable that they took offense whether or not they voted anyway.

Still, even at this stage of the postelection process of review and consultation, there has been a small advance in the demeaning process of name-calling that is supposed by some publicists to lead to instant success. It was reported immediately after the election results became known that a leading champion of the notion that Republican victories could be assured by denouncing all Democrats as liberals suffered a humiliating loss of face among his own clientele. Three of them who faithfully followed the party line by demeaning liberals were defeated.

It would seem, accordingly, that there still may be hope to salvage the eternal soul of W. S. Gilbert, who produced the following lyric that was set to music in the last century by Arthur Sullivan:

> That every boy and every girl
>   That's born into this world alive
> Is either a little liberal
> Or else a little con-serv-atyve.

Whatever difference advertising may or may not have made in assuring President Clinton's reelection, the first Democrat to do so since Woodrow Wilson in 1916 and Franklin D. Roosevelt in 1936, the marketing techniques of encouraging mass public patronage seemed to be of greater benefit to former Senator Dole, even in his losing cause. Whereas every major public-opinion poll save one had maintained President Clinton's lead well into double digits up to and including election day, the Republican nominee's actual vote total came within 8 points of the president, 49 to 41 percent.

Even as late as the last weeks of the campaign, some well-regarded polls had put Dole as far behind the president as 15 to 22 points, which is mainly what made the contest appear to be so much of a ho-hum affair to the reporters who were primarily responsible for passing the feeling of "no contest" along to the public at large for most of the campaign.

Not many close to the candidate went to the trouble of trying to dispute the evidence by contending that an attempt to change Dole's tactics of push, shove, and punch, or at least varying the monotony, might give him a chance at the great prize that he had sought at the end of his career of seven decades.

If Dole himself had had the barest notion that he was being under-polled, it would account at least in part for his alternate outbursts of rage and seeming despair ("Don't listen to the polls," "Make up your own minds," etc.) So far as is known, however, he never bothered to mount a determined campaign to complain that some of his poll figures toward the end were wide of the mark.

For the record, in any event, the only major feat at the end was by the great British agency, Reuters, which informed its American clientele just before election day that its final presidential poll gave Clinton 49 percent, Dole 41 percent, Perot, 8 percent, and other minor candidates 2 percent.

Although Dole was also accused after the fact of having run a poor campaign because he acted more like a legislative tactician than a presidential nominee and sometimes crossed up his own people by not taking their advice, there was also something to be said for the sacrifice that an elderly senator made for the sake of his party when, at age seventy-three, he voluntarily ended his Senate career as majority leader.

The surprise that more likely may have detracted from his campaign was his failure to sparkle on the stump. But then, there have been relatively few of presidential calibre who could compare with Clinton as a speaker or campaigner. On the Republican side of recent vintage, there was only Ronald Reagan; among Democrats, none since FDR, whose four terms won't soon be eclipsed.

When Dole voted early election day in his hometown, Russell, Kansas, he spoke his piece gracefully and finally while standing with his wife and daughter:

> We've been given endless encouragement and love. Seems we've shared the good days; we've had some that weren't so good; but at every stage, I've never walked alone; and that's important. . . . So I think from the earliest memories to the final hours of the campaign, your friends and your family are always your strength.

For President Clinton, there had also been a turnabout after losing the first great battle of his presidency, the kind of health insurance protection for all Americans that has been taken for granted in leading nations across the Atlantic. Even worse, that defeat in 1993 in a Democratic Congress was followed by the Republican sweep of both the Senate and the House in 1994, something that hadn't happened in forty years.

It hit the young president hard that he might be facing certain defeat in his fight for reelection; and, if he couldn't find a way out of the box in which he had placed himself by trying to go too far too soon without adequate preparation and a program on which he could depend, he might possibly have to engage in a primary election battle for the Democratic nomination.

The clue to his future came first from Dick Morris, who had worked for Republicans in the past, was familiar with their strategic purposes, and now gave the kind of counsel that must at first have made the president uneasy. To go the conservative route; to campaign at once for a balanced budget Republican style; to protect the entitlements, particularly Medicare, from the cuts that seemed almost certain to become necessary — such proposals as these required in the first instance a liberal about-face.

Perhaps Clinton hadn't at that precarious moment in his presidency been familiar with the story of Ronald Reagan's passage from a well-nigh radical Hollywood character as president of the Screen Actors Guild to become the conservative governor of California and the even more innovative Republican president of the United States. But as a Democratic president in deep trouble with his constituency, the inevitable change in Clinton's own outlook began under Morris's tutelage. One by one, the trappings of conservative Republicanism became a part of the Clinton White House, sometimes with confusion and even dismay among his loyal staff.

The pledge to balance the budget, along with the mandatory effort to reduce the national debt, was the first step; and it worked beautifully, particularly because Clinton's Treasury people were enthusiastic. The avoidance of the *liberal* label, strangely enough, was more difficult for some of the older Democrats to accept because of its association with both FDR and Truman. But despite Republican jeers, the public as a whole seemed unconcerned. And from then on, the Republican tactic for a Democratic president became the way to go, even when Morris had to resign and leave the White House.

Clinton, the "new" Democrat, had come into being; and the whole nature of his reelection campaign changed from then on. Even Hillary, the toughest liberal of all, voluntarily retreated into the background and contented herself with her interest in children for the duration of the presidential campaign.

Beginning with public outrage over the fateful bombing of the Federal Building in Oklahoma City in 1995, the president steadily moved away from the Left and, in his words, "back to the vital center," which is where he stayed, even when he discussed the necessary changes yet to come in the entitlements—Social Security, Medicare, and Medicaid—which somehow would have to be revised early in the next century with the growth of a considerably older America.

The greatest Republican mistake of all—twice shutting down the federal government in the weeks when the presidential campaign of 1996 was about to begin—became the starting point thereafter for a quite different but ultimately successful drive that was climaxed with Clinton's reelection.

Therefore, the Democratic revival toward century's end rested on solid though moderate Republican principles in a prosperous land that was at peace with itself and the world when it reelected William Jefferson Clinton. When the Republicans and their candidate tied their opposition campaign to monstrous abuse on television rather than a competing program for better governemnt, they sealed their own fate.

The end, as already has been shown, came with the merciful suddenness early on election night. Each hour, as various states closed their polls from 6:00 P.M. on, there was never any doubt of a Clinton victory.

As expected, the six New England states gave Clinton 35 undisputed electoral votes; but the first big tip-off came with Florida's 25 tallies that went into the Clinton column. Along the East Coast, another 87 votes went to Clinton from New York, New Jersey, Maryland, Delaware, Pennsylvania, and the District of Columbia. Clinton already had 147 votes—more than half the total he needed—the evening had barely begun, and most polls were still open.

By that time, Dole had only the southern Atlantic coast states—Virginia, North and South Carolina, and Georgia—with 48 votes. But with the closing of polls in the Midwest, he soon added Indiana, North and South Dakota, Nebraska, and Kansas, plus Mississippi and Alabama in the South, for 45 more votes, bringing his total to 93.

But from then on, it was all downhill for Dole because the heart of the country plumped for the president with a rush between 8:00 and 9:00 P.M. Seven of the so-called Big Ten states of Ohio, Illinois, Michigan, Wisconsin, Minnesota, Iowa, and Missouri added 100 points to his total, giving him 247. With 39 more from West Virginia, Kentucky, Tennessee, Arkansas, and Louisiana, the president was well over the 270 mark at 286; and the nation's TV screens that were in use lit up with the smiling face of the newly reelected president.

All Dole could counter with was the only big one on his list of nineteen, Texas, plus Oklahoma, Colorado, Utah, Wyoming, and Montana for 59 votes, giving him a total of 152.

The Pacific coast and intermediate states, plus Hawaii, just about cleaned up the rest of Clinton's column—California's 54, together with Washington, Oregon, New Mexico, Arizona, and Nevada—for a final total of 379 for the president, who by that time was already celebrating. As for Dole, following his concession, he added his last 7 votes from Idaho and Alaska for his total of 159.

Despite his losing campaign, there was consolation for Dole because he could fairly consider that he had helped maintain Republican control of Congress, something that he could only guess at when he telephoned his admission of defeat to the president. Regardless of its mistakes, the Republican Party remained a great power in the land both in Congress and in the states that had chosen Republican governors. Wisely or not, for at least the next two years, the electorate would continue to entrust its fate to another divided government.

37 State of the Union

Favored by a nation at peace amid the strongest American economy of the century and a record bull market in Wall Street, President Clinton opened his second term by winning agreement from his Republican opposition on a balanced federal budget.

To achieve that goal, however, required the approval of Congress for each successive session from 1997–1978 until 2002, by no means an assured accomplishment. Still, the prospect was so appealing that the president, beginning with his State of the Union message, called for a $51 billion program to boost public education. His public approval rating then was near an all-time high.

But as might have been expected in Washington, D.C., all was not wine and roses. Both major parties belabored each other with charges, first heard during the presidential campaign against the Democrats, that huge campaign funds for Clinton had been raised by every means from soliciting gifts from foreign sources to renting out even the American Valhalla, the Abraham Lincoln bedroom in the White House. In the postelection season, the Republicans also could not expect to escape blame for foreign solicitations, especially when they, too, had to return campaign gifts that might have been tainted.

And while both parties piously agreed that something should be done about campaign reform, and the president actually endorsed a Senate bill to that effect, the chances were very much against barring the free flow of cash without limit directly to the political leadership itself, regardless of limits that were placed on presidential contenders. To be sure, the Republicans promised a thorough investigation of shortcomings in the campaign funding process through their continued control of Congress; but few believed that process would do more than center on the scandalous conduct of the Democrats while holding aloof from Republican failings in the same much-abused process.

The on-again, off-again, on-again three-year Whitewater inquiry involving President and Mrs. Clinton, meanwhile, was nearing another decisive stage in the spring of 1997, with former Solicitor General Kenneth Starr openly accusing President Clinton of withholding evidence in the case. The White House, of course, denied Starr's right to whatever information it was that the investigator had sought. The general position of President and Mrs. Clinton throughout the past three years had been a denial of fault in their Whitewater real estate venture, dating back to the years when he was governor of Arkansas, that had cost them $35,000.

Starr's inquiry had also had its ups and downs throughout its history. In February 1996, in the midst of his work as a special prosecutor, Starr had announced that he was resigning to become the law school dean at Pepperdine University, Malibu, California, a forty-year-old institution with about 8,000 students and 300 faculty. In response to charges early in 1996 that Starr was stepping out because he didn't have a case against the Clintons, the special prosecutor issued an angry denial.

At that time in 1996, Starr still had not been able to persuade a reluctant jailed Whitewater witness, Susan McDougal, to corroborate charges of illegal Whitewater acts by Clinton while he was governor of Arkansas. Once real estate partners of the Clintons, the McDougals had since been convicted during the Starr inquiry; and it had been widely reported that, in a plea bargain, James McDougal had "changed his story." He began serving a shorter jail term.

Nevertheless, the reaction of press and public was so heated in early 1996 at what was termed Starr's "desertion" that he changed his mind, agreed to stay on to wind up his inquiry, and deferred accepting the Pepperdine offer. His next announcement early in the presidential campaign proved, however, to be somewhat of a relief to the White House, for the special prosecutor issued a one-hundred-page report upholding the verdict of suicide of still another Clinton regime "insider," Vincent W. Foster, on July 20, 1993. A previous independent counsel, Robert B. Fiske Jr., had also found that Foster had killed himself after he was found with a bullet hole in his head and a pistol in his hand in Fort Marcy Park in Virginia.

The president's enemies on the far right had insisted for years on a conspiracy theory in which Foster was supposedly murdered elsewhere and his body was later dumped in the Virginia park, only Starr and Fiske didn't see it that way. The question remained, however, how much longer Starr could operate as a special prosecutor without coming up with unchallenged proof of his frequent intimation that he had evidence of obstruction of justice by unnamed individuals in the Whitewater case.

His latest extension, granted by the courts, ran well into the fall of 1997.

The Republicans had their own political problem, Speaker Gingrich, who had come perilously close to becoming their political casualty of the postelection period but managed to save himself, even though his Republican colleagues in the House voted overwhelmingly to disapprove of his official conduct. The charges of wrongdoing lodged against him had been buried for two years in the House Ethics Committee but came to public notice mainly through the efforts of a few determined Democrats.

The position seemed far worse than the punishment he had taken for his acceptance of a $4.5 million advance in 1995 for his book *To Renew America*, published by HarperCollins. The Speaker got out of that scrape by agreeing to return the money and to take instead a $1.00 advance, with the rest coming from his book royalties as they occurred.

Even so, on December 12, 1995, the Ethics Committee rebuked him for the deal, charging that it

> creates the impression of exploiting one's office for personal gain. Such a perception is especially troubling when it pertains to the office of the Speaker of the House of Representatives, a constitutional office requiring the highest standard of ethical behavior.

Despite that, Gingrich emerged in the following year with a financial disclosure on May 15, 1996, that he had earned $1,244,239 in royalties in 1995 but also had $752,891 in expenses, which gave him a net profit on the book deal of $471,348 at the time. Not bad, considering that he also earned $171,600 a year as Speaker and had hefty savings in campaign funds as well.

The difference between the book deal and the more dangerous current charges before the Ethics Committee was that in the latter case the accusation involved lying to the Ethics group and thereby disgracing his own role in the House as well as the House itself. He was charged with using money from tax-exempt foundations for political purposes in helping to influence the election of a Republican congressional majority in 1994.

While the Democratic and Republican members of the Ethics Committee aired their differences, with the former demanding Gingrich's punishment, President Clinton, upon his return from vacation, busied himself instead by reshaping his cabinet, an arduous task that he completed on December 20. With the appointment of the first woman secretary of state, Madeleine K. Albright, the former US representative to the United Nations, and Republican William S. Cohen as secretary of defense, his revised cabinet made a favorable public impression, as did other replacements and holdovers.

The next day, Speaker Gingrich publicly admitted that he had disgraced the House with the false information that he had given the Ethics Committee about a college course that he had taught and some televised town meetings that were financed through political means and for political purposes. He argued only that his failings were not deliberate because he had not sought legal advice on his use of funds from tax-exempt foundations to advance a political objective. In addition, he agreed to accept whatever punishment the House would adopt on the recommendation of the Ethics Committee.

That same day, however, a Florida tourist couple, by complete accident, intercepted an over-the-air conversation between Speaker Gingrich and Republican House colleagues on a radio scanner, in which the Speaker seemed to be planning his own reelection, regardless of his admitted faults. The couple gave a tape of what they heard to a Democratic member of the Ethics Committee, the text of which subsequently appeared in two newspapers. Much as the Republicans protested, the tape injured the Speaker still more.

He also had bad luck when he consulted a New York *Times* columnist, William Safire, and drew in return a widely publicized column on December 26, in which an immediate resignation was advised, as follows:

> I wished him a Merry Christmas and told him that—for the sake of the country, the conservative cause, the Republican Party, and even his own long-term career—he should resign.

Instead, Gingrich decided to try to bull his way out of his increasing troubles, and the Republican high command backed him—to a point. On January 7, 1997, the first day of the One hundred-fifth Congress, which had been elected with President Clinton and Vice-President Gore, Gingrich squeaked through to reelection as Speaker, even though many Republicans were disturbed because they were given no specifics.

The report of the special counsel to the House Ethics Committee, James M. Cole, who had asked for a few days' more time, was postponed so that, as one participant said, "It was an Alice-in-Wonderland situation with the verdict being given in the trial before the evidence was presented."

In pleading for his reelection, Speaker Gingrich apologized profusely for embarrassing the House and pledged his best efforts to work with all members on a variety of issues. An opponent, Representative David E. Bonior of Michigan, the Democratic whip, noted that the Ethics Committee proceedings were unfinished, that the Republicans were rushing ahead anyway, and concluded, "There's an ethics cloud hanging over this House that will only get darker in the days to come."

When the vote was taken, 9 Republicans defected; but the Speaker received 216 votes, all Republican, while the closest Democrat, Representative Richard A. Gephardt of Missouri, received 205. Four members did not vote, which meant that Gingrich just barely achieved the necessary majority of the 431 members who were present and voting.

Dissatisfaction among the Republicans increased, however, when the Ethics Committee's special counsel was finally able to present his detailed report on Speaker Gingrich's wrongdoing. That came just before the deadline that the Republican high command had set for January 20, so that it was well-nigh a miracle that the report was presented with its Ethics Committee recommendation of a reprimand for the Speaker and the payment of a fine of $300,000.

Just before that unexpectedly strong recommendation for punishment, President Clinton had broken his silence on the case by demanding action from the House. "I want it to be over," he said. "The American people have given us larger responsibilities . . . . Way too much time and energy and effort are spent on these things, leaving too little time and emotional energy for the work of the people."

Referring specifically to Gingrich and his troubles, the president added,

> The Speaker should do whatever is appropriate; and we should get on with it, put it behind us, and go on with the business of the country.

In his inaugural address to the nation on January 20, while the Republican majority in Congress was preparing dolefully to accept the verdict of the Ethics Committee for Gingrich's punishment, the president again obliquely referred to the Gingrich affair in an appeal for unity addressed to the Republican Congress. With Speaker Gingrich sitting near him, Clinton coupled a plea for political harmony with the larger issue of racial discord, saying:

> The American people returned to office a president of one party and a Congress of another. Surely, they did not do this to advance the politics of petty bickering and extreme partisanship they plainly deplore. No, they call on us instead to be the repairers of the breach and to move on with America's mission. . . . America demands big things of us. And nothing big ever came from being small.

The showdown on Gingrich came the next day, January 21, when the Republican majority that the Speaker helped to create at last deserted him and accepted the Ethics Committee's punishment for him by a vote of 395 to 28—an overwhelming rebuke.

On still another matter vitally affecting Gingrich's future, the suggestion that he might pay his $300,000 fine in part or altogether from campaign funds and not from his personal savings, California Democratic Representative Nancy Pelosi seemed to speak for many others when she warned the Speaker against using campaign money to settle his debt to the House. For, as she said, that would serve only to increase the American public's cynicism about the way Congress conducts its affairs in the nation's capital.

The Speaker began paying off his $300,000 ethics fine with a $50,000 check from his own account on May 15, promised to pay the rest before January 3, 1999, and agreed to limit the $150,000 final payment as the extent of the loan he had been promised by Bob Dole, the Republican presidential candidate in 1996.

This was not only the first time in its history of more than two centuries that the House had ever imposed punitive sanctions against any presiding officer but it was also an act that barely stopped short of a vote of censure that would have been tantamount to a demand for his immediate resignation. The best that one of his few defenders could say of him was that he had "screwed up," a reference to his admitted use of nontaxable funds for political purposes that was offered by the Republican whip, Representative Tom DeLay of Texas.

Representative Benjamin L. Cardin of Maryland, the ranking Democrat on the House Ethics Committee, summed up the position against the Speaker by saying:

> Mr. Gingrich's case involves more than just giving false information to the committee. Mr. Gingrich has also admitted directing a political empire that made extensive use of tax-exempt entities for political fundraising purposes. As a result of these actions, the reputation of the House of Representatives has been damaged, and tax dollars have been lost.

Representative Porter J. Goss, a Florida Republican who was chairman of the Ethics subcommittee of investigation, was just as concerned in his concluding remarks:

> I found it extraordinarily imprudent of Mr. Gingrich not to seek and follow a less aggressive course of action in tax areas he knew to be sensitive and controversial. And even more troubling, I found the fact that the committee was given inaccurate, unreliable, and incomplete information to be a severe failure on his part.

Among other Democrats, there were five who did not vote and two others cast ballots against the Speaker's punishment on the ground that it hadn't been tough enough. They had apparently wanted him removed from office at once. As for the Republicans who objected, most of them believed that the fine was too stiff for the admittedly faulty conduct of the Speaker.

Gingrich did not remain in the House to witness his disgrace. Because he had won reelection in 1996 from his Georgia district, his two-year term in the House remained unaffected. As for the $300,000 fine, former Senator Dole offered him the loan, he accepted, and all else was left for the future. But meanwhile, there was no doubt that Senator Lott, as the majority leader of the upper house, now was the acknowledged Republican spokesman in Congress, and he accepted the role with tact, grace, and enthusiasm.

The way that President Clinton and Senator Lott operated to reach agreement on their budget-balancing deal demonstrated that the two major parties really could cooperate if they tried hard enough. Senator Lott's first move on the issue, once the second Clinton term began, was to sound out the president on a proposed budget-balancing amendment to the Constitution.

The president responded with a classic example of Clintonian double-talk: "I don't believe we need it but if we do, it ought to be able to be implemented." Questioned about what he meant, he replied easily that whatever was done about the Constitution should include an "escape hatch" if the proposal became unworkable.

Lott promptly concluded that the president might be "coming around" to the idea of budget balancing.

But Treasury Secretary Rubin then announced that the president opposed balancing the budget through a constitutional amendment. To which the White House issued a statement that the head of the Treasury was correct. After returning from a Hawaiian vacation, however, with the first lady, Hillary Rodham Clinton, the president issued an unexpected bid for budgetary cooperation from the Republicans, saying:

> I want to meet them [the Republicans] halfway on this and many other issues, And I hope they'll meet me halfway.

What he referred to was a previous Republican proposal to cut Medicare spending by $270 billion over seven years. His offer, which at once drew scattered Republican praise, moved up his own willingness to cut the growth of Medicare spending.

Still, like his much-criticized move toward the Republican position on curbing public welfare funding, the overture toward increased cuts in Medicare drew no cheers from Democratic leaders in Congress and elsewhere who would have to run for reelection. The president, being forbidden from seeking a third term, had greater freedom to act; but his centrist cause wasn't any the better for it.

The last heard from both sides previously, when budget talks were suspended on Medicare savings, President Clinton had offered a $116 billion cut over six years and had made an issue of the Republicans' insistence on the much higher figure of $158 billion. The presidential postelection approach toward the higher Republican figure, therefore, became the subject of a sarcastic tirade by at least one of his Republican opponents, Senator Phil Gramm of Texas.

Regardless of how the two sides eventually agreed to cut Medicare spending, it seemed to be the president's way in the immediate postelection era of serving notice that he meant to achieve a balanced budget in fiscal 1998. As a symbolic gesture toward his opponents, he bestowed the Medal of Freedom on his defeated opponent, former Senator Bob Dole, at a White House ceremony. The deal to balance the budget in 2002 followed.

As another postelection initiative, the president also tried to ease public doubts about Democratic fund-raising practices in the 1996 election by announcing that noncitizens resident in the United States would no longer be able to contribute money to the Democratic Party. But on the larger issue of accepting "soft money" for future campaigns — the unlimited corporate and other large gifts that go to the respective political parties for use wherever needed — the president limited them to $100,000 each but with this condition:

> Today, let us resume our call to our friends in the Republican Party. Together, let's stop accepting soft money, even before the reform becomes law. If you will do it, we will do it.

Despite that statement, he took a crack at Republican "soft money" practices anyway, arguing that the other party didn't seem interested in cleaning up the campaign-finance mess. He demanded:

> Why should they? They raise more money. They raise more foreign money. They raise more money in big contributions. But we take all the heat. It's a free ride.

Even so, he announced support for a pending bill in the Senate, sponsored by Republican Senator John McCain and Democratic Senator Russell Feingold, which would restrict campaign financing in general and huge "soft money" gifts in particular. Senator McCain, however, was not impressed. He denounced the Democrats for using "soft money" funds supplied by the AFL-CIO, which didn't elicit any support from the Democratic side.

Despite the president's attempt to shift the blame for campaign financing excesses to the Republicans, it didn't work out that way. Following up on the preelection-day disclosures about the foreign fund-raising activities of John Huang that obliged the Democratic National Committee to refund more than $1.5 million, the DNC gave back still more money after the president was reelected.

The largest single amount by the end of November was $450,000 from associates of an Asian enterprise that had also previously figured in Huang's fund-raising activities, the Riady family of Indonesia. The couple that were sent the refund reportedly live in Virginia and were friendly with James T. Riady, another large Democratic contributor.

At about the same time, the Democratic National Committee also announced the return of more than $250,000 from a woman in Bangkok and, previously, another $250,000 from a company in South Korea. The point about all these and other contributions from firms in Asia doing business in the United States was that fund-raisers like John Huang, as well as others working in the field, had given the Republicans a chance to intimate that the White House may have been influenced by such contributions in an improper manner, something both the Democratic National Committe and others promptly denied.

The Republicans, however, had not been idle in raising money from Asian sources that had to be returned. In early May 1997, the Republican National Committee said it was returning $100,000 in contributions from a company in Hong Kong that has an affiliate, a real estate company, in Coral Gables, Florida. A Republican official denied reports that the company had benefited a prominent Republican official, insisting that the only reason the money was returned was that it came from Hong Kong.

In similar vein, while criticizing the Democrats for rewarding big donors with White House visits, coffee hours with the president, and the like, the Republicans are known to have encouraged their own big donors with special designations and sessions with prominent Republican officials in Congress and elsewhere. There were published reports, for example, that several score large corporations each had contributed $250,000 to the Republican campaign of 1996, quite an advance from the usual $100,000 corporate gift that had been more or less a standard in previous years on the Republican side.

The difference for 1996 was the very real effort that the Clinton people made to market the president as a host at White House visits, entertainment, and with some even being granted the extraordinary privilege of sleeping in the Lincoln bedroom. Given such efforts as these by the two major parties, it is understandable that ambitious new fundraisers associated with the Democratic Party like John Huang should also have solicited large Asian contributions, some of which had to be returned for reasons that were seldom clearly spelled out.

It was not surprising, therefore, that the Republicans made such striking progress against fund-raising practices that became a national scandal in the postelection era. The Republican problem, however, developed in time, even though it wasn't as strongly emphasized on TV and in the newspapers as the Democratic scandal that had broken first in the closing month of the presidential campaign.

What President Clinton did to try to divert public attention from his party's shortcomings was to court still more Republican cooperation, this time for what he called "citizen service." To that end, on January 24, he welcomed former President George Bush to the White House, together with General Colin L. Powell, former chairman of the Joint Chiefs of Staff, to sponsor a drive to enlist volunteers for community service on a nationwide basis.

Former President George Bush, whom Clinton had defeated in 1992, was intrigued by the idea of citizen service, saying, "I'm proud to be a part of this and proud to be at your side in this effort."

It turned out that Bush had pleaded successfully for continued federal support for expanding citizen volunteerism for community service, which he had initiated just before Clinton took the oath of office for the first time. What both now sought to duplicate and expand was the then current Clinton program of Americorps volunteers, among them students who pay their way through college with part-time community services.

What the wider program was founded for, General Powell made clear as its prospective leader, was to mobilize the efforts of a large group of private charitable foundations to promote immunization for children, as well as broader health inspections; improve chances for community services among adult volunteers; and encourage greater advances in education, recreation, and job training among young people.

"This," General Powell said, "is about Americans getting out on the playing field and away from the sidelines."

To which President Clinton added, in praise of former President Bush, "He understands that much of what is good in America is being done outside Washington."

If Vice-President Al Gore was a thoughtful if relatively modest observer of these proceedings in the White House, there may have been reason for it. Having been quietly promoted since the most recent election day as "the man to beat" for the Democratic nomination four years hence, he hadn't been particularly enthusiastic about the prominence of General Powell as the leader of this Clinton-sponsored activity.

Gore also could not overlook the presence in Washington that day, though elsewhere on problems before Congress, of such other Republican future presidential prospects as Governor George W. Bush of Texas, the former president's son; Governor Jim Edgar of Illinois; and Governor George E. Pataki of New York.

The vice-president had already been represented publicly as also concerned over a prospective rival for the Democratic nomination in 2000, former Senator Bill Bradley of New Jersey. And then, there was a gaggle of Democratic governors and congressional leaders who might be quietly putting together campaign war chests just on the off-chance that a presidential nomination might come their way.

It was on this immensely practical echo of bipartisan collaboration that President Clinton's successful reelection celebration was concluded in the nation's capital while the somewhat anxious vice-president nursed his chances for the future. After all, in America it has always been open season for politics and politicians where the presidency is concerned; and, toward century's end, nowhere was this more true than in Washington, D.C.

Appendix
Index

Appendix
The 1996 Presidential Election Results

	Popular Vote			Electoral Vote
State	Clinton (D)	Dole (R)	Perot (Ref)	
Alabama	662,165	769,044	92,149	9-Dole
Alaska	80,380	122,746	26,333	3-Dole
Arizona	653,288	622,073	112,072	8-Clinton
Arkansas	475,171	325,416	69,884	6-Clinton
California	5,119,835	3,828,380	697,847	54-Clinton
Colorado	671,152	691,848	99,629	8-Dole
Connecticut	735,740	483,109	139,523	8-Clinton
Delaware	140,355	99,062	28,719	3-Clinton
District of Columbia	158,220	17,339	3,611	3-Clinton
Florida	2,546,870	2,244,536	483,870	25-Clinton
Georgia	1,053,849	1,080,843	146,337	13-Dole
Hawaii	205,012	113,943	27,358	4-Clinton
Idaho	165,443	256,595	62,518	4-Dole
Illinois	2,341,744	1,587,021	346,408	22-Clinton
Indiana	887,424	1,006,693	224,299	12-Dole
Iowa	620,258	492,644	105,159	7-Clinton
Kansas	387,659	583,245	92,639	6-Dole
Kentucky	636,614	623,283	120,396	8-Clinton
Louisiana	927,837	712,586	123,293	9-Clinton
Maine	312,788	186,378	85,970	4-Clinton
Maryland	966,207	681,530	115,812	10-Clinton
Massachusetts	1,571,763	718,107	227,217	12-Clinton
Michigan	1,989,653	1,481,212	336,670	18-Clinton
Minnesota	1,120,438	766,476	257,704	10-Clinton
Mississippi	394,022	439,838	52,222	7-Dole
Missouri	1,025,935	890,016	217,188	11-Clinton
Montana	167,922	179,652	55,229	3-Dole

Appendix (Continued)

State	Popular Vote			Electoral Vote
	Clinton (D)	Dole (R)	Perot (Ref)	
Nebraska	236,761	363,467	71,278	5-Dole
Nevada	203,974	199,244	43,986	4-Clinton
New Hampshire	246,214	196,532	48,390	4-Clinton
New Jersey	1,652,329	1,103,078	262,134	15-Clinton
New Mexico	273,495	232,751	32,257	5-Clinton
New York	3,756,177	1,933,492	503,458	33-Clinton
North Carolina	1,107,849	1,225,938	168,059	14-Dole
North Dakota	106,905	125,050	32,515	3-Dole
Ohio	2,148,222	1,859,883	483,207	21-Clinton
Oklahoma	488,105	582,315	130,788	8-Dole
Oregon	649,641	538,152	121,221	7-Clinton
Pennsylvania	2,215,819	1,801,169	430,984	23-Clinton
Rhode Island	233,050	104,683	43,723	4-Clinton
South Carolina	506,283	573,458	64,386	8-Dole
South Dakota	139,333	150,543	31,250	3-Dole
Tennessee	909,146	863,530	105,918	11-Clinton
Texas	2,459,683	2,736,167	378,537	32-Dole
Utah	221,633	361,911	66,461	5-Dole
Vermont	137,894	80,352	31,024	3-Clinton
Virginia	1,091,060	1,138,350	159,861	13-Dole
Washington	1,123,323	840,712	201,003	11-Clinton
West Virginia	327,812	233,946	71,639	5-Clinton
Wisconsin	1,071,971	845,029	227,339	11-Clinton
Wyoming	77,934	105,388	25,928	3-Dole
TOTAL:	47,402,357	39,198,755	8,085,402	379-Clinton 159-Dole

Source: Federal Elections 96: 1996 Electoral and Popular Vote Summary

Index

ABC-TV, 128, 162, 181, 205
Abortion issue, 36–37, 58, 65, 85–86, 153–54, 158–59, 219
Affirmative action, 58, 178, 257
AFL-CIO, 166, 211, 284
Agnew, Spiro, 208
Air Force, US, 96, 100–101
al-Aksa Mosque, Jerusalem, rioting at, 246–48
Alabama, 274
Alaska, 275
Albright, Secretary of State Madeleine K., 279
American Civil Liberties Union, 136, 140
Anti-tobacco issue. See Big Tobacco
Apple, R. W. Jr., 92
Arab summit, 96, 99, 101
Arafat, Yasir, 244–45, 250
Archer Daniels Midland Co., 264
Arizona, 222, 232, 275
Arkansas, 85, 90–92, 218, 267, 274
Associated Press, 59, 67, 269
Atomic testing, 33

Babbitt, Secretary of the Interior Bruce, 235
Baker, James A. III, 92, 93
Baker, Senator Howard H. Jr., 24, 51
Balanced budget amendment, 163
Balanced budget agreement, 78, 104–5, 183, 198–99, 276
Barbour, Haley, 130
Bauer, Gary, 86
Bayh, Evan, 187

Berke, Richard L., 63
Big Tobacco, 31; attacks on, 210, 256; in the campaign, 113–19, 162, 166; cigarette sales, 172–73
Bill Clinton Story, The, ix
Black, Charles, 44
Black churches, torching of, 173–74
Black hole, 63–69, 73
Blythe, William, 14
Bonior, David E., 279–80
Bosnia, US peacekeeping in, 33, 109
Boutros-Ghali, UN Secretary General Boutros, 34, 231
Bradley, Bill, 286
Brady, Jim, 186
Brady, Sarah, 186
Branscum, Herby Jr., 92
Brasseux, Barney, 93–94
Britain, 193
Broder, David, 166
Brown, Secretary of Commerce Ron, 64
Brown & Williamson Tobacco Corporation, 114, 118
Buchanan, Pat, 23, 25, 42–43, 44–45, 46, 50–51, 56, 67, 149, 156, 158
Buffalo, New York, 212
Burke, Edmund, 73
Bush, President George, 15, 41, 58, 75, 89, 193, 208, 283
Bush, Governor George W. (Texas), 286

Cable Network News (CNN), 128
Cairo, 96, 99–100
Califano, Joseph A. Jr., 234

California, 26, 107, 127, 229, 262, 266, 269, 270, 275
"Camel, Joe," 172–73
Campaign fund argument, 74–75, 88
Campbell, Senator Ben Nighthorse, 66
Campbell, Mayor Bill, 56
Canada, 187
Cardin, Representative Benjamin L., 281
Carter, Grady, 117–18
Carter, President Jimmy, 89, 178
Castellanos, Alex, 201
CBS's *60 Minutes*. *See 60 Minutes*
Census Bureau economic report, 13–14
Center for Responsible Politics, 115
Central Intelligence Agency (CIA), 197, 225
"Character issue," 25, 79, 107, 262
Chechnya, war in, 122, 222
Chernomyrdin, Prime Minister Viktor S. (Russia), 121, 124, 210
Chicago, 178, 179, 180–90, 220
Chicago *Tribune*, 65
Christian Coalition, 76, 106, 142, 150, 161, 219
Christopher, Secretary of State Warren, 96, 99, 210
Choate, Pat, 214
Church-state separation as an issue, 219
Cigarette sales, 172–73
Cipollone, Rose, 118
"Citizenship USA" campaign, 220
Cleveland *Plain Dealer*, 66
Clinger, Representative William F. Jr., 93–94
Clinton, Chelsea, 174, 188
Clinton, Hillary Rodham, 14, 15, 17, 66; on campaign trail, 229, 273, 282; criticism of, 68–69, 91–92, 162, 174; quoted, 188
Clinton, Roger, 14
Clinton, William Jefferson "Bill": administrative record, 28–30; analysis of the presidential contest, 207–14; apologizes for White House misuse of FBI files, 90–93; approves regulating cigarette sales, 172–73; approves welfare reform, health bill, and clean water act, 140–43; asks for more police, 225; Big Tobacco as an issue, 31–32; biography, 14–16; campaign to improve education, 79–80; Congress shuts down government and, 3, 4, 5, 6–12; criticism of Dole, 52–55; defends fund-raising practices but admits need for reform, 283; defends Medicare, 203; on economy, 13–19; gains in polls, 12; helped by Perot candidacy, 130–33; helps rebuild torched black church, 173–74; interview on CNN, 185; justifies missile attack on Iraq, 193; lead in polls in closing of campaign, 229–30; and Middle East peace conference at White House, 244–50; as "new" Democrat, 77–83; opens campaign on Labor Day, 193–201; opposes Dole's proposed 15-percent tax cut, 149–52; opposes Dole's view of tobacco nonaddictiveness, 114; peacekeeping missions, 33–34; quoted, 8; reelected by large vote, 268; on reform, 283; renominated at Democratic Convention, 180–90; signs Congress's $256.6 billion spending bill, 230; State of the Union address, 9, 276–80; view of opponent Dole, 27; war on terror, 135–36; on welfare reform, 74; wins balanced-budget amendment for 1997–2002, 276; wishes Dole well on leaving Senate, 84–85
Clinton's "Twenty-first Century Express," 185
Cohen, Secretary of Defense William S., 278
Cole, Arnold, 94
Cole, James M., 279
Colorado, 66, 127, 231, 275
Columbia University, 212
Common Cause, gifts to by Big Tobacco, 115–17
Community service programs, 285
Congress, US: approves welfare reform and funds to rebuild torched black churches, 142–48; Gingrich's "Contract with America," 22; gridlock, 21; hits a low in polls, 28; measures against terrorists, 137; political divisions outlined, 27; Republicans again win control in 1996, 268; shuts down government, 3, 4, 5, 6, 12; summary of One hundred-fourth Congress, 237–43

Coolidge, President Calvin, 208
Corporation for Public Broadcasting, 239
Coughlin, the Reverend Charles E., 45
Couric, Katie, 113–14
Crime, 95, 182, 233
Crime and prison reports, 141
Cuba, 34, 137, 225
Cuomo, Mario, 180, 187

Daiwa Bank Ltd., 264
Dale, Billy R., 93, 94
Daley, Mayor Richard M. (Chicago), 66, 181
Dallas *Morning News,* 64
D'Amato, Senator Alfonse, 16, 58, 59, 144, 252
DeBakey, Dr. Michael E., 123
Debates, 236; Clinton/Dole, October 6, 251–53; Clinton/Dole, October 16, 255–58; Kemp/Gore, October 9, 253–55. *See also* individual listings
Defense, Department of, 217, 223–24
Delaware, 274
DeLay, Representative Tom, 281
Democratic fund-raising criticism, 262, 265, 266, 276, 284–85
Democratic National Committee, 76, 115, 180–90; charges against Speaker Gingrich, 22–23
Democratic Party, 22, 268
Democrats, "new," 133–34, 142–45, 178, 180–90
Denver *Post,* 65
Detroit *News,* 64
Dewey, Thomas E., 55, 133
Dhahran, US troops killed in, 100, 103, 138
Disaster relief, 26
District of Columbia, 76, 268, 274
Dodd, Representative Christopher, 177, 189
Dole, Elizabeth, 66, 71, 113–14, 161, 266
Dole, Senator Robert "Bob": acceptance speech of, 162; analysis of vice-presidential contest, 207–14; as anti-abortionist, 37; appeals to Perot to drop out, 121, 130–32; attacks cigarette regulation, 172–73; attacks White House use of FBI files, 90–93; backs US move against Saddam Hussein, 200; balks at speech before NAACP, 109; Big Tobacco and, 113–19; calls for party unity, 59; career of, 6–7; Chicago *Tribune*'s assessment of his chances, 65; criticism of media coverage, 6–9; criticizes Clinton record, 34; criticizes Clinton tax plan, 88; debates leave poll standing unchanged, 261, 266; denounces black church burning, 174; detaches himself from GOP platform, 158; disputes polls, 204; ducks attack on Big Tobacco, 32; falls from platform in California, 235; farewell to the Senate, 84–85; fights Clinton vetoes, 22; funding troubles of, 73–75; General Powell rejects place on GOP ticket, 35–36; loses to Clinton, 272; physical condition, 68; plans major tax-cut proposal, 105–6; pleads for African-American support, 178; primary battles, 27; proposes 15-percent tax cut, 149–52; proposes retirement from Senate, 71; raises character issue against Clinton, 79; receives government campaign funding, 157; relations with Speaker Gingrich, 21; Republican Convention nominates him for president, 156–64; rivals for the nomination, 23–26; role in congressional shutdown, 7–12, 20; says US economy is in "bad shape," 235; seeks GOP presidential nomination, 21; as Senate majority leader, 20; shakes up staff for fall campaign, 201; supports war on terror, 135–36; wins GOP presidential nomination, 53
Dornan, Representative Robert, 25, 43
Dow-Jones Industrial Averages, 25, 70, 104–5, 133–34, 203, 264
Downsizing, 26
Drugs, war on, 140, 182
Dubail, Jean, 66
Duke, David, 42

Earnings, average hourly, 203
Economy, US, 13–19, 133, 182, 202
Edelson, Naomi, 235

Edgar, Governor Jim (Illinois), 286
Education as Clinton campaign issue, 79, 182
Education funding program, 276
Egypt, 193, 222
Eisenhower, President Dwight David, 52, 73, 89, 206, 208, 212
Emergency aid, 26
Environmental safeguards, 30, 188
Escalante Canyon Park, Utah, 231
Ethics Committee, House, 22, 238, 279–80. *See also* Gingrich, Speaker Newt
Ethics issue, 257–58

Family Research Council, 86
Farley, James A., 27
Farrakhan, Louis, 212
FBI files at the White House, 87, 88, 90, 95, 269
Federal Aviation Administration, 108, 225–26
Federal Election Commission, 8, 75, 76
Federal Housing Administration, 81
Fiedler, Tom, 66
Fifth Amendment invoked, 91, 94
Financing presidential elections, 18, 76
Flat tax proposal, sponsored by Dole, 149–52
Florida, 26, 203, 218, 229, 274
Flynn, Kathleen, 226
Food and Drug Administration, 87, 172–73
Food stamps, cuts in, 177
Forbes, Steve, 18, 24–25, 43, 47, 57, 58, 149
Ford, President Gerald R., 89, 178, 208
Foster, Vincent, suicide of, 17, 277
Flowers, Gennifer, 15, 25, 211
Frahm, Sheila, 85
France, 222
Fraternal Order of Police, 233
Freedom Forum, 64
Freeh, FBI Director Louis J., 90, 91, 95
Freemen gang, 67
Funk, Sherman, 40, 41

Gays in the military, 67
Gaza Strip, 97, 101, 244
Georgetown University, 14
Georgia, 21–22, 57–58, 203, 218, 274

Gephardt, Representative Richard, 242
Gilbert and Sullivan, 65, 271
Gingrich, Speaker Newt: apologizes, 279; book advance, 22, 278; career, 21; fined $300,000, 281; other matters, 136, 159, 188; rebuked by House Ethics Committee, 278; reelected, 211, 230, 237, 242, 268; on shutdowns, 5, 6, 7, 12; wins vote to remain as Speaker, 280
Gorbachev, President Mikhail (USSR), 121
Gore, Vice-President Albert Jr., "Al," 54, 55; analysis of, 207–14; on campaign trail, 229, 267; helps rebuild torched black church, 174; "man to beat" in 2000, 286–87; plans for security against terror, 136; quoted, 188–89; renominated at Democratic National Convention, 180
Gore, Albert III, 209
Gore, Karenna, 209
Gore, Kristin, 209
Gore, Sarah, 209
Gore, Tipper (Mrs. Albert Jr.), 174, 209, 267, 270
Goss, Representative Porter J., 281
Gramm, Senator Phil, 6, 10, 18, 22, 42–43; loses in Iowa primary, 44; position, 55–56, 67
Grand Canyon of the Colorado, 231
Great Depression, 70, 77
Greenberg, Stanley B., 88
Greenspan, Federal Reserve Chairman, Alan, 133
Gridlock, 21, 230
Gulf War, 25, 96, 100–103, 196, 227
Gun control law, 16, 108, 186, 252

Harding, President Warren G., 68, 208
Hardy, Thomas, 65
Harlem, 204, 212
Hamas, anti-Israeli Arab organization, 139
HarperCollins, 278
Harvard Law Review, 139–40
Harvard University, 66, 213
Hatch, Senator Orrin, 94, 225
Hawaii, 275
Head Start program, 240
Health and Human Services, Department of, 240

Health insurance, 16, 28, 78, 146, 240
Hebron, scene of Palestine violence, 245–46, 250
Helms, Senator Jesse, 183
Helprin, Mark, 163
Hezbollah, anti-Israeli Arab organization, 139
Hill, Robert M. Jr., 92
Hinson, David R., 107
Hitler, Adolf, 193
Hoover, President Herbert, 4
Hope, Arkansas, 14, 183
Hope scholarships, 79, 81
Horton, Nathan, 118
Housing and Urban Development, Department of, 81, 213
Houston *Chronicle*, 67
Huang, John, 265, 266, 285
Hussein, king of Jordan, 244, 245–50
Hutchison, Senator Kay Bailey, 159, 230

Idaho, 232, 275
Illinois, 190, 218, 274
Immigration and Naturalization Service, 220, 239
Immigration as an issue, 168, 220
Indiana, 274
Indonesia, 97
Inflation, 104
"Infomercials," by Perot, 205, 267
Iowa, 42–45, 274
Iran, 96, 101, 135, 137
Iraq, 96, 101, 135
Israel, 32, 96–100, 101–2
Israeli-Arab relations, 96–103
Israeli-Palestinian Peace Accord, 97

Jackson, the Reverend Jesse, 180, 187
Jennings, Peter, 43
Jerusalem, 97–98, 99–100, 101–2, 244
Joffe, Robert, 218
Johnson, President Lyndon, 78, 85, 208
Jones, Paula C., 25
Jordan, Kingdom of, 193, 222

Kamisiyah, Iraq, 227–28
Kansas, 272, 274

Kassebaum, Senator Nancy, 82, 146, 176
Kelly, Virginia, 40
Kemp, Jack, 58, 150; biography, 212–14; GOP candidate for vice-president, 153–54; criticizes Clinton, 217; loses with Dole, 272; nominated, 161–62, 204
Kennedy, Senator Edward, 15, 78, 82, 146, 176, 180
Kennedy, President John F., 15, 208, 270
Kentucky, 87, 115, 190, 203, 218, 274
Keyes, Alan, 25, 43, 53, 56
King, Dr. Martin Luther Jr., 204
Ku Klux Klan, 42, 59
Knight-Ridder syndicate, 67
Kohut, Andrew, 221
Koop, Dr. C. Everett, 113, 114, 173
Kurds, Iraq atrocities to, 191, 197–99, 223–24
Kuwait, 100–101, 193, 228

Lacy, Bill, 201
Lamm, Richard D., 38–40, 166–71
Landon, Alfred M., 49, 70
Larry King Live, 128, 130, 170
Las Vegas, 95
Lebed, General Alexander, 121, 124, 125, 126
Lehrer, Jim, presidential debate moderator, 255
Lewis, Representative John, 143
Liberal label, 273
Libya, 96, 135, 137–38
Lincoln, President Abraham, 4, 52, 276
Lindsey, Bruce R., 92
Linn, Roger, 10
Literacy program, 182
Literary Digest, 70
Livingstone, Craig, 92–94
London, 97, 261
Long, former Governor Huey (Louisiana), 45
Long Island, New York, 138–39
Los Angeles, 85, 213
Los Angeles Times, 213
Lott, Senator Trent, 85, 147, 183, 242, 282
Louisiana, 42, 87, 203, 218, 274
Lugar, Senator Richard G., 24, 43, 47

Madison Guaranty Savings and Loan, 16, 18, 91
Marceca, Anthony, in FBI inquiry, 91, 92–94
"Marlboro Man," 172–73
Maryland, 68, 120, 274
Mason-Dixon Line, 85, 173–74, 218
Massachusetts Institute of Technology, 98
McCaffrey, General Barry R., 140, 233
McCain, Senator John, 232
McCain-Feingold bill to outlaw "soft money" campaign funds, 283–84
McDougal, James B., 16, 19, 277
McDougal, Susan, 91, 277
McInturff, Bill, 217
Medicaid, 114, 203, 220, 274
Medicare, 78, 85, 87, 203, 220, 256, 273, 274, 283
Mexico, 187
Mfume, Kweisi, 109
Miami *Herald,* 66, 67
Michigan survey of rich and poor, 104, 218, 274
Middle East, 96–103, 193–98, 244–50
Miller, Governor Zell (Georgia), 79
Minimum wage, 26, 56, 65, 73, 104, 146, 176
Minnesota, 274
Mississippi, 118, 274
Missouri, 190, 199, 267, 274
Molinari, Representative Susan, 79, 154–59
Money magazine, 19
Montana, 67, 232
Moody's credit-rating service, 11
Morales, Victor, 67
Morgan, Stanley & Co., 134
Morocco, 97
Morris, Dick, 143, 181, 202, 211, 273
"Motor voter" law, 16
Mottola, Chris, 201
Moynihan, Senator Daniel P., 142, 143, 144
Mubarak, President Hosni (Egypt), 96, 99, 247–48
Murdoch, Rupert, 22, 261
Murphy, Mike, 201, 202
Muslim nations in Middle East disputes, 97, 99–100, 138, 198, 222

Nashville *Tennessean,* 67, 87, 209
National Association for the Advancement of Colored People (NAACP), 108, 109, 178
National Association of Black Journalists, 178, 213
National Baptist Convention, 203, 204
National debt, 10, 12, 133, 263–64
National Institute of Health, 240
National Rifle Association, 140, 142, 166, 252
NBC-TV, 113, 160, 162, 205
Nebraska, 274
Neilsen Media Research, 251
Netanyahu, Benjamin, 32, 96, 97–99, 100; visits United States, 101–2; at White House, 244–45
Nevada, 95, 275
New Deal, 4, 77, 78
"New" Democrats, 77–83, 143, 180–90
New England states, 26, 274
New Hampshire, 48–53, 262, 267
New Jersey, 262, 279
New Mexico, 275
New York City, 212, 220
New York State, 220, 274
New York Stock Exchange, 70, 119
New York *Times* and New York *Times/*CBS News, 63, 64, 68, 106, 160, 202
Nixon, President Richard M., 208
Nobel Prize, 66
Nomo, Hideo, Japanese pitcher, 235
North American Free Trade Agreement, 16, 168, 214
North Atlantic Treaty Organization (NATO), 193, 263
North Carolina, 115, 203, 218, 274
North Dakota, 274

Oak Ridge, Tennessee, 217
Ohio, 218, 274
Oklahoma, 275
Oklahoma City Federal Building blast, 138, 169, 273–74
Olmert, Mayor Ehud (Jerusalem), 247
Olympic Games in Atlanta, 131, 135–36, 139
Oregon, 67, 275
Oslo Peace Accords, 244–50
Oxford University, 14

Pakistan, 97
Palestine Liberation Organization (PLO), 97, 99–100
Pam Am flight 102, 137
Panetta, Leon, 91
Pataki, Governor George E. (New York), 286
Peacekeeping, 25, 32–33, 109
Pelosi, Representative Nancy, 281
Peña, Secretary of Transportation Federico, 107, 226
Pennsylvania, 274
Pentagon, 91, 138, 200, 224
Pepperdine University, 277
Peres, Shimon, 32, 97, 99
Perot, H. Ross, 15, 37–38, 39, 40–41, 63, 106; barred from presidential debates, 229; becomes candidate of the Reform Party, 165–71, 205; his opponent in the Reform Party, Richard D. Lamm, 127–28; runs for president again, 127–29; total vote received, 268, 274
Perry, Secretary of Defense William J., 138, 222, 224
Perry County (Arkansas) Bank, 92
Philip Morris, 119
Pickering, Thomas, 121
Platform, Democratic, 184–85
Platform, Republican, 158, 159
Political funds from government, 205
Polls in presidential race, 17, 28, 37, 52, 60, 65, 69, 70–73, 85–86, 90, 106; Clinton resumes lead, 175, 176, 181, 201, 261, 266; Dole bulge at GOP Convention, 175
Poverty in America, 104–6
Powell, General Colin L., 36, 52, 84, 152, 157, 200, 285
Pratt, Larry, 51
Princeton University, Clinton speech at, 79
Puerto Rico, 206
Pulitzer Prizes, 65

Quinn, Kenneth, 225

Rabin, Yitzhak, 97
Rahman, Sheik Abdel, 138

Rayburn, former Speaker Sam, 85
Reagan, Nancy, 157
Reagan, President Ronald, 73, 86, 89, 157, 186, 272, 273
Reed, Ralph, 158
Reed, Scott, Dole campaign manager, 53, 58, 71, 76, 201, 216
Reform Party, 37, 38, 106, 127–29, 130; the campaign, 205, 268–69, 272; the two conventions, 165–71
Reno, Attorney General Janet, 140
Republican campaign funds returned, 276, 284–85
Republican National Committee, 75, 84, 115, 221
Republican National Convention, 43, 49, 156–64; analysis of delegates, 160–61; Dole's acceptance speech, 162–64; platform, 162
Republican primaries, 27, 42–43, 51, 53, 57, 59, 60, 65
Reston, James, ix
Reuters final poll, 272
Rhodes scholars, 14, 24
Riady, James T., Indonesian magnate, 284
Riyadh, Saudi Arabia, 100
RJR Nabisco, 119
Robertson, the Reverend Pat, 76
Roosevelt, President Franklin D., ix, 4 (quoted), 8 (quoted), 27, 70, 77, 89, 144, 167, 180, 208, 261, 271
Roosevelt, President Theodore, 15, 52, 89, 130, 208
Roper, survey, 64
Rose law firm, Little Rock, 14
Royko, Mike, 65–66
Rubin, Secretary of the Treasury Robert E., 10, 282
Russell, Kansas, 272

Saddam Hussein, 135, 193–96, 202, 217, 222, 224
Safire, William, 11, 279
San Diego, 149, 156–64
Saudi Arabia 96–97, 99–100, 101, 193
Schroeder, Representative Pat, 66
Secret Service, US, 93–94
Seelye, Katharine Q., 68
Shalikashvili, General John M., 83

Shays, Representative Christopher, 221
Shutdowns, federal government, 8–12, 71, 183, 237, 274
Sipple, Don, 53, 201
60 Minutes, 15
Snowe, Senator Olympia, 158
Social Security, 78, 87, 144, 185, 220, 274
Soros, George, 241
South Carolina, 117, 274
South Dakota, 274
Starr, Kenneth, Whitewater investigator, 68, 91–92, 93–94, 277
State Department, US, 40–41, 225
State of the Union message, 9, 279
Stevens, Greg, 201
Stevens, Supreme Court Justice John Paul, 76
Supreme Court, US, 76
Sweeney, AFL/CIO President John J., 198

Taft, President William Howard, 130, 131
Taiwan, US defense of, 33–34
Talbott, Strobe, 123
Tamposi, Elizabeth M., 40
Tax cut plans, 77, 88, 149–52, 171, 254, 262
Taylor, Morrie, 25, 43
Teachers Union, 163
Telecommunications Act, 30
Tennessee, 25, 85, 87, 190, 203, 217–18, 274
Texas, 26, 85, 275
Thompson, Governor Tommy (Wisconsin), 28, 74
Tobacco as a campaign issue, 31, 87. See also Big Tobacco
Trans World Airlines flight 800, 135, 138–39
Truman, President Harry, 22, 55, 77, 132, 199, 208, 267
Tucker, Governor Jim Guy (Arkansas), 91
TV advertising, 87, 107, 160, 262

Unemployment rate, US, 104, 203
United Nations in the Middle East, 96–103

United Nations, US role in, 33–34, 137, 229, 231
Utah, national park created in, 231, 275

Valujet air crash, 107–8
Vanderbilt University, 209
V-chip, 30
Verney, Russell J., 236
Vietnam War, 179, 180, 206, 222
Virginia, 115, 218, 274
Voter News Service (VNS), 269
Voters, elderly, 219–20

Walesa, Lech, 66
Wall Street Journal, 51, 73, 106
Washington *Post,* 37, 68, 106
Washington (state), 275
Weld, Governor William (Massachusetts), 150, 158
Welfare reform, 28, 78, 142–43, 144–45, 177, 241
West Bank, 97, 99, 101, 244
West Virginia, 218, 274
White House Travel Office dismissals, 16–17, 269
Whitewater case, 16, 18, 25, 68, 79, 90–94, 262, 269, 276–77
Whitman, Governor Christine Todd (New Jersey), 84, 150
Whitney, Justin, 186
Wilson, Governor Pete (California), 53, 107, 150, 158
Wilson, President Woodrow, 130, 131, 271
Wisconsin Workfare program, 28, 74, 199, 218, 274
Women's vote, 150, 219
World Trade Organization, 137
Wright, former Speaker Jim, 23
Wyoming, 232, 275

Yale Law School, 14
Yellowstone National Park, 232
Yeltsin, President Boris (Russia), 33, 109, 120, 125–26, 210

Zyuganov, Gennadi A., 120